THE PEOPLE'S FARM

Malcolm Chase

The People's Farm

English Radical Agrarianism

1775-1840

BREVIARY STUFF PUBLICATIONS

2010

Published by Breviary Stuff Publications,
BCM Breviary Stuff, London WC1N 3XX
www.breviarystuff.org.uk
First published in 1988 by
Oxford University Press

A CIP record for this book is available from
The British Library
ISBN: 978-0-9564827-5-4

Contents

Abbreviations

BAPCK	British Association for Promoting Co-operative Knowledge
BL Add. MSS	Additional Manuscripts, British Library
CRO	County Record Office
EHR	*Economic History Review*
GNCTU	Grand National Consolidated Trades' Union
HL	House of Lords
HO	Home Office Papers, Public Record Office
HWJ	*History Workshop Journal*
LCS	*London Corresponding Society*
NMW	*New Moral World*
NS	*Northern Star*
NUWC	National Union of the Working Classes
PC	Privy Council Register, Public Record Office
PMG	*Poor Man's Guardian*
PP	*Parliamentary Papers*
PRO	Public Record Office
RC	Royal Commission
SC	Select Committee
TS	Treasury Solicitor's Papers, Public Record Office
WFP	*Weekly Free Press*

Acknowledgements

While I was an undergraduate at the University of York, and before I seriously considered pursuing historical research, I was introduced to the study of property, and of radical politics, by Gerald Aylmer and Ted Royle respectively. It has taken little hindsight to appreciate my good fortune: my debt to them both is greater than they — or indeed I — probably realize. The research on which this book is based was begun at the University of Sussex in 1979-81, helped by a studentship from the then Social Science Research Council. I am grateful to both institutions, as well as to the many friends I made through the Graduate Division of History at Sussex.

Then and since History Workshop (the 'movement' rather than the journal) has played a significant part in my involvement in historical study. I should like to thank the various workshop groups with whom I have had the opportunity to discuss aspects of work now presented here. I am also grateful to members of research seminars at the Universities of Exeter and York, and to the 1986 annual conference of the Social History Society.

I have made extensive use of a number of libraries and repositories. Thanks are particularly due to the staffs of the British Library, Bloomsbury and Colindale; the Public Record Office, Kew and Chancery Lane; the Goldsmiths' Library of the University of London; Bishopsgate Institute; and the university libraries of Sussex and Exeter. Special mention must be made of the staff of the Brotherton Library, University of Leeds, who have coped cheerfully with a voracious long-distance borrower.

I must especially thank the following individuals for their interest, help, and encouragement: Iain Bain, Ken Dueck, David Goodway, Alun Howkins, Iain McCalman, Iorwerth Prothero, Robin Thornes, Ray Watkinson, Roger Wells, and Eileen Yeo. John Harrison was the most generous, and at the same time searching, of supervisors. For his help and inspiration thanks expressed in words alone cannot suffice. Lastly, but very far from least, Shirley Chase has helped so much to nurture *The People's Farm*, both as a friend and as a fellow historian. Never once has she questioned an enthusiasm to get back to the land that has so rarely taken me out into our own, much overgrown, garden.

M.S.C.

Preface (2010)

I am naturally delighted that *The People's Farm* has stood the test of time sufficiently well to justify this new edition.[1] The purpose of this preface is briefly to indicate how our understanding of English radical agrarianism has been extended since it first appeared in 1988, particularly concerning Thomas Spence (whose thought and influence is a central theme of this book). The prevailing interpretation in the 1980s, as chapter 2 argues, was that Spence was a marginal eccentric who had had little practical bearing on radical politics. It is now generally accepted (to quote for example the editors of Horne Tooke's prison diary) that 'Spence's views ... formed a coherent political philosophy which endured after his death'.[2] Recognition that his influence extended beyond 1814 to constitute a significant strand in radical thinking about property in land has been extended and consolidated in a range of publications. The Spenceans themselves have been the subject of important studies,[3] also receiving their due in the *Oxford Dictionary of National Biography*.[4] The years since this book first appeared have also witnessed the discovery of a surviving copy of Spence's seminal 1775 lecture which I had confidently asserted (in chapter 2, footnote 7) 'does not survive'. Retired physician and Tyneside local historian, Dr David Gardner-Medwin, stumbled across *Property in Land*

1 I would like to thank Paul Mangan at Breviary Stuff Publications for making this new edition possible and Shirley Chase for her continuing help and enthusiastic interest (even though my disinclination to put agrarian theory into practice alas persists).

2 A. V. Beedell and A. D. Harvey (eds), *The Prison Diary (16 May-22 November 1794) of John Horne Tooke*, (1995), p. 25 n20.

3 I. McCalman, *Radical Underworld: Prophets, Revolutionaries and Pornographers in London, 1795-1840* (1988); D. Worrall, *Radical Culture: Discourse, Resistance and Surveillance, 1790-1820* (1992); M. Chase (ed.), *The Life and Literary Pursuits of Allen Davenport, with a Further Selection of the Author's Work*, (1994). On Spencean poetry see M. Scrivener, *Poetry and Reform: Periodical Verse from the English Democratic Press, 1792-1824* (1992); A. Janowitz, *Lyric and Labour in the Romantic Tradition* (1998); S. K. Weiner, 'Public and private occasion in 1820s radical poetry: Paine commemorations and Davenport's *Muse's Wreath*', *Nineteenth-Century Contexts* 30: 4 (December 2008), pp. 323-42.

4 There are entries for William Benbow, Allen Davenport, George Edwards, Janet and Thomas Evans, Alexander Galloway, W. J. Oliver (Oliver the Spy), Thomas Preston, Arthur Thistlewood, James Watson, and Robert Wedderburn, plus a collective entry on the Cato Street Conspirators.

Every One's Right (to give the lecture its full title) in the library of the Newcastle Literary & Philosophical Society in 2007. It had never been catalogued and was bound into a volume of miscellanea inaccessible to general readers.[5]

Dr Gardner-Medwin's discovery prompted a useful article for the general reader in the magazine *History Today*.[6] It also gave a fillip to a campaign by the Thomas Spence Trust for a permanent memorial to him in his native Newcastle. This reached its fruition in June 2010 with the placing of a plaque recording Spence's achievements near his birthplace on the city's Quayside.[7] Another factor in raising awareness about Spence has been a lively website.[8] This indispensable resource is further evidence that Spence's life and thought have become part of the common currency of our thinking about land reform at the close of the long eighteenth century. While it is unlikely that there ever will be adequate material from which to construct a full-length biography of Thomas Spence, there is certainly scope for further and more-detailed appraisal of his life and influence. I hope that this new edition of *The People's Farm* will stimulate this.

Eighteenth-century British history is a lively field and several publications since 1988 cast further light on Spence and the development of his ideas. An insight into the society into which he was born has been offered in an important work by Kathleen Wilson, *The Sense of the People* (though his place within 'the people' as she defines them, and even more so his parents', was precarious). The cumulative portrait of Spence's mentor James Murray that emerges in her work is the best we have.[9] By demonstrating that, under Murray's leadership, anti-Catholicism on Tyneside 'was shared by men and women of all ranks', Wilson offers a powerful corrective to any tendency to regard Spence as unequivocally politically progressive. Spence supported the Newcastle Protestant Association, led by Murray, and the tenets of the petition it presented to Parliament in the year of the infamous Gordon Riots, 1780.[10] This

5 It is among the last items in volume 1 of 'The Reports, Papers, Catalogues etc. of the Lit & Phil, collected by the Revd Anthony Hedley', kept in the Librarian's Room at the Society. See also A. Bonnett, 'Thomas Spence, *Property in Land Every One's Right*', *Labour History Review* 74:1 (April, 2009), pp. 134-36.

6 A. Bonnett, 'The Other Rights of Man', *History Today*, (September 2007), pp. 42-8.

7 The driving force behind the Trust, Keith Armstrong, edited two useful pamphlets to raise awareness of the life and work of Spence, *Bless'd Millennium* (2000) and *The Hive of Liberty* (2007).

8 http://www.thomas-spence-society.co.uk/

9 See also K. Wilson, *The Sense of the People: Politics, Culture and Imperialism in England, 1715-85* (1995), pp. 207-8, 273, 348-50, 354, 358-60, 366-8, 373. See J. Smith, 'James Murray (1732-1782): radical dissenter', *North East History* 32 (1988), pp. 55-79.

10 Spence's token coins included nine variants commemorating Gordon: A. W. Waters, *Notes Gleaned from Contemporary Literature, &c. Respecting the Issuers of Eighteenth Century Tokens. Struck for the County of Middlesex* (1906), p. 41.

demanded that penal laws against Roman Catholics be restored to 'preserve the succession of the illustrious House of Hanover … and to secure our civil and religious liberties'.[11] The strongly Calvinist household in which Thomas Spence was raised, and his close association in early adulthood with Murray, make his anti-Catholicism explicable. Furthermore, as Wilson reminds us, militant Protestantism of this nature, was 'bound up with arguments and fears about the nature of arbitrary power and its relationship to Catholicism that had been engraved in public consciousness for two centuries. Equally important … [it] was a vehicle for a number of dispossessed or excluded communities in Newcastle and its environs to assert their status as members of the body politic'. Among these excluded communities were both religious dissenters and Scottish immigrants, the latter a group that 'in particular retained an "outsider" status in Newcastle as in the nation more generally'.[12]

This perspective on Spence is helpful in making sense of one of the textual variations between the recently discovered 1775 lecture and his 1793 *Rights of Man* (hitherto the earliest known version).[13] In *Property in Land Every One's Right*, each parish is to maintain from its revenues a 'building, clergymen etc. for the established religion of the country'; and in a remark that suggests a definite wish to efface his dissenting Calvinist roots, Spence also proposes that, 'dissenters if they set up any other religion, must bear the expenses of it themselves'. The 1793 and subsequent editions of the lecture, however, are devoid of any mention of religious activities. Instead, precisely where the original text specified the maintenance of the established church, later versions set out proposals for the 'humane protection' of 'poor strangers' and 'people from distant countries who by sickness or other casualties should become so necessitous as to require relief'. This switch is by some way the most substantial, both spatially and ideologically, of the changes that Spence made in later life to his 1775 lecture.

Most of Spence's later amendments to the 1775 text simply refined his prose and there were only two other changes of significance. First, later versions excised the power of parishes to apply the death penalty to criminals (the implication being not that this power should be held by government nationally, but that the Spencean polity would not need capital punishment). Second, later editions substituted or supplemented the word *Parliament* with *Senate, or Congress*, *National Congress* or *house of representatives*. Overall, the changes made by Spence in the 1790s to his original 1775 text reflect a definite internationalization of his perspective,

11 Petition in the National Archives, TS 11/388, quoted by Wilson, pp. 366-7.

12 Wilson, pp. 366 and 369.

13 Bonnett, 'Thomas Spence *Property in Land Every One's Right*', p. 335; T. Spence, *The Rights of Man, as Exhibited in a Lecture Read at the Philosophical Society, in Newcastle* (1793).

but also the final emergence of a robustly independent-minded political writer. (His proposal to relieve the poverty of strangers should be seen in the context of debates around poor law reform which, while muted two decades earlier, were increasingly heated by the 1790s.) By contrast in 1775 his admittedly bold ideas for property reform nevertheless emphasized (for a combination of deeply personal as well as pragmatic and tactical reasons) that they were compatible with the central ideological tenets of Protestant England and the British State.[14]

Thomas Spence, then, was an outsider in several senses of the word and not in terms of social class alone (which is where *The People's Farm* places most emphasis). Social exclusion, however, remained the prime driver of his political philosophy and several works published since 1988 help substantiate our understanding of this. The social purpose of Spence's spelling reforms, only touched on in chapter 2, is abundantly demonstrated by Joan Beal in her study of Spence's phonetic publications. In a different way, though his specific references to Spence are sparse, Jonathan Rose has much to say concerning the general intellectual milieu from which he emerged, especially in his discussion of the influence of *Robinson Crusoe* on autodidact readers.[15]

Social purpose was also an underpinning consideration in Spence's striking choices of non-print media to disseminate his message. 'The period is distinctive in the development of a popular style of political discourse', it has been argued, '"democratical" writing is important for the way it constructs its reader, making accessible to all political issues which were customarily shrouded in a refined language which confined them to an educated elite'.[16] But as Marcus Wood has pointed out, 'Spence was a multi-media artist' who extended political discourse beyond conventional print.[17] To the characteristically blunt slogans carried by the token coinage discussed here in chapter 3, should be added the terse exclamations he literally hammered into legal and other coinage: 'SPENCE'S PLAN AND FULL BELLIES YOU ROGUES'; 'LAND IN PARTNERSHIP AND FAT BAIRNS'; 'SMALL FARMS AND LIBERTY'; 'NO LANDLORDS'.[18] Wood has also discussed how Spence produced cheap etchings developing icons and slogans from his tokens. He also argues the graffiti that Spence

14 For the centrality of Protestantism and anti-Catholicism to the emergence of the ideas about Britain and Britishness at this time see L. Colley, *Britons: Forging the Nation, 1707-1837* (1992).

15 J. Beal, *English Pronunciation in the Eighteenth Century: Thomas Spence's "Grand Repository of the English Language"* (1999); J. Rose, *The Intellectual Life of the British Working Classes* (2001), pp. 106-11.

16 M. Philp, 'The fragmented ideology of reform', in M. Philp (ed.), *The French Revolution and British Popular Politics* (1991), p. 69.

17 Marcus Wood, *Radical satire and print culture, 1790-1822* (1994), p. 76.

18 A. Judd, 'Spence's Countermarked Tokens' (first published in the *Condor Society Journal*), accessible via http://www.thomas-spence-society.co.uk/

chalked around London should not 'be written off as an impotent or small-scale operation' but constitute further evidence, alongside his poetry and lyrics, of how 'Spence constantly questioned and stretched the resources of late eighteenth-century English'.[19] Their impact is evident in a contemporary claim that, 'When Mr. Malthus published his Essay on Rent, it seems to have been partly with a view to *answer* the cry of "No Landlords," which then "stood rubric on the walls," to stand up in defense of that class, and to prove that they were not like *monopolists*'. This commentator added, 'No Landlords' did not necessarily mean, 'that there ought to be *no such thing* as rent, but rather that it ought to be equally divided among the people, according to what was called "Spence's plan."'[20]

Beyond historical writing, Spence's ideas have also become a tool to think with for some political analysts. 'The agrarian socialism of Thomas Spence', has been analysed from a libertarian perspective.[21] It has also been argued that his proposals to distribute revenues from the public ownership of land constitute 'primitive versions of citizens' dividend as espoused today'.[22] Citizens' dividend attracts contemporary scrutiny not least because of the controversial 'Permanent Fund Dividend' operated by the Alaskan state legislature, with which it has some similarities. Spence's proposals have similarly been invoked as a precursor of 'universal grants', a concept featuring in recent social philosophy and policy discussions on 'stakeholding' and 'basic income'.[23]

Clearly, understanding and appreciation of Thomas Spence has come a long way since even so empathetic an historian as E. P. Thompson could conclude that 'it is easy to see Spence ... as little more than a crank'.[24] However, *The People's Farm* is not exclusively focused on Spenceanism. Chapters 5 and 6 were especially concerned to capture radicalism's communitarian impulse. A comparative analysis of British and American radical agrarianism, and a substantial study of Owenism's Hampshire community, now explore this area in depth.[25] In particular, the 1990s saw

19 Wood, pp. 76-9, 85.

20 *An Inquiry into those Principles Respecting the Nature of Demand and the Necessity of Consumption* (1821), p. 108. 'Stood rubric on the walls' is a quotation from Alexander Pope. Malthus is also coupled with the 'Spence's Plan' graffito in *A Brief Vindication of the Principles of Mr. Malthus, in a Letter to the Author of an Article in the Quarterly Review* (1813), pp. 32-3.

21 B. Morris, *Ecology and Anarchism* (1996).

22 J. Marangos, 'Thomas Paine (1737-1809) and Thomas Spence (1750-1814) on land ownership, land taxes and the provision of citizens' dividend', *International Journal of Social Economics*, 35: 5 (2008), p. 323.

23 J. Cunliffe and G. Erreygers (eds.), *The Origins of Universal Grants. An Anthology of Historical Writings on Basic Capital and Basic Income*, (2004); J. E. King and J. Marangos, 'Two arguments for basic income: Thomas Paine (1737-1809) and Thomas Spence (1750-1814)' *History of Economic Ideas*, 14: 1 (2006), pp. 55-71.

24 E. P. Thompson, *The Making of the English Working Class*, 2nd edn (1968), p. 177.

25 J. L. Bronstein, *Land Reform and Working-Class Experience in Britain and the United States, 1800-62*

the rehabilitation of the Chartist Land Plan, to the point that in 1997 the last unmodernized cottage, complete with its canonical four acres, was rescued from redevelopment by the National Trust.[26] 'It is tempting to dismiss such projects as pastoral and nostalgic', the most authoritative survey of English history during this period comments, 'but the enthusiasm shown for these and similar schemes ... indicates how deeply felt was the desire for self-sufficiency and for independence of the business cycle'.[27] Beyond the 1840s, the radical agrarian tradition continued to have some purchase upon popular politics. (This was most evident in the Freehold Land Movement, briefly touched on in chapter 6 below.[28]) Finally, a range of recent work, on the land question and land nationalization in later nineteenth- and early twentieth-century Britain, has confirmed the continuing vitality of popular agrarian ideas.[29]

Malcolm Chase, August 2010

(1999); E. Royle, *Robert Owen and the Commencement of the Millennium: A Study of the Harmony Community* (1998).

26 Bronstein, *Land Reform*; M. Chase, '"We wish only to work for ourselves": the Chartist Land Plan', in M. Chase and I. Dyck (eds), *Living and Learning: Essays in Honour of J. F. C. Harrison*, (1996), pp. 133-48; I. Foster, *Heronsgate: Freedom, Happiness and Contentment* (1999); A. M. Hadfield, *The Chartist Land Company* (new edition 2000); A. Messner, 'Communication: land, leadership, culture and emigration: some problems in Chartist historiography', *Historical Journal* 42 (1999); D. Poole, *The Last Chartist Land Settlement: Great Dodford, 1849* (1999). See also M. Chase, '"Wholesome object lessons": the Chartist Land Plan in retrospect', *English Historical Review* vol. 118 (2003), pp. 59-85.

27 B. Hilton, *A Mad, Bad, and Dangerous People? England, 1783-1846* (2006), p. 490.

28 For a full-length study, see M. Chase, 'Out of radicalism: the mid-Victorian Freehold Land Movement', *English Historical Review* 106 (1991), pp. 319-45.

29 M. Cragoe and P. Readman (eds.), *The Land Question in Britain, 1750-1950* (2010); I. Packer, *Lloyd George, Liberalism and the Land: the Land Issue and Party Politics in England, 1906-1914* (2001), esp. pp. 1-32; P. Readman, *Land and Nation in England: Patriotism, National Identity, and the Politics of Land, 1880-1914* (2008), esp. pp. 13-39; Antony Taylor, '"Commons-Stealers", "Land-Grabbers" and "Jerry-Builders": Space, Popular Radicalism and the Politics of Public Access in London, 1848–1880', *International Review of Social History* 40 (1995), pp. 383-407; Chase, '"Wholesome object lessons".

1

Agrarianism

> Draw near if you would understand,
> The Rights of Man art in the Land,
> Let feudal Lords say all they can;
> A Nation is the People's Farm,
> They build, they plant, 'tis their strong arm,
> That till the clod, defend their clan.
>
> Broadside ballad, *The Wrongs of Man* [?1816]

In 1845 the young radical journalist George Julian Harney addressed an audience of Greenwich and Deptford Chartists at the George and Dragon, Blackheath. He was, he declared, 'a first principle man … his creed was — and Thomas Spence had taught it him — that "the Land is the people's farm", and that it belongs to the entire nation, not to individuals or classes'.[1] That Harney, speaking close to the heart of Cobbett's Great Wen, should have given the land priority in his political creed is instructive; so too is his reference, without need of any explanation, to the now somewhat unfamiliar reformer Thomas Spence (1750-1814). Unconsciously echoing the popular song which heads this chapter, Harney consciously invoked a political pedigree which, through Spence, pre-dated the French Revolution. He was one of many radical reformers who were drawn to the concept of 'the people's farm' as a means of expressing support for the redistribution of property in land. Spence himself had not used the formula, though it was anticipated in a comment, encapsulating his views, that 'The land with all its appurtenances is the natural common or estate of the inhabitants.' Thomas Evans, formerly a secretary of the London Corresponding Society and leader of Spence's followers after his death, should probably be credited with coining the felicitous phrase, perhaps in a letter to the *Independent Whig* (27 August 1815), though the *Wrongs of Man* broadside was published about the same time. The concept figured prominently in the publications of Spence's closest followers. Evans brought his own peculiar

1 *The Wrongs of Man by Feudal Landlords* [?1816]; BL Add. *MS* 27817, fo. 223; *NS*, 30 Aug. 1845.

slant:

> The territory of the nation is the people's farm, provided for them by their great Creator, who, when he sends an individual into the world, sends an equal to those already there, — a partner, — a proprietor; and whoever set themselves up to withhold, set aside, or oppose this claim, this his just system of policy, are declared enemies of God, and are not Christians.

The argument of the infidel Robert Wedderburn, on the other hand, was entirely secular, urging 'that all feudality or lordship in the soil be abolished, and the territory declared to be the people's farm; that there be no other tenure than the leasehold of the public'.[2]

Among Spence and his followers, as we shall see, a systematic argument for public ownership of the land was constructed for the first time in the early labour movement. However, as Harney's Blackheath speech indicates, the concept of the people's farm was confined neither to the immediate post-war period nor to the Spencean Philanthropists. According to the free-thinker Richard Carlile, seldom inclined to defer to the views of his radical contemporaries, 'The sentiment of Thomas Spence, that THE LAND IS THE PEOPLE'S FARM, is incontrovertible by any other argument than that of the sword.' Henry Hetherington, the important publisher of the unstamped press, 'considered that the land was the people's farm, and he was for demanding restitution from both temporal and spiritual lords'. His one-time editor Bronterre O'Brien, subsequently a leading Chartist, urged that the first responsibility of a self-governing people would be to 'make the land the inviolable property of the people … what God intended it to be — *the people's farm*'. The slogan was also employed in the *English Chartist Circular*, and by members of the breakaway 'Owenite' community at Manea Fen, Cambridgeshire. Later in the 1840s communities of the 'People's First Estate', the Chartist Land Plan, were likewise referred to as 'the People's Farm'.[3]

In itself the multiplication of these examples is of limited value. What they demonstrate, however, is the endurance of proposals for a radical redistribution of landed property within early nineteenth-century popular politics. At their historical core lay the thought of Thomas Spence. The present study is therefore concerned to a great extent with the development and influence of Spenceanism; but also, more broadly, it seeks to explore popular radical perceptions of land and property and suggest why

---

2 T. Spence, *Constitution of a Perfect Commonwealth* (2nd edn., 1798), 16; T. Evans, *Christian Policy the Salvation of the Empire* (1816), 9; *Axe Laid to the Root*, 3 (1817), 45-6

3 *Gauntlet*, 1 (10 Feb. 1833), 2; *PMG* 41 (24 Mar. 1832); *Operative*, 25 Nov. 1838; *English Chartist Circular*, 26 (1841), 104; *Working Bee*, 1/1 (20 July 1839), 2/10 (8 Aug. 1840); *NS*, 22 Aug. 1846, 14 Aug. 1847.

agrarianism is central to an understanding of the social history of the first industrial nation. It will already be apparent that the term 'agrarian' is not employed here as the inappropriate synonym for 'agricultural'; nor does 'agrarianism' signify the views of rural labour. It is rather with the industrial working class that we are concerned, and with those of their responses to economic, social, and political dislocation which sought solutions in and on the land. In contrast with America, the literature on this topic in England is not extensive.[4] This reflects the contrasting historical experiences of the two nations, and differing historiographical interests. Yet it is interesting to note how contemporary commentators not infrequently sought English antecedents for American agrarianism, 'being nothing more than English Chartism transplanted to this country'.[5] This doubtless yielded the consolation of shifting ultimate responsibility but it also recognized, however clumsily, that certain fundamental political concerns were shared by the two societies. This was not particularly through the agency of British exiles: if anything, American agrarianism became in the 1840s an exemplar for British radicalism. Rather, agrarians on both sides of the Atlantic shared a common intellectual inheritance, particularly in the thought of Harrington and Locke. They shared also the context of legal systems especially tender to private property rights in land. Paradoxically, the easy availability of land in America stimulated debate over its ownership and distribution no less than did the absence of the same in England.

The readiness of American historians to respond to agrarian issues is of course bound up with perceptions of the past. Historians of modern England have long debated 'the industrial revolution', its causes, course, and consequences. In the United States the space occupied by this debate has been filled by other problems. The tendency among English social historians until recently has been to concentrate upon those reactions to industrialization which most evidently prefigured concerns of the present. At the same time attention has been focused on those elements and personalities in politics which most obviously, or allegedly, contributed to the evolution of the modern labour movement. From this perspective the land question can seem irrelevant, and working-class absorption in it even mildly embarrassing. Yet at a time of unprecedented economic change and urban growth, attachment to 'the land' persisted among the working class, profoundly influencing the radical politics of the period. The explanation for this does not lie in nostalgia alone, nor merely in the desire to escape to

4 I have found particularly useful P. K. Conkin, *Prophets of Prosperity: America's First Political Economists* (1980), L. Marx, *The Machine in the Garden: Technology and the Pastoral Ideal in America* (1964).

5 *Washington Intelligencer*, 16 Aug. 1844, cited in H. Sperber and T. Trittschuh, *American Political Terms: An Historical Dictionary* (1962), 6.

a less disagreeable environment. Rather, agrarianism was the product of a particular perception of social and economic change, widely held during what posterity alone designated as industrial *revolution*. The popular heroic view of 'the industrial revolution' depends upon a foreshortened historical perspective: industrialization was not achieved precipitately, nor was it a straight-forward linear progression. For these reasons the economy appeared potentially more capable of accommodating the culture and values of labour than was in fact to be the case. The cognate concept of 'agricultural revolution' likewise impairs historical perception. Belief in the viability of small-scale agricultural enterprise was underpinned by the endurance of a phenomenon which contemporary 'experts' belittled and subsequent historians ignored: peasant farmers, sustained largely outside the cash nexus by agricultural undertakings in which the family as a whole was the production unit.[6]

Industrialization did not then replace the landlord with the capitalist as the object of radical scorn. Rather, it led to an enhanced awareness of how inequality in the ownership of land, 'the womb of wealth', reinforced inequalities in all other spheres of economic activity.

> We look to the possession of land by the Working Classes as the means of organising them into a perfectly distinct and wholly emancipated body … we consider that the monopoly of land is the source of every social and political evil — when we reflect that every law which 'grinds the face of the poor' has emanated from this anomalous monopoly — when it is borne in mind that our national debt, our standing army, our luscious law church, our large police force, our necessity for 'pauper'-rates, our dead weight, our civil list, our glorious rag money, our unjust laws, our game laws, our impure magistracy, our prejudiced jury system, our pampered court, and the pampered menials thereunto belonging, are one and all so many fences thrown round the poor man's inheritance.[7]

As the metaphor of enclosure so vividly suggests, land monopoly and its attendant injustices were mutually reinforcing. There is much in this demonography which links its anonymous Chartist author with the radicalism of the previous fifty years, and indeed with 'country party' ideology of the previous century. Resonant with earlier outcries against 'Old Corruption', popular politics in the 1830s and 1840s continued to rail against long-established targets: misappropriation of the land and of the wealth derived therefrom. On this simple basis it has plausibly been claimed that almost all English radicals were agrarians, tracing the root

6 On the endurance of peasantry see especially M. Reed, 'The Peasantry of 19th Century England: A Neglected Class?', *HWJ* 18 (Autumn 1984), 53-76.

7 *PMG* 148 (5 Apr. 1834); *NS*, 22 Mar. 1845.

cause of social, economic, and political injustice back to the pattern of land ownership.[8] It is less misleading, however, as well as more useful, to confine agrarianism to responses which not only saw a cause of economic and social dislocation in the land but also sought solutions on and through it. This was the customary usage among contemporaries, Thomas Paine's tract of 1797, *Agrarian Justice*, being the most obvious example. Other reformers, however, proposed considerably more far-reaching reforms than did Paine, notably the Spenceans: 'If nations wish to be happy, they must have recourse to the *earth*, the "untaxed earth": do but wed *her* and you will have a happy family, but this will never take place until there is a *radical political and agrarian reform*.' It was perhaps to counteract the reputation of Paine as a specifically agrarian reformer that Spence's most influential biographer took care to promote him as the 'author of the Spencean System, or Agrarian Equality'. Such usage can be supported by examples from outside radical politics, as the *Oxford English Dictionary* shows.[9]

It is curious that labour historians, whose particular province has been the processes of resistance and negotiation through which workers have interacted with capitalism, should so often have neglected popular agrarianism. It is odd not least because of the vigour of historical scholarship directed at 'the longest chapter in the history of democracy', from which emerged a distinctive ideology 'based upon an experience of dispossession, and focused around the "deep-rooted tradition of lost freedom and rights"'.[10] Recourse to the land was a means of resisting the imposition of increasingly capitalistic work-forms; to campaign for such access was one means by which labour sought to negotiate what shape industrializing society should assume. It will be argued in subsequent chapters that this was as logical and integral a part of popular politics as machine-breaking, trade-unionism, or the demand for universal suffrage. Yet, with certain honourable exceptions, English labour historians have paid scant attention to the agrarians. Significantly, European historians accounted for much of the early interest, reflecting, perhaps, the concern of the Second International with the agrarian question but also indicating the greater flexibility of less institutionalized approaches to labour history.[11]

8 W. Thomas, *The Philosophic Radicals: Nine Studies in Theory and Practice, 1817-1841* (1979), esp. pp. 95-6.

9 *Medusa*, 27 (21 Aug. 1819); A. Davenport, *The Life, Writings, and Principles of Thomas Spence, Author of the Spencean System, or Agrarian Equality* (1836); cf. T. Evans's *A Brief Sketch of the Life of Mr Thomas Spence, Author of the Spencean System of Agrarian Fellowship or Partnership in Land* (1821). See *OED*, s.v. 'agrarian'.

10 R. Johnson, 'Culture and the Historians', in J. Clarke *et al.*, *Working-class Culture* (1979), 55. Johnson is here quoting Dona Torr's seminal study, *Tom Mann and His Times* (1956).

11 A. Menger, *Das Recht auf den vollen Arbeiterstag in geschichtlicher Darstellung* (Stuttgart, 1891), published in English as *The Right to the Whole Produce of Labour* (1899), with an introduction by H. S.

More recently, certain studies of early nineteenth-century radical politics have included sensitive appraisals of popular agrarianism,[12] but there is still no full-length consideration of the issue. This volume is therefore concerned with those who were led from an agrarian analysis of the causes of inequality to agrarian prescriptions for them; who posited a relationship between man and soil of peculiar profundity; and who sought, through a return to the land, to negotiate the form and future of industrializing society. The volume takes its shape from the history of Spenceanism, and therefore concentrates on the period before 1840, when Spencean and similar agrarian ideas made their most vital contribution to radical politics. However, it steps into the 1840s to offer some thoughts towards understanding the Chartist Land Plan, an extraordinary phase in Chartism's history which can be fully comprehended only in terms of English radicalism's persistent agrarian theme, to which the scheme was largely heir. There is great need of a study of Chartism that will fully integrate the Land Plan with the experience of the movement generally. Such a work would need to consider the whole spectrum of Chartist thinking about property, as well as the relationship between the movement and the contemporary free trade and freehold land movements. This lies, however, beyond the scope of the present book.

Though some of the implications of 'the industrial revolution' can encumber historical understanding, the pace and consequences of economic change in the period can scarcely be belittled. The context of popular agrarianism has to be sought first at the work-place. What prompted the desire to return to labour, where, arguably, intellect and manual dexterity were at a lower premium than basic physical strength — at least relative to skilled industrial work? What was enticing about an occupation many associated with narrower horizons of education and opportunity, and with deference and subservience? It was, after all, no working-class radical but John Stuart Mill who spoke of allotments as a 'method of making people grow their own poor rate', and it was the *Communist Manifesto*, not any indigenous publication of the British labour movement, which referred scathingly to 'the idiocy of rural life'.[13] It was

---

Foxwell; G. Adler, 'Der altere englische Sozialismus und Thomas Spence', introd. to T. Spence, *Das Gemeineigentum am Boden* (1904); H. Niehuus, *Geschichte der englischen Bodenreformtheorien* (1910); F. Bachmann, *Die Agrarreform in der Chartistenbewegung* (1928).

12 e.g. E. P. Thompson, *The Making of the English Working Class* (2nd edn., 1968), 253-6; J. Saville, introd. to R. G. Gammage, *History of the Chartist Movement* (1969 edn.), 48-62; J. F. C. Harrison, *Robert Owen and the Owenites in Britain and America* (1969), *passim*; I. J. Prothero, *Artisans and Politics in Early Nineteenth Century London* (1979), *passim*; J. Epstein, *The Lion of Freedom* (1982), 249 ff.; D, Thompson, *The Chartists* (1984), 299-306.

13 J. S. Mill, cited by F. E. Green, 'The Allotment Movement', *Contemporary Review*, 114 (1918), 90; Marx-Engels, *Selected Works* (1968), 39.

certainly not from any desire to evade labour that the working class turned to agrarianism. Though belief in the almost unrestrained fertility of the soil was a feature of the agrarian response, so too was an enduring emphasis upon the productive agency of labour harnessed to the land. The almost universal espousal of spade husbandry against ploughing is one example of this. The working class were no strangers to hard work, and it was not the physical input of energy into tasks which was actually an issue. Even among a highly organized trade such as the flint-tailors, paid by the stint (or day) rather than by piecework, 'there was a stigma attached to slacking'.[14] It was rather the manner, or more precisely the form and timing, of work which was at issue in the nineteenth-century work-place. Agricultural work, under the social relations which would pertain in an agrarian polity, would offer a sense of real control over production: what was produced, when, and how. Agrarianism was centrally concerned with skill, security, independence, and status. These were perhaps the greatest constituent of working-class grievances and trade disputes, as new studies increasingly confirm.[15] So, far from being some retarded throwback to pre-industrial, 'traditional' society, agrarianism can — and indeed must — be located precisely in the experience of labour during industrialization. Neither the sometimes fragmentary nature of the evidence nor the differentiation of working people's experiences under the capitalization of industry obscures the general pattern of these years. Security was precarious, skill on the defensive, and status and independence frequently beleaguered. This was true of more than merely artisan groups. A sense of pride, indeed property, in skill extended beyond the occupations conventionally defined as skilled trades. As the compilers of an exhaustive survey of working-class autobiographers observe,

> 'Skill' here is not simply to be equated with the traditional crafts which required apprenticeship: a sense of possessing skill is found much more widely among textile workers and miners, among some domestic servants, shop assistants, and farm labourers — occupations which rank low in the hierarchy of labour. What seems important in determining satisfaction is the degree of discretion which a worker had over the task, whether he had control over the way it was carried out and responsibility for the end product.[16]

---

14 T. M. Parssinen and I. J. Prothero, 'The London Tailors' Strike of 1834 and the Collapse of the Grand National Consolidated Trades Union', *International Review of Social History*, 22 (1977), 64-107.

15 See e.g. C. Behagg, 'Custom, Class and Change: The Trade Societies of Birmingham', *Social History*, 4/3 (Oct. 1979), 455-80; D. Goodway, *London Chartism, 1838-1848* (1982); R. Price, *Masters, Unions and Men: Work Control in Building and the Rise of Labour, 1830-1914* (1980); id., 'Labour Process and Labour History', *Social History*, 8 (1982), 57-75; id., *Labour in British Society: An Interpretative Essay* (1986); Prothero, *Artisans*, esp. chs. 2 and 11; Parssinen and Prothero, 'The London Tailors' Strike'.

16 J. Burnett, D. Vincent, and D. Mayall, *The Autobiography of the Working Class: An Annotated Critical Bibliography*, i (1984), p. xxvii.

Furthermore, trade societies, the fiercest guardians of custom and practice, far from being hermetically sealed expressions of narrow particularism, 'grew directly from the pressures created by rapid industrialization. They also developed from within the working-class community, sharing its values, attitudes and above all its forms of expression.'[17] Agrarianism, then, reflects features common to occupations, and to trades organizations and the radical political movement, rather than offering evidence for a compartmentalist interpretation of labour's experiences during the period. Its endemic appeal evolved from a perceptible decline in status and security, and from the devaluation of skill.

However, these are necessary but not sufficient explanations for the agrarian strand within popular politics. Fundamental changes at the work-place were not at this point matched by comparable developments in the environment. It is a simple point, yet worth restating, that few places in early Victorian England were truly urbanized in the modern sense of the word. Even the uncompromising townscapes of London, Birmingham, or Manchester were punctured by open spaces, their centres still relatively close to the countryside that encircled them, and their streets peopled by many who were recent migrants from rural areas. 'When I was a child,' wrote Frederic Harrison of the 1830s, 'in every city of the kingdom and even in most parts of London, an easy walk would take a man into quiet fields and pure air.'[18] Extensive kinship networks in even the fastest-growing industrial centres further cushioned the impact of urban employment. Moreover, until the middle of the century the urbanization of England was achieved as much through the multiplication of towns as by substantial increases in population density. As late as 1841 the median English urban unit had a population of between only two and three thousand, while infilling and ribbon development — the principal modes of urban growth — ensured the continuing spatial proximity of town-dwellers to rural hinterlands.[19] Tramping (not common vagrancy but systematized touring in search of work, usually sponsored by a trade society) even brought workers who were born and bred in towns deep into the countryside, often introducing them to occasional fieldwork.[20] The economy too was still one which depended on industrial workers for fieldwork at harvest peak times,[21] whilst making available opportunities for

17 Behagg, 'Custom, Class and Change', p. 479.

18 F. Harrison, *Autobiographic Memoirs*, i. 4, quoted by W. E. Houghton, *The Victorian Frame of Mind 1830-1870* (1957) 79.

19 See particularly M. Anderson, *Family Structure in 19th Century Lancashire* (1971); F. Vigier, *Change and Apathy: Liverpool and Manchester During the Industrial Revolution* (1970), 16, 18, fig. 3.

20 See E. Hobsbawm, 'Tramping Artisans', in id., *Labouring Men* (1964), and R. A. Leeson, *Travelling Brothers* (1979).

21 See e. g. Reports from Assistant Hand Loom Weavers' Commissioners, *PP* 1840 (43-11), xxiii. 460-1,

dual employment, especially among domestic out-workers.[22]

Moreover, in its heyday the putting-out system was accompanied by wider social participation in the land market. Though further research is needed to establish how prevalent popular participation in the market for land was, it may be suggested that the numerous radical land societies of the 1830s and 1840s were in one sense purely the culmination of authentic tradition. 'Ever since I was eight years old', recalled a former Birmingham stockinger in the 1790s, 'I had shewn a fondness for land; often made enquiries about it; and wished to call some my own. This ardent desire after dirt never forsook me.'[23] For those without a directly personal property in the land, extensive remaining commons could still be exploited for agriculture as well as recreation. For some they represented additional income (as many as a quarter of Coventry's freemen may have directly exercised their rights in this way, with more of them nominally graziers of non-freemen's cattle) and, no less crucially, they constituted status. Even seasonal rights of grazing on Michaelmas or Lammas lands were a right of access to the land, and in effect a form of property in it.[24]

Thus, the industrial working class was rarely, if ever, totally divorced from the land; and the physical and mental world of the early nineteenth-century urban dweller was therefore fundamentally different from our own. This fact was also reflected in recreation, and there is abundant

---

536; ibid. 1840 (639), xxiv. 11; D. Bythell, *The Handloom Weavers* (1969), 59; W. Scruton, *Bradford Fifty Years Ago* (1897), 95; R. Samuel, 'Comers and Goers', in H. J. Dyos and M. Wolff (eds.), *The Victorian City* (1973) i. 134; RC Framework Knitters. appendix part : *PP* 1845 (618), xv, q. 4607; E. I. T. Collins, 'Migrant Labour in British Agriculture in the 19th Century', *EHR* 29 (1976), 38-59.

22 SC Emigration, 2nd Report, *PP* 1826-7 (237), qq. 2262-8; RC Framework Knitters, appendix, part 1, qq. 4013-15, 3233, 3239; J. Holt, *A General View of the Agriculture of the County of Lancashire* (1795), 81; R. W. Dickson, *General View of the Agriculture of Lancaster* (1815), 106 ff.; J. Aikin, *A Description of the Country from Thirty to Forty Miles around Manchester* (1795), 23, 43, 93-4; Bythell, *Handloom Weavers*, pp. 16, 45, 58-60; id., *The Sweated Trades* (1978), 70 ff., 130 ff.; H. Heaton, *The Yorkshire Woollen and Worsted Industries* (2nd edn., 1965), 290-2; W. Cunningham, *Growth of English Industry and Commerce in Modern Times* (5th edn., 1910-12), 1. 564 ff.; D. M. Smith, 'The Hatting Industry in Denton, Lancs', *Industrial Archaeology*, 3 (1966), 1-7; J. R. Wordie, 'Social Change on the Leveson-Gower Estates, 1714-1832', *EHR* 27 (1974), 601; J. M. Neeson, 'Common Right and Enclosure in 18th Century Northamptonshire', Warwick University Ph.D. thesis (1977). *passim.*

23 Aikin, *Description*, p. 23; Dickson, *General View*, pp. 107, 117; W. Radcliffe, *Origin of the New System of Manufacture* (1828), 59 ff., 67; Wordie, 'Social Change', p. 601; J. Chapman, 'Land Purchasers at Enclosure; Evidence from West Sussex', *Local Historian*, 12 (1977), 339; id., 'The Parliamentary Enclosures of West Sussex', *Southern History*, 2 (1980), 73-91; W. Hutton, *The Life of William Hutton* (1816). 107.

24 J. Prest, *The Industrial Revolution in Coventry* (1960), 21-9, 32, 39-41, 57, 76 ff.; P. Searby, *Coventry Politics in the Age of the Chartists* (1964); id., 'Chartists and Freemen in Coventry, 1838-1860', *Social History*, 2 (1977), esp. p. 777; SC Public Walks, *PP* 1833 (448), xv, qq. 164-81 (London), 599 ff. (Leeds), 782-95 (Manchester); M. Beresford, 'The Face of Leeds: 1780-1914'; in D. Fraser, (ed.), *A History of Modern Leeds* (1980), 72; H. Cunningham, *Leisure and the Industrial Revolution* (1980), 92; C. S. Davies, *A History of Macclesfield* (1961), 280-1.

documentary evidence for continuing 'rural' leisure pursuits in the towns of this period. Indeed, the concept of 'rational' recreation was partly directed against pursuits whose rural origins were unmistakable, such as cock-fighting and bull-baiting. In the 1820s open land to the east of Tottenham Court Road was a favourite resort for Londoners:

> You might see the working classes of London flocking out into the fields on a Sunday morning, or during a holiday, in their dirt and dishabille, deciding their contests and challenges by pugilistic combats. It was no uncommon thing, at that time, on taking a Sunday's walk to see about twenty such fights. Dog-fights and cock-fights were equally common.

The same area was used for duck-hunting and badger-baiting.[25] This, indeed, was part of 'the urban problem': the corollary of increasing middle-class concern at the lack of open spaces within towns was a desire to regulate usage of the spaces outside them. For example, the parliamentary Select Committee on Public Walks (1833) has been commended for its foresight in considering the provision of open spaces for urban areas; but its purpose was essentially reactionary, to reinforce the privatization of property by preventing popular leisure-time use of open adjoining urban areas, and to promote 'public' recreational spaces as a further instrument for the social control of the work-force:

> Your committee feel convinced that some Open Spaces reserved for the amusement (under due regulations to preserve order) of the humbler classes, would assist to wean them from low and debasing pleasures. … The spring to industry which occasional relaxation gives, seems quite as necessary to the poor as to the rich … Neither would your Committee forget to notice the advantages which the Public Walks (properly regulated and open to the middle and humbler classes) give to the improvement in the cleanliness, neatness, and personal appearance of those who frequent them. A man walking out with his family among his neighbours of different ranks, will naturally be desirous to be properly clothed, and that his Wife and Child should be also; but this desire duly directed and controlled, is found by experience to be of the most powerful effect in promoting Civilisation and exciting Industry.

Great emphasis was placed upon 'due regulations to preserve order', upon direction, and upon control because of the high incidence of trespass on privately owned land adjoining built-up areas:

---

25 SC Public Libraries, *PP* 1849 (655), xviii, q. 2782; SC Education, *PP* 1835 (465), vii, qi 804; SC Public Walks, q. 100. In the 1850s the Birmingham wakes calendar was still 'suggestive of a traditional, harvest orientated pattern': D. A. Reid, 'Interpreting the Festival Calendar', in R. D. Storch (ed.), *Popular Culture and Custom in Nineteenth-century England* (1982), 133.

> In the neighbourhood of many large towns it is shown in evidence that much damage is done by trespass on the fields adjoining footpaths, owing to the people having no other spot to which they can resort, and the damage is continually increasing as the population are more confined.[26]

Among the evidence laid before the Committee of this kind of behaviour were accounts of East Enders bathing in the canal east of Limehouse and the River Lea; of the working classes 'very frequently' trespassing on the fields around Birmingham; of 'considerable damage' done in this way on land at Bradford; and of the immense popularity of walking the footpaths near Blackburn. Evidence was also advanced of similar 'nuisances' in Bolton, Leeds, Walsall, and Manchester. William Cooke Taylor, in his *Notes of a Tour in the Manufacturing Districts*, commented: 'It is quite enough to say that a "Foot-path Protection Society" exists in Manchester: the necessity for such an institution at once establishes not merely the want of sympathy for the pleasures of the poor, but something like a determination to deprive them of their pleasures by robbery and usurpation.' Complaints were likewise voiced to the 1842 Enquiry into the Sanitary Condition of the Labouring Population,[27] and to the 1844 Select Committee on the Inclosure of Commons. Particularly interesting is the evidence from Nottingham given by a civil engineer, who opined 'that the want of inclosure is in every case detrimental'. On Lammas lands adjacent to the town it was not just popular recreations which were offensive (cricket was specified), nor mainly the commoners' tenacity in exploiting the economic benefits of their seasonal rights. Rather it was the very fact of there being common rights at all, and the manner in which those who enjoyed them chose to exercise them, which offended notions of *private* property. Asked 'Do you think that the present state of the common lands in the neighbourhood of Nottingham has an effect upon the morals of the parties living there?', the respondent replied:

> A very prejudicial effect certainly … It occasions very great disrespect to the laws of the country generally; as an instance, I may say, that when the day upon which the lands become commonable arrives, which, with respect to a considerable portion is the 12th of August, the population issue out, destroy the fences, tear down the gates, and commit a great many other lawless acts which they certainly have a right to do, in respect of the right of common to which they are entitled.[28]

---

26 SC Public Walks, pp. 8-9; W. Ashworth, *Genesis of Modern British Town Planning* (1954), 110.

27 SC Public Walks, qq. 113, 322, 374-7, 599 ff., 647-9, 684-7, 705, 722, 782-95; W. C. Taylor, *Notes of a Tour in the Manufacturing Districts of Lancashire* (1841), 133; *Enquiry into the Sanitary Condition of the Labouring Population* (1842), 275-8.

28 SC Commons' inclosure, *PP* 1844 (583), v, qq. 3199, 3203 ff.

This unconsciously ironic emphasis on allegedly 'lawless acts' perpetrated by those to whom is conceded a right to commit them underlines how notions of private possession had yet to eclipse those of commonable ownership in popular understanding — not only of property law, but of the very meaning of the term 'property' itself. Vestigial, but none the less real, communality in land considerably influenced popular radical thinking. Arguably, the use of unenclosed land for recreational purposes was as significant in this respect as was its use for agriculture.

Official endeavour, locally and centrally, could not succeed totally in enclosing popular recreation. Established habits and cultural preferences died hard; the continual appeal of whippets and greyhounds to working-class dog-fanciers was a residual reflection of the popularity of rabbiting. Like ferreting for rats (a pastime of unquestionable utility in the nineteenth-century town), hunting rabbits continued wherever the opportunity persisted. It was one way in which 'rural' recreation would contribute to urban subsistence. Brewing with nettles and dandelions, fishing, blackberrying, and mushroom-gathering were others. A useful recourse in periods of acute distress, rural recreations could always support living standards and should be seen in the context of diets in which meat was a relative rarity and food often adulterated. Continued access to the countryside was hence an important element in workers' attempts to retain control over their environment and general quality of life. Those familiar features of the modern townscape, allotments, are another facet of this aspect of the rural residuum. So too were the oft-deplored urban pig-sties of the nineteenth century. Keeping them was a practice by no means confined, as was often suggested, to Irish immigrants. For example, in addition to his success as a radical journalist and politician, the Huddersfield Chartist Joshua Hobson (a joiner by trade) achieved modest local fame as a breeder of prize pigs: his 1847 sow weighed in at over 41 stones. It is almost impossible to assess how many strove to emulate such achievements, though a figure of 9 per cent has been suggested as the proportion of West Bromwich families keeping pigs in 1837. Allotment cultivation, pig-keeping, hen-raising, or pigeon-fancying offered absorbing, cheap, and even profitable recreation. Not only the environment but the nature of the tasks involved (especially the absence of supervision) contrasted agreeably with the industrial work-place. There was space too for the competitiveness of sport without its intense physical input. Both leisure and table were enhanced, and generations of urban children continued to grow up in closer proximity to raw nature than is now the case.[29]

29 S. Chadwick, *'A Bold and Faithful Journalist', Joshua Hobson, 1810-1876* (1976), 46; J. Benson, *The Penny Capitalists: A Study of Nineteenth Century Working Class Entrepreneurs* (1983), 22 f., 28 ff.

In many respects the ways in which 'the land' impinged on the working class may seem mundane, but the fabric of this popular culture contained much that was ostensibly mundane, an urban weft woven to a rural warp. This was the cultural context of popular agrarianism. From time immemorial the vast majority of the common people had been rural workers. It is understandable, then, that even those deviating from this pattern should have retained so much that was involved with the values and habits of the countryside. For such people 'Nature' retained a profound meaning, not sentimental or Arcadian in character, but ingrained, realistic, and born of continuing proximity (spatial and psychological) to the land. Virtually the only consistent element in the long and varied career of William Cobbett was his attachment to, and concern with, the land — a clue, surely, to his immense popularity as well as an indication of his acute awareness of his audience's situation and interests. It can be detected at its strongest (yet most elusive) in folk remedies, herbalism, homoeopathy, nature superstitions, and arguably astrology. John Wesley's *Primitive Physic, or an Easy and Natural Method of Curing Most Diseases*, first published in 1747, was scarcely less popular than his hymnal, and it was the most widely circulated of this genre (at least thirty editions by 1832). Imbibing in youth the ethos of a pre-industrial natural order, even the most determined rationalist found it difficult to shake off its formative influences: 'It was many years after I came to London before I became a sceptic in ghosts,' wrote William Lovett.[30]

Similar influences permeated humour, language, and popular literature. Again, it is not to be expected that industrialization could have reversed at once the traditions of centuries, especially not an industrialization that accommodated, as Britain's did, so many continuities of culture and custom. Moreover, a powerful stimulus was derived from the trinity of the most widely read works of the time: the Authorized Version of the Bible, the Book of Common Prayer, and Bunyan's *Pilgrim's Progress*. The principal sources of imaginative literature for the common reader, all three are redolent with pastoral imagery, and thus spoke to an early nineteenth-century audience with a freshness and vitality which has only subsequently diminished. Culturally, the preference for such imagery is most clearly apparent in the working-class poetry of the time. It is obvious in the poetical works of almost all those radicals who took to verse to make private or political statements. To attack, as did the Teesside 'printer, radical and poet' Henry Heavisides, 'the strange and unnatural mania for

30 W. Lovett, *Life and Struggles of William Lovett in his Pursuit of Bread, Knowledge and Freedom* (1876), 9; J. F. C. Harrison, *The Second Coming* (1979), 52; D. Vincent, 'The Decline of the Oral Tradition in Popular Culture', in Storch (ed.), *Popular Culture and Custom*, pp. 20-47; K. Thomas, *Man and the Natural World* (1983), 85 and *passim*; on the importance of herbalism in an early 20th-cent. working-class community (Middlesbrough) see Florence Bell, *At the Works* (1907; repr. 1985), 90.

Pastoral', was not to turn one's back upon the poetry of nature.[31] Rather, the nature poetry of early nineteenth-century autodidacts, though heavily rhetorical, is on the whole refreshingly straightforward and free of the customary conceits of pastoral verse. In her study of working-class literature Dr Vicinus concludes that the function of pastoral in this context was to effect an 'escape through poetic imagination'. The result, in her opinion, was 'a poetry little attuned to working-class life'.[32] Yet it would have been remarkable if such poets had *not* exhibited a predilection for the pastoral, representing as it did a still-felt rural reality, an environment at harmony with the individual, as well as in its form and spirit a link with almost all that was read and admired in English literature. If working-class poets continued to represent nature as an escape in their work, it was chiefly because this was precisely one of the functions fulfilled by the countryside in their lives. This poetry, then, was very much attuned to one of the most cherished realities of working-class life. In the following verses by William Whitmore, a Leicester house-painter, self-educated from the age of 10, the initial theme of escape from the town is developed into a second of greater significance and sophistication: the poet belongs to the countryside, and it in turn belongs to him — a relationship very much like that of the peasant farmer, and one which (as we shall see) underlay the political preference of popular agrarianism.

To one who hath long pined, shut from the sky,
Immured amid bare walls, how full and strong
The feel of life, how wild the bounding joy,
At length, released, to roam at large among
The woods and hills, imbathed with sunshine, flowers, and song!

I come unto mine own, engirt with powers
Old as the world and man. This green expanse
Of heavenly earth with all its starry flowers,
Is my inviolable inheritance,
To share with all who will in free participance.

Mine the first-fruits of earth; these fields for me
Yield their ripe harvests. Bounteous Nature knows
No patent save the power to feel and see,
To own her joy and share the love that flows
Through all her works, in all her aspects glows.

O my co-mates and yoke-fellows come hither!
Leave sorrow and the weary town behind.
Come ye and gather, sweets before they wither,

31 H. Heavisides, *Centennial Edition of the Works of Henry Heavisides* (1895), 1, 151.

32 M. Vicinus, *The Industrial Muse* (1974), 144, 147.

> 'Drink the free air', and feel through heart and mind
> The throb of a new life, intense and unconfined![33]

Aspects of the quest for that 'new life, intense and unconfined', from the substance of the chapters that follow, beginning with the first and foremost theorist of agrarianism, Thomas Spence. Not all whose views are considered would have styled themselves, as Spence's followers did, 'agrarians': but this study is equally concerned with the agrarian ideas which were a facet of radical politics generally. Their popular appeal can be understood only in the context of the working and living environments of the period. It seemed to many that issues in contention at the work-place might be resolved through the land, the relevance of which to working-class experience was only slowly eroded by the course of industrialization.

---

33 W. Whitmore, 'Respite Hours', *Firstlings* (1852), 26-8. Biographical details from the preface to his *Gilbert Marlowe, and Other Poems* (1859), pp. iii-iv.

2

Thomas Spence: Newcastle, 1750-1787

Thomas Spence lived and died in poverty. In spite of this his life and thought are relatively well known: he attracted the attention of four contemporary biographers[1] and, though to some extent interest in him declined during the mid-Victorian period, it revived from the 1880s. Spence's legacy of ideas was disproportionate both to the size of his following and to the ephemeral nature of much of his published output. Though his work, unlike that of his contemporary Thomas Paine, went unpublished after his death, Spence's contribution to radical thought was one of substance, vitality, and longevity. From the society which took his name, the Spencean Philanthropists, there emerged, in the years following his death, a cadre of dedicated propagandists. A significant factor in ensuring that agrarianism remained high on the radical agenda in the 1820s and 1830s was the large number of Spencean members of key labour organizations, among them the London Co-operative Society, the British Association for Promoting Co-operative Knowledge, and the National Union of the Working Classes. Several Spenceans survived long enough to make their mark upon Chartism. In the absence of any reprinting of Spence's work, this transmission of his ideas through personal connections was especially important; its function is most evident, for example, in the way the young Harney was introduced to Spence's work through the latter's biographer the shoemaker Allen Davenport, a tireless agrarian campaigner. Because this, rather than the printed word, was the process by which his posthumous influence was sustained, an acquaintance with Spenceanism can sometimes only be inferred. It is known for certain, however, that Robert Owen was familiar with Spence's ideas, from his proposal to make land 'the public property of each succeeding generation' by dividing it among 'Townships or model republics. By this change, the

1 T. Evans, *A Brief Sketch of the Life of Mr Thomas Spence* (1821); E. Mackenzie, *A Descriptive and Historical Account of the Town and County of Newcastle upon Tyne* (1827), i. 399 ff., printed separately as [E. Mackenzie], *Memoir of T. Spence* (1826); A. Davenport, *The Life, Writings, and Principles of Thomas Spence* (1836); F. Place, 'Collection for a Memoir of Thomas Spence' (unpublished), BL Add. MS 27808, fos, 138 ff.

use of land will remain for ever for those born upon it, to the number that it will maintain in the highest state of comfort, when it shall be laid out and cultivated in the best manner.' Significantly for the evaluation of later awareness of Spence, Owen took for granted in his readership a knowledge of 'Spence, author of the Agrarian system' in his autobiography of 1858. He did so in a most revealing anecdote. On a mail coach journey in the early 1820s Owen struck up a conversation with a fellow passenger on the subject of his political philosophy: 'I entered fully into its principles and practices, and these we discussed with animation and interest for nearly three hours, when at last he said, I am sure you are Spence … or else Owen.'[2]

Spence's advocacy of the case for common ownership of the soil was a bench-mark to which a variety of nineteenth-century reformers referred. 'The vagaries of Spenceanism', in J. S. Mill's view, were something to avoid. For Ernest Belfort Bax they were part of socialism's central philosophical heritage; in Ebenezer Howard's view they were an early and authoritative argument in favour of municipal ownership of land. In the 1880s, as interest in both land nationalization and socialism gathered momentum, H. M. Hyndman's discovery of Spence (through the British Museum Reading Room) was particularly significant. At the insistence of Henry George he reprinted Spence's 'practical and thoroughly English proposal for the nationalization of the land'. It was the first republication of his work in over sixty years, and was later followed by further editions issued by the English Land Restoration League and the Independent Labour Party. Subsequently Max Beer confirmed Spence's place in the history of land reform, not only in his *History of British Socialism* (1919) but in *Pioneers of Land Reform* (1920), an expansion of the assessment he had made there of the agrarian writings of Spence and two of his contemporaries, Paine and William Ogilvie.[3]

For the historian this late nineteenth-century renaissance of interest in Spence is problematic; our view of Spence has come dangerously close to being refracted solely through the prism of land nationalization — a concept Spence, with his suspicion of centralized authority and at times almost anarchical leanings, would have had some trouble comprehending. It is interesting to note that among earlier historians G. D. H. Cole, with

2 R. Owen, *The Revolution in the Mind and Practice of the Human Race* (1849), 121; id., *The Life of Robert Owen, Written by Himself* (1856), i. 227, 389.

3 J. S. Mill, in *Tait's Edinburgh Magazine*, 3 (1833) 352; for Bax see S. Pierson, *Marxism and the Origins of British Socialism* (1973), 91; E. Howard, *Garden Cities of Tomorrow* (1902; 1st edn. 1898), 106-9; H. M. Hyndman, *The Nationalisation of the Land in 1775 and 1882* (1882); H. George, 'Science of Political Economy', in *Complete Works*, vi (1904), 185; F. Verinder, *Land for the Landless* (English Land Restoration League, 1896); J. M. Davidson, *Concerning Four Precursors of Henry George and the Single Tax* (*Labour Leader*, 1900); M. Beer, *A History of British Socialism*, i (1919), 106-9; id. *The Pioneers of Land Reform* (1920).

little interest himself in land reform, and writing at a time when its political momentum had subsided, concluded that Spence had 'little practical bearing on the contemporary development' of radical politics.[4] Some recent commentators have come to the same conclusion, albeit for different reasons.[5] For it is not just the whig interpretation of labour history which has impaired understanding of Spence. The fact that his followers plausibly constituted 'the revolutionary party' in London in the years 1816-20 has caused their activities in other spheres to be obscured, and the resilience of Spencean ideas in the period after Cato Street (1820) to be overlooked. Inevitably this has distorted understanding of Spence himself. A further disabling factor has been an unwillingness to accept on their own terms his apparent idiosyncrasies of language and behaviour. These are all points to which the present study will return: in the next chapter particularly with reference to Spence's millenarianism, and subsequently in analysing early nineteenth-century agrarianism and the place of Spenceanism within it. This chapter focuses upon the core of Spence's political views and their derivation.

A brief biographical résumé may first be helpful.[6] One of nineteen children, he was born in 1750 of Scottish parents in Newcastle upon Tyne; his father was a pious Aberdonian net-maker and his mother a stockinger, originally from Orkney. Thomas grew up in a domestic environment saturated with the biblical fundamentalism of Scottish Calvinism. With a few exceptions details of his education are obscure; by 1775, however, he was a member of the Philosophical Society of the day in Newcastle, to whom he read a paper in November of that year. In it he outlined his view of the injustice of existing property relations and made proposals for their improvement, which he would advocate consistently thereafter until his death. The paper met with a hostile reception, which increased when the author had it published.[7] Spence was expelled from the Society but

4 T. M. Parssinen, 'Thomas Spence and the Origins of English Land Nationalisation', *Journal of the History of Ideas*, 34 (1973), 135-41; G. D. H. Cole, *A History of Socialist Thought*, i. (1953; new edn. 1977), 25.

5 T. M. Parssinen, 'Thomas Spence', in J. O. Baylen and N. J. Gossman (eds.), *Biographical Dictionary of Modern British Radicals* (1979), i. 458; T. R. Knox, 'Thomas Spence: The Trumpet of Jubilee', *Past and Present*, 76 (1977), 75.

6 See O. D. Rudkin, *Thomas Spence and his Connections* (1927; repr. 1966); P. M. Kemp-Ashraf, *Life and Times of Thomas Spence* (1984); H. T. Dickinson, *Political Works of Thomas Spence* (1982); G. I. Gallop (ed.), *Pigs' Meat* (1982); also Parssinen, 'Thomas Spence', in *Biographical Dictionary*; Knox, 'Thomas Spence'; and M. S. Chase 'Thomas Spence', in J. Bellamy and J. Saville (eds.), *Dictionary of Labour Biography*, viii (1987).

7 This edition does not survive. The authors claim that it was published is substantiated by his Newcastle biographer Mackenzie, who adds that it was printed 'in the manner of a halfpenny ballad and ... hawked about the streets' (*Memoir*, p. 5). Its title is unclear: Davenport, *Life, Writings, and Principles*, p. 3 (followed by Rudkin, *Spence*, p. 42) quoted it as being 'On the mode of Administering the Landed Estate of the Nation as a Joint-Stock Property, in Parochial Partnerships by dividing the Rent', but this is a

remained on Tyneside, where he worked as a schoolmaster, publishing proposals for the reform of the alphabet into phonetic characters, a dictionary using these, and a political allegory developing ideas from his lecture, based on Defoe's *Robinson Crusoe*.

In December 1787 (or early the following year) Spence moved to London. This seems partly to have been prompted by financial considerations, but probably no less important was his failure to make significant headway as a reformer in Newcastle. His early years in London passed in poverty, and he was mainly dependent on casual earnings as a printer's deliveryman; but by the winter of 1792 at the latest Spence had taken a stall at the corner of Chancery Lane and Holborn selling books and saloop, a cocoa-like beverage made from powdered sassafras bark. Here his customers included the young Francis Place. His stock presumably included some of the popular religious ephemera circulating at the time; it also included works by the radical dissenter Richard Price, Thomas Paine, London Corresponding Society publications, and his own work, notably a third edition of the 1775 lecture published under the title *Rights of Man*. No copy of this edition survives, but Place includes it among an otherwise verifiable list of Spence's publications, and it was a work of that title by him that agents of John Reeves's Loyal Association purchased from Spence under the impression that it was Thomas Paine's work of the same name. This was on 6 December 1792. Four days later Bow Street Runners did buy Paine's *Rights of Man*, but at his subsequent trial Spence was acquitted of selling seditious material. Meanwhile, though, he was subjected to verbal and physical abuse at his stall, and on Christmas Eve was served with an eviction notice.[8]

Despite this setback, Spence was very shortly able to resume trading in permanent premises at No. 8, Little Turnstile, an alley connecting Lincoln's Inn Fields to High Holborn. He was by now well integrated into London radicalism, apparently the leader of Division no. 30 of the London Corresponding Society.[9] His position within the Society, combined with the modest fame that attended his arrest twice in December the previous year, was probably the factor which most encouraged him to issue a fourth edition of his original lecture, again under the title *The Rights of Man*, together with his first venture into periodical literature, the remarkable *One*

---

direct quotation from T. Evans's *Brief Sketch of the Life of Spence*, p. 2 (used extensively by Davenport), where it is neither cited as the title nor capitalized. The terminology, moreover, is Evans's. The lecture was subsequently republished by Spence under the following titles: *Poor Man's Advocate* (1779), of which no copy survives; *Rights of Man* (1792), of which no copy survives; *Rights of Man* (1793); 'The Lecture ...', in *Pigs' Meat*, iii (1796), 220-41; *Meridian Sun of Liberty* (1796).

8 BL Add. MS 27808 fos. 152, 174; the December 1792 débâcle is fully described by Spence in *The Case of Thomas Spence, Bookseller* (1792; 2nd edn. 1793).

9 List of members of LCS Division 30, 'No. 1, Thomas Spence Bookseller No. 8 Little Turnstile Holborn', PRO PC 1/23/A38 (n.d., but similar lists for other divisions dated 1792-4).

Pennyworth of Pigs' Meat, issued in weekly parts, 1793-5, and twice reprinted. To judge from the account of his brush with the Loyal Association and Bow Street runners, Spence had started compiling this late in 1792.[10]

The next dramatic incident in Spence's life, and the last before his writings assume an overtly millenarian character, was his arrest in May 1794 and examination before the Privy Council on suspicion of high treason. There was, of course, a general internment of prominent radicals in that year and it was not unexpected that Spence should be arrested; but he was arraigned specifically in connection with a shadowy radical military group, the Lambeth Loyal Association. It is not clear whether Spence was a member, but he allowed it to meet for armed drilling on his premises. The Government, unable to prove a general conspiracy in England, used the Loyal Association to embarrass the defence of Thomas Hardy, secretary of the LCS. An indictment against Spence was prepared in the expectation that his conviction would be secured with ease once Hardy had been convicted. This plan was frustrated when Thomas Hardy was acquitted and proceedings against Spence were pursued no further.[11]

Involvement in London radicalism during 1794 appears to have prompted Spence to make his first substantial re-evaluation of his proposals, or more precisely of the method by which they were to be put into effect. From the *End of Oppression*, first published anonymously the following year, until his death, Spence's writings explicitly conceded the possible need for physical force to assist in carrying out reform. Spence argued the need for constitutional propriety to be observed, with a committee appointed in each parish to oversee the resumption of the land by the people:

> Every Landholder should immediately, on pain of Confiscation and Imprisonment, deliver to the said parochial Committee, all Writings and Documents relating to their Estates, that they might immediately be burnt; and that they should likewise disgorge at the same time into the Hands of the said Committee, the last payments received from their tenants, in order to create a parochial Fund for immediate use, without calling upon the exhausted People.

Thus far Spence was articulating a position very like that of the moral economy of crowd action; but he then goes on to propose:

---

10 When he was searched following his arrest there were found in his pocketbook extracts from Locke, Pope, Swift, Leviticus 25, Pufendorf, and More's *Utopia*.

11 Information on the Lambeth Loyal Association contained in PRO FC 1/23/ A38; PC 2/140, pp. 169, 170, 173, 174, 177, 252, 316-18; TS 11/951, printed indictment for high treason, R. v. Spence; cf. *The Trial of Thomas Hardy*, 305-37, for Crown attempts to implicate the defendant in the activities of the Association.

> If this Proclamation was generally attended to, the business was settled at once; but if the Aristocracy arose to contend the matter, let the People be firm and desperate, destroying them Root and Branch, and strengthening their Hands by the rich Confiscations. Thus the War would be carried on at the expense of the wealthy enemy, and the Soldiers of Liberty beside the hope of sharing in the future felicity of the country, being well paid, would be steady and bold.[12]

It is not surprising that Spence should have reached such conclusions, having lived throughout the French revolutionary wars and himself expressly endorsed armed drilling by radicals by permitting regular practices at his shop. It is difficult, then, to endorse Knox's conclusion that Spence 'stopped short of violent and conspiratorial revolution. London changed neither the end nor the means. The French Revolution and metropolitan Jacobinism should, perhaps, have … yielded a mature revolutionary. But his obsession with his plan, well rooted by his middle-age, stunted Spence and produced instead a radical crank.'[13] With his continuing concern for the necessity of securing educated public opinion, and his emphatic prescription of a federal network of supervisory committees, it is true that Spence was no violent iconoclast; few, if any, revolutionary English radicals in this period were. In particular, one should underestimate neither the ubiquity of the committee structure in English radicalism at all levels nor the premium placed on education; nor should the historian overlook the vigorous and vivid dimensions millennial belief lent to radical thought. ('Crank' is an unhelpful epithet in this connection.)

Spence was again detained without trial in 1798. Yet despite these interruptions he maintained a steady output of new work, together with two further editions of the 1775 lecture, the one in *Pigs' Meat*, vol. iii, the other under the title of *The Meridian Sun of Liberty*. He was eventually brought to trial in 1801 on account of his own published opinions, the offending article being a passage from his longest work, *The Restorer of Society to its Natural State*:

> Now citizen if we really want to get rid of these evils from amongst men we must destroy not only personal and hereditary Lordship but the cause of them, which is private property in Land, for this is the pillar that supports the Temple of Aristocracy … [Landlords] are now like a Warlike Enemy quartered upon us for the purpose of raising contributions, and William the Conqueror and his Normans were fools to them in the Arts of Fleecing, therefore anything short of the total destruction of the power of these Samsons will not do … in plain English, nothing less than complete extermination of the present system

12 Spence, *End of Oppression* (1795), 7; cf. E. P. Thompson, 'The Moral Economy of the English Crowd in the Eighteenth Century', *Past and Present*, 50 (1971), 76-136.

13 Knox, 'Thomas Spence', p. 75.

> of holding land ... in the manner I propose will ever bring the World again to a state worth living in.[14]

Spence was found guilty of seditious libel and imprisoned for a year, but the trial, and his exploitation of the privileged status of legal proceedings, allowed him to reprint both his spirited defence and the offending pamphlet. This secured for him a wider following. A formal Spencean society was founded in 1811, though it had met informally for something like a decade before then. It was this society, under its new title of 'Spencean Philanthropists', which buried Thomas Spence with due ceremony after his death in September 1814.

Spence's ideas deserve careful attention; the passages already quoted convey something of their flavour. His mature political position was subtle and distinctive, and may be seen as evolving from the interplay of a number of factors. The intellectual vigour of his thought derived from the popularization of seventeenth-century and Enlightenment ideas, especially the neo-classical concept of natural law. Spence was also influenced by a radical and iconoclastic Calvinism, and its emphatic scriptural fundamentalism, although the extent of this has been overestimated. An indigenous English tradition, at once both powerful and elusive, with strong millenarian overtones can also be discerned in his thought; and unquestionably Spence's experiences in later eighteenth-century Newcastle were a crucial formative influence.

Intellectual life in Newcastle at this time greatly benefited from its Scottish connections, felt at only a short remove through its burgeoning book trade, its ministers trained over the border, and through passing travellers. Among the latter, Jean-Paul Marat paused to make a contribution to Tyneside radicalism, presenting copies of his *Chains of Slavery* (1774) to certain of the city guilds, about the time that he obtained a degree in medicine from St Andrews.[15] The Scottish connection was particularly obvious in dissenting chapel culture: Spence, himself the son of immigrant Scots, was closely connected with at least one congregation of Scottish Calvinists, a point to which we shall return.

However, there was also much indigenous to Newcastle that helped to

14 *The Restorer of Society to its Natural State* (1801), 11, 16.

15 J. Feather, *The Provincial Book Trade in Eighteenth Century England* (1985), 29, 107. There was an oral tradition in late 19th-c. Newcastle that Marat had been involved in a Philosophical Society there, presumably the one to whom Spence lectured, since the Frenchman had left the city by the time the second (and still extant) society was founded: see J. Clephan, 'Jean-Paul Marat in Newcastle', *Monthly Chronicle of North-country Lore and Legend*, 1/2 (Apr. 1887), 49-53; also H. S. Allen, 'Jean-Paul Marat, MD.', *Alumnus Chronicle* (St Andrews) 18 (1936), 30-9; J. Massin, *Marat* (1960), ch. 3, 'Un prophète chez les Anglais', pp. 28-43; and R. Watkinson, 'Thomas Bewick', in L. M. Munby (ed.), *The Luddites and Other Essays* (1971), 26-8.

create a lively intellectual atmosphere: its position as an important port, and the vigour of its local politics, helped by the fact that the city was a provincial capital of some eminence. It was a notable centre for publishing, supporting five newspapers and several journals during the period 1750-1800; perhaps the liveliest of these was *The Freemen's Magazine*, edited by Spence's close friend and mentor, the Scottish dissenting pastor James Murray.[16] Around the premises of Newcastle's printers, publishers, engravers, bookbinders and booksellers, there flourished an informal artisan intelligentsia, usefully portrayed in the autobiographical *Memoir* of its most notable 'graduate', Thomas Bewick. One of the focal points of this culture was the workshop of the bookbinder Gilbert Gray, where Bewick first met Spence during one of many winter evenings of convivial discussion held there.[17] Thomas Spence's reformed alphabet was, in a sense, the joint product of this informal school. Spence probably had access to Gilbert Gray's own library, and his keen appreciation of how an inability to read held back the poor is concordant with Bewick's portrait of Gray's beliefs and works. Bewick himself cut the punches for Spence's phonetic characters at the workshop of his master Ralph Beilby, who then struck the matrices from them. These types were used to print Spence's *The Grand Repository of the English Language*, his *Real Reading-made-easy*, and *A Sŭplĭmĭnt too thĭ Hĭstĭre ŏv Rŏbĭnsĭn Kruzo*. The printer and publisher of these was Thomas Saint, one of the foremost publishers of radical broadside ballads in the city.[18]

In considering how the more general environment of Newcastle influenced Spence's political thought, it is necessary to make the imaginative leap back to a society in which urbanization and industrialization were essentially modest in scale. This is particularly important in the case of Thomas Spence, for it remains doubtful whether his thirty-eight years on Tyneside, thriving commercial centre though Newcastle was, could ever have provided him with experience of the industrialized society only then beginning to emerge in the Midlands and North. The fusion of town and country, noted in the previous chapter, was therefore very much part of Spence's formative environment. This had two important consequences, the second of which, as we shall later see, was

16 Rudkin, *Spence*, p. 13; *The Freemen's Magazine: Or, the Constitutional Repository, Containing, A Free Debate Concerning the Cause of Liberty* (1774).

17 T. Bewick, *A Memoir of Thomas Bewick, Written by Himself*, (ed. I. Bain 1979), 43-5, 52-3. See also Watkinson, 'Thomas Bewick', pp. 11-32.

18 Bewick, Memoir, pp. 44, 53; T. Spence, *The Grand Repository of the English Language* (1775); *Real Reading-made-easy* (1782); *A Sŭplĭmĭnt too thĭ Hĭstĭre ŏv Rŏbĭnsĭn Kruzo* (1782); there was probably a fourth publication concerning Spence's alphabet, a periodical *Repository of Common Sense and Innocent Amusement* advertised in *The Grand Repository*, though no copy is extant. Saint, the publisher of all Spence's Newcastle works, seems himself to have been a radical: the singing of his broadside ballads was suppressed by a sensitive Newcastle magistracy; see Bewick, *Memoirs*, p. 41.

that the experience of London had a fundamental effect on him; firstly, however, the barrier between town and country being virtually negligible, Spence did not perceive it as inimical to his 'Plan for Parochial Partnership in the Land … the only effectual Remedy for the Distress and Oppression of the People'.[19] This is evident in the *Supplement to the History of Robinson Crusoe* (1782), where Spence elaborated his proposals through the time-honoured medium of a Utopian travelogue. The principal town of Crusonia shares more similarities with eighteenth-century Newcastle than coincidence can adequately explain, but under the Spencean polity its residents share the rents of the land with their rural neighbours:

> This Town is built on each side of a commodious Harbour, a considerable River falls into it, and at the upper End of the Harbour, there is a most elegant Bridge. The Town extends about a Mile on each Side along the Shore, and about half a Mile outward towards the Country, and contains about fifty thousand Inhabitants. Four Parishes meet and have their Churches in it, two on each Side, whose Steeples are very magnificent, and a great Ornament to the Town. It is full of superb and well furnished Shops, and has every Appearance of Grandeur, Opulence, and Convenience, one can conceive to be in a large Place, flourishing with Trade and Manufactures.

The fusion of rural and urban landscape is underlined in the author's observation that the one is 'properly a Continuation of [the] Gardens and Orchards' of the other.[20]

Spence did not venture detailed proposals for reform in the ownership of non-agricultural production, doubtless because of his limited experience of industrialism. Spenceanism was not, however, an ideology of mere pastoral simplicity: a continuing role for non-agricultural economic activity is anticipated even in Spence's allegorical Utopias. Significantly, the one form of large-scale industrial production with which Spence, as a Tynesider, was familiar, namely mining, appears to have been accommodated explicitly within the scheme of his proposed land reforms. It is also implied that the organization of production in other non-agricultural activities could be similarly reformed:

> You know that all things which cannot be divided justly among a number of proprietors can yet be enjoyed with the nicest exactness in partnership. As for instance, shipping, collieries, mines, and many other great concerns.[21]

19 The title of a handbill issued in 1816 by the Society of Spencean Philanthropists, BL Add. MS 27809, fo. 93.

20 T. Spence, *Supplement to the History of Robinson Crusoe* (1782), 10-11, 19-20.

21 'A Dream', in *Spence's Songs*, iii [?1811], 3.

It is worthwhile to dwell for a moment on this passage, from an allegory called 'A Dream'. As the only explicit statement of Spence's views on the ownership of the means of industrial production, it has had to bear much analytical weight, as it does in the most recent biography, which is anxious to fit its subject into an apostolic succession of socialist thinkers.[22] Two bibliographical points may be in order here. First, the passage may not be by Spence: there is nothing else by him in the publication from which it is taken. Second, the conventional dating of its publication, 1807, is unacceptable, given that every surviving copy is printed on paper watermarked 1811: this clearly increases the chances of it post-dating Spence's death. Against this it can be argued plausibly that its small jobbing printer was unlikely to carry large stocks of paper, making publication within a year or so after 1811 likely. More pertinently, Spence's Newcastle-published *Robinson Crusoe* allegory (1782) hints at arrangements similar to those in the later publication: 'The parish treasuries are supplied … by the rate they lay upon the houses, lands, mines, etc.' If Spence is to be held up as an innovative critic of industrial capitalism, much depends on the interpretation of 'etc.', in this passage, and of 'many other Great Concerns' in the later work. If Spence did write the latter, it is also surely not without significance that he did so towards the end of his life when his contacts with the working class were most extensive, and drawn from a wider spectrum of artisan trades than the highly skilled and independent bookbinders, engravers, and silversmiths of Newcastle.[23]

Yet, if the authenticity of 'A Dream' is accepted (and on balance it is likely), attention to the exact context of the oft-quoted passage makes clear its essential *agrarian* thrust, for it continues: 'Partnership in trade is now well understood. What great difficulty then would there be in a parish managing its own territory or landed property, as a joint stock in partnership?' So, far from arguing *outwards* from agrarian to industrial equality, Spence used the example of joint stockholding (familiar from shipping, mining, and commerce) to demonstrate the feasibility of communal land ownership. The passage concludes:

> If you adopt that, then will you be your own masters and landlords. And then you may return to your natural occupation of tillage, until the whole earth be as the Garden of Eden. Every land then will literally be a land flowing with milk and honey. Trade will then be genuine, unforced and natural. For none will be in trade and manufactures, but those who can live well by them, because tillage would then be open to all in the case of difficulty.

Hence, once we have stripped away an anachronistic concern with Spence

22 Kemp-Ashraf, *Life and Times*, p. 212.

23 Spence, *Supplement* (1782), 28.

as a harbinger of socialism, the essential agrarian focus of his thought becomes clearer. It is concerned not just with the reform of landed property, but with a superabundant nature and with the scale and setting of society. The notion that open access to the land was a guarantee of full employment, and could thus undermine the basis of low wages, lay at the very core of nineteenth-century popular agrarianism. 'Tillage is a trade that never fails, therefore the way to it ought to be easy to every man when all other trades fail.' The innovatory quality of Spence's thought derived principally from his identification of the ownership of land as the basis of economic and political power: 'here lies the rub, — for a mistake on this point is the rock on which all the liberties of the world have been wrecked.'[24]

Spence's preoccupation with landed property, and his creative use of analogy from contemporary commercial practice in shipping and mining, reflected his formative years in mid-eighteenth-century Northumberland. The Newcastle experience also shaped the particular reforms he proposed. The details of Spence's plan, and how it would be secured, will be considered later: it is his ideas on the mechanism of redistribution which especially reflect the years spent by him in Newcastle. Having taken the land into their joint possession, the inhabitants of each parish form themselves into a corporation: 'The public then is Lord of the Manor, and has an indefeasible right to the rents.' These are paid to the corporation by those cultivating the land. After deductions to cover the costs of government this rental income is then redistributed equally throughout the population of the parish. On his own admission, Spence formulated this proposal in the light of how a dispute over the enclosure of the Newcastle Town Moor was resolved. The Mayor and Corporation of Newcastle attempted to enclose the Town Moor in 1771, ignoring the grazing and wooding rights which the city's freemen enjoyed there. The resulting dispute was a protracted and bitter one, which did much to shape Newcastle local politics during the 1770s. Eventually the dispute was settled in favour of the freemen, who gave up their direct property rights in the Moor in return for an assured income from the rents of the enclosed area. 'Now I took a lesson from this affair', said Thomas Spence, 'which I shall never forget.'[25]

The enclosure of the Town Moor was an influential element in the formation of Spence's political thought; it was not, however, the only one. It provided a mechanism for achieving agrarian equality, but not its philosophical and historical justification. That property which the

24 'A Dream', in *Spence's Songs*, iii. 3; Spence, *The Reign Of Felicity* (1796), 6.

25 Spence, *Reign of Felicity*, p. 8; *The Important Trial* (2nd edn., 1807), 27, part of his defence speech. For the Newcastle enclosure dispute see T. R. Knox, 'Popular Politics and Provincial Radicalism: Newcastle-upon-Tyne, 1769-1785', *Albion*, 11/3 (1979), 224-41.

Newcastle freemen had in the Town Moor was essentially a private, restrictive one; by definition, non-freemen were excluded. In proposing the universal right of property in land Spence was developing ideas from two areas of Newcastle intellectual life as he experienced it: the popular enlightenment and biblical fundamentalism.

'Popular enlightenment' might seem to be both vague and voguish, but it can be employed with some precision to denote certain developments in plebeian thought and culture in this period: firstly, the popular reception of Enlightenment, and especially deistical, ideas; and secondly, the developing legacy of English seventeenth-century political thought. Thomas Spence's first and most central political statement, the lecture given at Newcastle's Philosophical Society in 1775, is wholly explicable in these terms. The centrality of millenarian ideas in Spence's thinking is therefore open to exaggeration, as is the contention that he is notable chiefly 'as one of the last of the Christian revolutionaries in the style of Winstanley or the Fifth Monarchy Men'.[26] Spence framed his initial lecture in answer to a typical philosophical enquiry: 'Whether mankind in society reap all the advantages from their natural and equal rights of property in land and liberty, which in that state they possibly may and ought to expect.'[27] The lecture of 1775 contained only one reference to God, and that ironic,[28] whilst the biblical authority which Spence would later emphasize was not Genesis but the early Hebrew republic under Moses. For Spence the original state of nature is a simple axiom:

> That property in land and liberty among men, in a state of nature, ought to be equal, few, one would fain hope, would be foolish enough to deny. Therefore, taking this to be granted, the country of any people, in their native state, is properly their common, in which each of them has an equal property, with free liberty to sustain himself and family with the animals, fruits and other products thereof.[29]

Spence's use of the idea of an original state of nature owed little to divine intervention, except in so far as it accepted uncritically Locke's proof of the equality of property in the natural state. Spence does not seem to have been greatly concerned with this issue, instead concentrating on the construction of further moral and practical arguments in favour of community of property.

Much of the distinctiveness of Spence's thought was derived not from

26 Parssinen, 'Thomas Spence', in *Biographical Dictionary*, p. 458; cf. Knox, 'Thomas Spence', p. 98.

27 Spence, 'Lecture', in M. Beer (ed.), *The Pioneers of Land Reform* (1920), 5. All further references will be to this edition.

28 Ibid. 8.

29 Spence, 'Lecture' in M, Beer (ed.), *The Pioneers of Land Reform* (1920), 5-6.

Locke but from his contemporary James Harrington, a subtler and ostensibly more unusual source of inspiration. Direct references to Harrington occur only in the writing of Spence's London years. His influence, however, is more appropriately considered as part of the ideological context in which Spence grew to political maturity. Critical opinion of Harrington has recently been significantly revised, emphasizing the longevity of his influence on English and American political thought.[30] This process, however, has yet to percolate through to the historiography of nineteenth-century English radicalism, though the indebtedness of the latter to the attitudes of the country party a century before has begun to be recognized.[31] There are indeed elements common to Spence and Harrington which should more properly be considered as the legacy of country party ideology to Spence, though their appeal may well have been reinforced by his reading of Harrington. The right, indeed the obligation, of all Spensonian citizens to bear arms is one example. It is part of the very basis of the Spensonian polity: 'The general forces of the commonwealth are composed of the whole people ... All the Spensonians are soldiers; they are all exercised in the use of arms.' The bearing of arms is an essential element in the assertion of political responsibility in Harrington's *Oceana*, in Spensonia, and in English radicalism generally. 'It was delightful to behold so many thousand citizen soldiers in arms only of defence; an army of "men, who their duties know, and know their rights; and, knowing, dare maintain".'[32]

Radical and country party ideology shared too a profound suspicion of wealth, corruption, and luxury. There are points in Spence's writing where one senses a call to flee from commerce and Whiggery: 'Good God! Is there to be no end or stop to this traffic? Must nothing be held sacred from commerce? No! It seems not. But in order to give full scope to the speculations of these people of property, all bounds must be thrown down and every thing must be vendible.' What particularly links Spence's thought to Harrington's here is a concern to isolate property in land as the key to political power, and therefore the one element in which trade should be forbidden. The distribution of landed property, rather than political

30 See esp. J. G. A. Pocock, *The Machiavellian Moment: Florentine Political Thought and the Atlantic Republican Tradition* (1975); id., *Politics, Language, and Time* (1971), ch, 4; id., *Virtue, Commerce, and History: Essays on Political Thought and History, Chiefly in the Eighteenth Century* (1985); I. Hampsher-Monk, 'Civic Humanism and Parliamentary Reform: The Case of the Society of the Friends of the People', *Journal of British Studies*, 18 (1979), 70-89. However, see also I. Kramnick's critique, 'Republican Revisionism Revisited', *American Historical Review*, 87/3 (1982), 629-64.

31 G. S. Jones, 'Rethinking Chartism', in *Languages of Class: Studies in English Working Class History, 1832-1982* (1983), esp. pp. 102-3.

32 Spence, *Second Edition. A Receipt to Make a Millenium or Happy World. Being Extracts from the Constitution of Spensonia* [1803], arts. 132, 134; *Supplement*, 17-19; 'Lecture', p. 14; 'A Further Account of Spensonia', in *Pigs' Meat*, ii (1795), 205.

systems, dictates the real character of a nation and its liberties. 'What does it signify whether the form of a government be monarchical or republican while estates can be acquired?' A democracy of landholders, on the other hand, maintains a self-stabilizing balance: 'after this empire of right and reason is thus established, it will stand for ever. Force and corruption attempting its downfall, shall equally be baffled, and all other nations struck with wonder and admiration at its happiness and stability.'[33] To this end Spence and Harrington confidently shared a belief that landed property was capable of a meaningful and enduring redistribution. Likewise, they were dismissive of the claims of mobile property to form the basis of political citizenship or national fortune or stability. The terms in which this belief was expressed by Spence suggest a close acquaintance with Harrington's work. Both objected to mobile property because it *was* mobile — 'Lightly come, lightly go' in Harrington's phrase; or, according to Spence, 'of a fluctuating and evaporating nature … apt like the moisture of the earth, to take wings and fly away'.[34]

Spence seems to have felt a special affinity with Harrington, whom he quotes in his works more frequently than any other author. He chose, at his trial in 1801, to read out lengthy extracts from the *Examination of James Harrington, Taken in the Tower of London by the Earl of Lauderdale* and from the same author's *Prerogatives of Popular Government*. The very titles of the allegorical societies the two thinkers conjured up are resonant: Oceana and Crusonia/Spensonia. Significantly, Spence avoided models which mirrored the more nearly contemporary allegories of Jonathan Swift. Furthermore, Spence followed Harrington in the creation of lengthy model constitutions ('Orders' in Oceana), though for the late eighteenth-century republican the French Constitution of 1793 was also a powerful exemplar. Generally, as one seeks out affinities between Spence and Harrington, it is the purpose and character of their agrarian reforms which arguably are most significant; and they are an element which clearly links Spence's thought with the wider Atlantic republican tradition. Radical agrarianism was not a crude attempt to escape back to nature. The state of nature to which Spenceanism aspired was not that of John Locke, nor was it an Arcadian wilderness. Rather, it was an economic and social democracy, in which an active civic life was made possible for all: 'Thus each parish is a little polished Athens.'[35]

Spence's case for agrarian equality rested upon two pillars. On the one hand (after Harrington), it is the guarantee of political liberty. On the other (after Locke), it is the concomitant of the equality of property enjoyed in

33 Spence, *Restorer*, 6; 'Lecture', p. 16.

34 Harrington, *Prerogatives of Popular Government* (1658), in *The Political Works of James Harrington*, ed. J. G. A. Pocock (1977), 405; Spence, *The Reign of Felicity* (1796), 10.

35 *Important Trial* (2nd edn., 1807), 64-6; *Supplement*, p. 30.

the state of nature. Spence argued the case for agrarian equality in a series of logical deductions. If 'the country of any people, in a native state, is properly their common' (an echo of the Newcastle Town Moor here), then they jointly reap its fruits and advantages, 'For upon what must they live if not upon the productions of the country in which they reside? Surely to deny them that right is in effect denying them a right to live.' It follows from this that one generation cannot, through a personal appropriation of the land, deny to those that come after them the selfsame right that they had themselves enjoyed: 'For the right to deprive anything of the means of living, supposes a right to deprive it of life; and this right ancestors are not supposed to have over their posterity.'[36] It is here that Spence breaks free from the Lockian schema, and it is here that the radical thrust of his philosophy lies: the denial that time conferred innocence upon private property in land. Later, Spence supplemented this argument from the inalienable right to life with a specific rejection of any concept of social contract:

> I enquired whether men left that rude state voluntarily for greater comforts in a state of civilisation, or whether they were conquered, and compelled into it for the benefit of their conquerors. My experience led me to conclude the latter, for I could observe nothing like the effects of a social compact, wherefore I concluded that our boasted civilisation is founded alone on conquest.[37]

Whether the initiation of private property in land was peaceable or won by force, therefore, Spence was covered by one of two arguments. Both concluded that no generation could arrange a private distribution of landed property that was in any way binding on another. Spence, therefore, was formulating a critique of private property that was qualitatively different from the customary radical attack on property for its tendency to induce effeminate and corrupting luxury or to cause owners to abrogate their reciprocal obligations to society at large. Similarly, his case for the overthrow of private property in land rested on a relatively sophisticated philosophical basis rather than crude anti-landlordism; nor was it necessary for him to invoke any right of just resistance based on constitutional or scriptural authorities:

> Let it be supposed, then, that the whole people in some country, after much reasoning and deliberation, should conclude that every man has an equal property in the land in the neighbourhood where he resides. They therefore resolve that if they live in society together, it shall only be with a view that every one may reap all the benefits from their

36 Spence, 'Lecture', pp. 5-6.

37 Spence, *Rights of Man* (1793), 34. The material appended to this edition of the 1775 lecture is the nearest Spence left to an autobiography.

> natural rights and privileges possible. ... Therefore a day [is] appointed on which the inhabitants of each parish meet, in their respective parishes, to take their long-lost rights into possession ...[38]

Spence's position was not one that held all property to be theft; on the contrary, he permitted the accumulation of property in chattels as a necessary inducement to industry. Effectively, he proposed a return to Lockian principles and in doing so deployed a concept of property very similar to Locke's own. Property is an extension of the person, and Spence follows Locke in using the term to embrace selfhood: 'there is no living but on land and its productions, consequently, *what we cannot live without we have the same property in as our lives*'.[39] It is this right to one's life which is for Spence the most important of all property rights, and upon which the right to property in land is contingent. For Spence, therefore, the so-called right to private property in land is not a right of property at all, but its very antithesis — a pretence and usurpation sanctioned at best only by the apathy or ignorance of the population at large as to their true rights. Hence the importance of education and discussion in preparing the way for a Spencean polity, the restoration of society to its natural state, 'That gives to all their Sum, of Property'.[40]

This is the keystone to Spence's justification for the overthrow of existing society: and it is this inalienable right of property in one's life that sanctions the unequal accumulation of chattels, for the right to them is secured by labour and industry, which are an extension of the self: 'The right of property is that which belongs to every Citizen to enjoy and dispose of according to his pleasure, his property, revenues, labour and industry.'[41] Furthermore, movable property does not confer political power; as has already been pointed out, Spence followed Harrington in believing movable property, unlike land, 'apt like the moisture of the earth, to take wings and fly away, unless restored by the showers of industry'. The argument is essentially that of Locke's labour theory of value, with the obvious and crucial Harringtonian exception that the land is inalienable.

> All Men, to Land, may lay an equal Claim;
> But Goods, and Gold, unequal Portions frame:
> The first, because, all Men on Land must live,

38 Spence, 'Lecture', p. 10.

39 Spence, 'Lecture', p. 7 (the emphasis is mine: cf. Locke, *Second Treatise of Government*, ix, para. 123, 'Lives, Liberties and Estates, which I call by the general Name, *Property*').

40 T. Spence, 'Jubilee Hymn', verse 1. The centrality of this resumption of lost property rights is emphasized in the title of Spence's most substantial work, *The Restorer of Society to its Natural State* (1801).

41 Spence, *Constitution* (1798), art. 20, repeated as art. 19 of *The Constitution of Spensonia* (1803) and *Something to the Purpose* (1803). It is also reprinted in *The Important Trial*.

> The second's the Reward Industry ought to give.[42]

Spence's attitude to movable property, therefore, was wholly in unison with the emphasis on the right to the whole produce of labour in the early radical movement. It highlights, too, a consistent theme sometimes overlooked in agrarianism, namely the extent to which it was thought compatible with continued non-agricultural activities; indeed it was held to provide a securer social and economic base for such economic pursuits. The agrarian polity made a return to the land viable, and more easily secured, for those who desired it; but agrarianism was not simply or purely a call back to the land.

Spence's views on 'the Reward Industry ought to give' must be linked to the development of a theoretical basis for the concept of the right to the whole produce of labour, one of the most obvious manifestations of the popularization of Enlightenment ideas in England. Reading Spence, however, one senses a more self-conscious participation in the 'progress of reason'. It is clear in his concern with the spread of education, which is the vehicle by which the overthrow of existing society will be achieved; it is reflected in Crusonian religious toleration, and in the codification of laws which is a central feature of Spence's London publications. The codified constitution proposed for Spensonia or the 'Perfect Commonwealth' was an avowed imitation of the French Jacobin Constitution of 1793, but 'amended, and rendered entirely conformable to the WHOLE RIGHTS OF MAN'. Spence published it six or seven times during the years 1798-1807, once in the phonetic alphabet to facilitate a wider circulation.[43]

The influence of Enlightenment ideology is also manifest in Spence's faith in reason and the idea of progress. The lecture of 1775 ends with the assured prediction

> that after this empire of right and reason is thus established, it will stand for ever. Force and corruption attempting its downfall shall equally be baffled, and all other nations, struck with wonder and admiration at its happiness and stability, shall follow the example; and thus the whole earth shall at last be happy and live like brethren.[44]

The proposal for a reformed alphabet is an example of the popularization of the Enlightenment *par excellence*:

> I only intend to free the Poor and the Stranger, the Industrious and the

---

42 Spence, *Reign of Felicity* (1796), 10; 'The Crusonian Creed on Matters of 'Property'', in *Supplement*, p. 35.

43 *Constitution* (1798), quotation from the title-page; phonetic version of the 'Constitution of Spensonia' printed as an appendix to the phonetic edition of Spence's *Important Trial* (1803), 70-92; *Something to the Purpose* [?1805]; *A Receipt to Make a Millenium or Happy World* ('4th edn.', [1803]).

44 Spence, 'Lecture', p. 16.

> Innocent from vexatious, tedious, and ridiculous Absurdities … I intend to print both Testaments, and Bibles, Prayer-books, and such other Books as my Friends, the industrious Part of Mankind require: (and why should not the circumstances and convenience of such People be studied).[45]

Spence's idea was not the device of an eccentric amateur, but 'a genuine, scientific, phonetic alphabet' which has recently attracted the serious attention of academic philologists. *The Grand Repository of the English Language* was one of the earliest English pronouncing dictionaries.[46] The phonetic alphabet further underlines the extent to which Spence was a self-conscious participant in the progress of reason and directly influenced by the dissemination of Enlightenment ideology. He supposed, somewhat naively but in a manner fully consistent with this influence, that by the application of reason he was reducing the sum of necessary knowledge to a single coherent corpus:

> When I began to Study I found every Thing erected upon certain unalterable Principles. I found every Art and Science a perfect Whole. Nothing was in Anarchy but Language and Politics: But both of these I reduced to order: The one by a New Alphabet, and the other by a New Constitution … Locke's Essay on Government and many other eminent Works as well as the Bible, have contributed to strengthen my confidence in this my Millenial form of Government … Whether we consider natural Reason … or Revelation … it is very clear that God … has given the Earth to the Children of Man: given it to Mankind in common. This Gentlemen is the Rights of Man! and upon this Rock of Nature have I built my Commonwealth, and the Gates of Hell shall not prevail against it.[47]

This is the first occasion in the present examination of Spence's political philosophy that a millenarian motif has occurred. It is important to comprehend the extent to which his thought was secular in character and derivation. The lecture of 1775, the kernel of his work, several times reprinted by him but never substantially amended, was based not upon divine, but upon natural writ.[48] This offers an important insight into

45 T. Spence, *Sŭplĭmĭnt* (1782), p. iii: this passage is transliterated into phonetic characters in the original.

46 D. Abercrombie, 'Forgotten Phoneticians' in *Studies in Phonetics and Linguistics* (1965), esp. p. 68; A. F. Shields, 'Thomas Spence and the English Language', *Transactions of the Philological Society*, 61 (1974), 33-64. *Grand Repository* was reprinted as no. 155 of the English Linguistics 1500-1800 collection of facsimile reprints, ed. R. C. Alston (1969). See also O. Smith, *Politics of Language, 1791-1819* (1984), 96-109.

47 Spence, *Important Trial*, pp. 59, 60. Spence is here quoting Locke's *Second Treatise*, v, section 25, 'Whether we consider … given it to Mankind in common'.

48 Rudkin includes an analysis of the variations in the texts of the three surviving editions of the lecture in *Spence*, pp. 250-1. They are none of them substantial variations, and none introduce any millenarian

Spence's mind and purpose, as well as into the factors which influenced them. The tendency recently has been to depreciate the influence of the secular on Spence's thought. This chapter has so far adhered to an opposing view; the derivation of Thomas Spence's political philosophy is a complex issue, however, and cannot be explained in terms of any one set of influences. This is clear if one considers the place of religious ideas in his political philosophy.

Spence grew up in a home environment unusually pious, perhaps, even by the standards of the time. Though in later life a schoolmaster, he himself apparently received no formal schooling. Instead, 'my Father used to make my brothers and me read the Bible to him while working in his Business, and at the end of every chapter encouraged us to give our opinions on what we had just read'. The Scriptures, then, dominated Spence in his formative years, but it is surely noteworthy that his father encouraged more than mere rote learning. 'By these means I acquired an early habit of reflecting on every occurrence which passed before me as well as on what I read.'[49] The influence of religious ideas on Thomas Spence, however, extended further than this, and can be traced through his association with dissenting sectarianism.

Contrary to received opinion, Spence was not a Sandemanian (Glassite), nor were his parents at any time members of that sect.[50] If the chronology offered by Mackenzie, the nineteenth-century historian of Newcastle dissent, is correct, then there was no Sandemanian congregation in the city until 1757 at the earliest. It may reasonably be assumed that the family were members of some Scottish sect before that date, but which is not known. Sometime after 1765 they joined the congregation at the High Bridge Meeting House built in that year for the Revd James Murray, who had moved south from Alnwick following a dispute with the minister there, whose assistant he had been. Spence's younger brother Jeremiah became a prominent member of Murray's congregation. Jeremiah Spence, 'a man of the most distinguished worth', led a substantial part of the High Bridge congregation to the Sandemanian chapel in Forster Street sometime after Murray's death (1782), probably in 1785, when the latter's chapel formally acceded to the Scotch Presbyterians.[51]

The formal connection between the Spence family and the

---

element into the discourse.

49 *Important Trial*, pp. 56-7; cf. *Rights of Man* (1793), 32.

50 E. P. Thompson, *The Making of the English Working Class* (2nd edn., 1968), 39; Parssinen, 'Thomas Spence and the Origins of English Land Nationalisation', p. 135; and id., 'Thomas Spence', in *Biographical Dictionary*, p. 455.

51 Mackenzie, *Newcastle*, i. 399, 'the small community has existed in this town for nearly 70 years'; on the High Bridge Meeting House, see *ibid.* 387.

Sandemanians would seem, therefore, to have been formed about a decade *after* Thomas had first published his political views, and only a couple of years before he moved south to London. Quite probably he had no part in it: his biographer Eneas Mackenzie does not mention any connection in his memoir of Spence's life, originally published as a footnote to a history of the Sandemanian congregation. The only connection, we are left to assume, was through Jeremiah. There is nothing, furthermore, in Spence's Newcastle publications that suggests distinctive piety on the part of their author, and the only reference that survives of his attendance at any religious establishment is to his frequenting the Anglican parish church of All Saints 'every Sunday morning', in 1775.[52] As a corollary to this argument, it may be pertinent to suggest that the critical reading of the Scriptures encouraged in his children by Spence senior seems incompatible with the unusually strict fundamentalism upon which contemporary observers of the Glassites commented.[53] It is this fundamentalism which has fuelled speculation upon the sources of Spence's apocalyptic thought, yet Spence's millenarian tendencies were most pronounced when he was furthest from Newcastle, and presumably free from its religious environment.

This is an important argument, relevant to more than biographical minutiae, for it helps to put into perspective the central contribution of popular enlightenment and seventeenth-century political ideas to Spence's philosophy. It also enables considerable clarification of Spence's millenarianism, as will be seen later. The argument in favour of Spence's supposed Sandemanianism rests not on any direct evidence (there is none), but on a connection easily made between the Sandemanian doctrine on property and the reformer's. It must be said in fairness that it is a plausible juxtaposition:

> The distinguishing tenet of the Sandemanians is, the perpetual obligation of every precept of the Scriptures taken in the most literal sense. This induces them to maintain such a community of goods, that every member of the church must consider his property subject to the claims of the body …[54]

Yet such comments should not be taken to indicate that the Sandemanians actually practised a form of communism. On the contrary, community of goods, like a vow of poverty, impaired the believer's capacity to fulfil the obligations of charity. Detached from pride, ambition, and avarice, the

52 Mackenzie, *Memoir*, p. 6.

53 D. Bogue and J. Bennett, *History of Dissenters*, iv. (1812), 133; J. Evans, *A Brief Sketch of the Denominations into which the Christian World is Divided* (1795), 33; Mackenzie, *Newcastle*, p. 399; W. Wilson, *History and Antiquities of Dissenting Churches* (1810), iii. 261-76.

54 Bogue and Bennett, *History of Dissenters*, p. 133.

Sandemanian was free to pursue business. This many believers successfully did, notably the music publishers Boosey, and a branch of the Sandeman family who were wine shippers. In the closed environment of Tyneside Scottish sectarianism Spence was doubtless aware of Sandemanian doctrines, and it is possible they were debated within his family about the time of Jeremiah's move from the High Bridge to the Forster Street Chapel. Certainly the brothers remained in touch after Thomas moved to London, and to judge from the token coinage the latter struck for Jeremiah, the two shared similarly radical political opinions.[55]

For all the radical implications of their beliefs (and arguably these have been overstated), the Sandemanians were politically quietist: 'they would reject from their communion all who should refuse submission to the civil government, or the conscientious payment of customs and taxes'. Christ, according to the sect's founder, John Glas,

> does not allow his subjects to disturb the kingdom of this world, by taking the sword to advance or defend his interest and kingdom in the world, but calls them to be subject to the powers that be, to pay tribute to them, to pray for them, and to lead quiet and peaceable lives in all godliness and honesty.[56]

It is clear from this, but more particularly from the later involvement of his family with the Sandemanians (an involvement in which Thomas did not share), that the radicalization of Spence in the matter of religion has to be sought elsewhere. It was the Revd James Murray, pastor of the High Bridge Meeting House which the family attended, who provided the radical religious element to complement the young Spence's discovery of Reason.

James Murray (1732-82) was a central figure in mid-eighteenth-century Newcastle politics and one of the mediators between 'the Scottish Enlightenment' (he was a graduate of Edinburgh University, 1760) and the indigenous Tyneside culture. He was the editor and publisher of the lively *Freemen's Magazine: Or, the Constitutional Repository, Containing, A Free Debate Concerning the Cause of Liberty*. A vigorous satirist, especially at the expense of the Church of England, he had to flee Newcastle for a while in 1773 to avoid arrest after preaching a series of stridently anti-Catholic sermons that implicitly endorsed violence. Possibly this incident was the origin of his persistent advocacy of the right of just

55 e.g. halfpenny token inscribed 'J. Spence * Slopseller * Newcastle', bearing on the reverse one of Thomas's political dies, 'Rouse Britannia', showing a seated Britannia and a French cap of liberty. The edge is stamped 'Spence, dealer in coins, London'. See R. Dalton and S. Hamer, *The Provincial Token Coinage of the Eighteenth Century* (1910-18), ii. 217-18.

56 Bogue and Bennett, *History of Dissenters*, p. 113; J. Glas, *Testimony of the King of Martyrs* (1727), in *The Works of John Glas*, 5 vols. (Perth, 1782), 115. (I am grateful to Geoffrey Cantor for this reference.)

resistance, the theme of a volume of sermons (published in 1781) of which Spence made much use during his London journalistic career. Murray was also the author of a pro-rebellion history of the American War of Independence. His *Sermons to Asses* (text, Judges 3: 22, 'and the dirt came out'), are thinly veiled political tracts; first published in 1768, they were reprinted with a memoir of the author by William Hone in 1817.[57]

That Murray made more than a passing impression on Spence is certain. Thomas Evans, the earliest biographer, suggested that it was Murray who persuaded Spence to publish the lecture delivered to the Philosophical Society in 1775.[58] If this is true, it would imply that Murray's influence was not decisive upon Spence, but rather that the minister took an active interest in his ideas only after they had been formulated independently. Murray was the only defender of Spence's lecture whose opposition to his expulsion is recorded. His contribution to the debate is noteworthy for employing a concept not invoked in the lecture, but upon which Spence would in time lean heavily: jubilee. Here are Murray's key questions:

> Do people ever act contrary to any divine law, when they resume their rights, and recover their property out of the hands of those who have unnaturally invaded it?
>
> Was the jewish jubilee a levelling scheme?
>
> Would it be inconvenient to the Philosophical Society to read the 25th chapter of Leviticus?[59]

Spence had based his lecture on natural, not divine, writ. He had not invoked the agrarian polity of the Old Testament Hebrews. Murray's questions underlined the possibility of achieving a synthesis of Reason and Revelation with profoundly radical implications, and in a subsequent edition of the lecture Spence included them as an appendix. However, he did not turn to the issues they raised for nearly eighteen years — except for a passing reference to jubilee in the Utopian travelogue of Lilliput appended to the *Supplement to the History of Robinson Crusoe* of 1782.[60] If Thomas Spence was 'the trumpet of jubilee', this aspect of his message was a muted one until well after Murray's death, some time after he had

---

57 J. Murray, *Lectures to Lords Spiritual* (1774); *Sermons for the General Fast Day* (1781); *An Impartial History of the Present War in America* (1778); *Sermons to Asses* (1768; 1817). Biographical details are taken from Mackenzie, *Newcastle*, p. 387, Bewick, *Memoir*, p. 77, and R. Welford, *Men of Mark 'twixt Tyne and Tweed*, iii. (1895), 212-19; the latter also contains a full bibliography of Murray's works and a list of attributions (Hone's memoir of Murray is inaccurate). It is possible that Spence may first have introduced Murray's *Sermons to Asses* to Hone: they patronized each other's bookselling businesses; see Hone to Place, 23 Sept. 1830, BL Add. MS 27808, fo. 315.

58 T. Evans, *Brief Sketch of the Life of Spence*, p. 2.

59 Spence, *Rights Of Man* (1793), 36, ff.

60 Spence, 'An History of the Rise and Progress of Learning in Lilliput', in *Supplement*, p. 47.

left Newcastle, and long after he had first ventured to promote his scheme for property reform in public. The millenarian and jubilee elements in Spence's thought emerge only after his arrival in the very different environment of London, after his first spell in prison, and (most significant of all) after the French Revolution. The chronology is instructive, and the next chapter begins by considering it.

3

Spence in London, 1788-1814

In the previous chapter Thomas Spence's political philosophy was considered within the context of the environment of his formative years: the artisan-radical milieu of late eighteenth-century Newcastle. The derivation of his ideas was examined under three headings; Newcastle influences, the popularization of Enlightenment ideas, and religion. It was suggested that the emphasis placed upon the latter as a key to understanding Spence in this period has been exaggerated. In particular his writings at this time reveal no evidence of millennial inclinations; and in conclusion it was proposed that Spence's apocalyptic vision was the product of the very different metropolitan environment in the years following the French Revolution.

The first point to be clarified is the date at which Spence moved south to London. As with his alleged membership of the Sandemanian sect, it is necessary to re-examine the received tradition concerning his life. The conventional view is that Spence left Newcastle in, or about, 1792; yet significantly, all four of his contemporary biographers are silent on the date he moved to London. In fact there is much evidence to suggest that he arrived in the capital in 1787 or 1788. For example, the minutes of the Newcastle Common Council record that Thomas Spence was dismissed from his post as under-master at St Anne's School on 17 December 1787. There is also evidence of crown currency countermarked with radical slogans by Spence, a tactic he pursued in London prior to issuing his own token coinage. All the coins that have come to light bear the date of 1787 or earlier, yet one would reasonably expect more coins of later date had Spence not commenced countermarking until 1792 or 1793.[1] Finally, and crucially, we have written evidence in a letter to Thomas Bewick from his brother John, a London wood-engraver, dated April 1788:

---

1 *Newcastle Common Council Book*, 17 Dec. 1787, cited by F. J. G. Robinson in 'Trends in Education in Northern England during the 18th Century', Newcastle University Ph.D. thesis (1972), app.; A. W. Waters, *Notes Gleaned from Contemporary Literature, etc., Respecting the Issuers of the 18th Century Tokens, Struck for the County of Middlesex* (1906), 50-2.

> Your old Friend Mr. Spence has been in Town some time, not in the most affluent circumstances you may be shure, he has frequently called upon me. I generally fild his Belly and gave him something to drink when so, [he] is as hearty as a Cracket and as full of his Coally Tyne Poetry as ever he refers people to me for his Caracture Poor Fellow and I say as much in his favour as I possible can, I spoke to Mr. Cooke, Publisher Pater Noster — roe — he has been a friend to him and Employ's him at present doing little odd jobs.[2]

The importance of determining when Spence moved to London lies in the assistance it lends in establishing more precisely the historical context of Spence's millenarianism. T. R. Knox concluded that 'London changed neither the end nor the means', whilst its author failed to mature in the radically different post-French revolutionary world.[3] This chapter argues that the experience of both metropolitan life and the French Revolution did indeed change Spence, and that this is partly reflected in the millenarian character his writings assumed after he had left Newcastle. The force of this argument rests on the proof that Spence experienced the French Revolution in London, rather than in the less heady climate of Tyneside.

Of course, Newcastle furnished Spence with a firm grounding in biblical matters and in Murray he had a friend who wrote a ponderous two-volume exegesis of the Revelation of St John the Divine (a point which Knox most surprisingly overlooks). Murray's treatment of Revelation, however, is notably restrained. He concentrates upon the first three chapters, and particularly upon Christ's 'epistles', conveyed through John to the churches of Asia: these are treated as 'practical' rather than eschatological, and Murray accordingly draws from them direct conclusions which he applies to the modern church. 'The rest of the visions in this book', he explains, 'are of the *Prophetic historical character*, and do not lead our views so much to practical points of divinity.' Not unexpectedly, given Murray's anti-Catholicism, he was more interested in Revelation as a prefigurative history of the Church of Rome, rather than as an account of the Second Coming. His comments on the millennial prophecies are in fact few, but given they agree with the views first developed by Spence in the 1790s they have a particular interest. Murray clearly equates the growth of equality with the millennium:

> Religion when it is rightly understood, and believed, makes the hope of Christians so strong, that the object thereof is, in a manner, present, and makes them actually enjoy heaven while on earth ... To see them

2 John Bewick to Thomas Bewick, 9 Apr. 1788, Hack MSS, cited in T. Bewick, *A Memoir of Thomas Bewick, Written by Himself*, ed. I. Bain (1979), 236. I am grateful to Iain Bain for giving me the full text and original orthography of this letter; also for his assurance (most helpful since the Hack MSS are not at present accessible to students) that there are no further references to Spence in the collection.

3 T. R. Knox, 'Thomas Spence: The Trumpet of Jubilee', *Past and Present*, 76 (1977), 75.

> giving and receiving, as those that belong to one family, and calling nothing their own that may do good to another, is a true image of this millenium, when there shall be but one sheepfold and one shepherd. In this millenium state of the world, there will be no need to hoard up wealth … for the holy church of Christ will take of all her children … This will be truly a golden age.[4]

Thus Spence arrived in London with an extensive knowledge of the Scriptures, having thought sufficiently highly of them to propose publishing the Bible in an edition printed according to his phonetic alphabet, and, although millenarian ideas apparently did not figure in his religious experience to any significant extent, he would doubtless have been familiar with his mentor Murray's equation of the millennium with equality. However, these were obviously not sufficient preconditions of millennial belief, no hint of which is present in his Newcastle writings. The clue to Spence's subsequent millenarianism must lie in his London experience, an experience which embraced the years of the French Revolution.[5]

All questions of religion aside, there can be little doubt of the indelible impression which the transition to metropolitan life made upon the provincial immigrant. Compared with Newcastle, in essence a county town with a harbour, the already sprawling, cosmopolitan conurbation of London must have had a profoundly disorientating effect on a man such as Thomas Spence. This contrast would have been thrown into all the more stark relief by the unaccustomed poverty and isolation in which he found himself, reduced to seeking casual employment with a printer when he had been, just a few months before, a grammar-school master. London, moreover, was an environment in which, as contemporaries noted, millenarian religious belief thrived. During the eighteenth century the capital was an important centre for Muggletonians and Swedenborgians: it was here too that the Camisards, or French prophets, came in the early years of the century and attracted an immediate following. The resilient traditions they founded resurfaced in the 1790s when new and powerful prophetic voices made themselves heard, particularly those of Richard Brothers and Joanna Southcott. For both prophets London provided a crucial element in their mission, Brothers particularly being drawn to millenarianism only after his arrival there in the late 1780s. There was an abundance of prophetical, mystical, homoeopathic, and astrological chapbooks and other ephemera for sale on the London streets, while the city — with its multi-faceted religious life — was an important centre for

4 J. Murray, *Lectures upon the Book of the Revelation of John the Divine: Containing a New Explanation of the History, Visions, and Prophesies, Contained in that Book*, 2 vols. (1778), vol. i, p, iv; vol. ii, lecture ix *passim*; quotation from ii. 362-4.

5 The proposal for a phoneticized Bible is made at the end of *Supplement*.

seekers after truth. Millenarianism prospered there: nearly a third of all known Southcottian believers, for example, lived in the capital.[6]

Thomas Spence established himself in this environment shortly before the French Revolution and the renewed incentive which it gave to millenarian sensibilities. Many 'respectable' and academic minds turned to speculation upon the date of the millennium, including that of Joseph Priestley. The French Revolution, an unprecedented upheaval involving the overthrow of both pope and princes, seemed to many a fulfilment of biblical prophecy. It is important to avoid a modern, secular, attitude when dealing with this aspect of the 1790s, and instead to seek to understand Spence's later writings in a context in which they are fully intelligible.

Spence came to an apocalyptic viewpoint later in the decade than many, but significantly his interest was sustained from 1795, when Richard Brothers's popularity was at its peak, and following a general quickening of the millenarian pulse. This was the year in which Brothers was questioned before the Privy Council on suspicion of fomenting unrest, as well as being the year in which he predicted that the millennium would commence. There is only slender evidence, however, that Spence was connected with Brothers's circle. Quite probably he knew of groups such as the Hoxton 'Ancient Deists', 'made up of Alchymists, Astrologers, Calculators, Mystics, Magnetizers, Prophets, and Projectors, of every class … it almost immediately yielded to the stronger impulse of the French Revolution.' His premises from 1801 (and maybe earlier) in Great Castle Street, near Oxford Street, were only a few yards from another deistical assembly in Margaret Street where the French Revolution produced a similar ferment. Then there were the seemingly innumerable 'Field-Disputants. These consisted of Mystics, Muggletonians, Millenaries, and a variety of eccentric characters of different denominations.' William Reid, a former infidel from whose book, *The Rise and Dissolution of the Infidel Societies*, these quotations are taken, sketched the intellectual links between infidelism, millenarianism, and radicalism, noting how 'the French system of politics insensibly attached itself to the auxiliary ideas of prophecies fulfilling on the Continent.'[7] It is likely that Spence was influenced by the same process; indeed, all the internal evidence of his later writings suggests this was so. It is evidence which clearly demonstrates the cross-fertilization of popular radical, infidel, and millenarian cultures, exemplified in Spence's associate of these years, the printer Arthur Seale. Seale, also a member of the London Corresponding Society, printed works by both Spence and Brothers. Something more than a purely business relationship is implied by Spence's consistent patronage

6 J. F. C. Harrison, *The Second Coming: Popular Millenarianism*, 1780-1850 (1979), 2-9.

7 W. Reid, *The Rise and Dissolution of the Infidel Societies in the Metropolis* (1800), 14, 19, 90-2, reprinted in V. E. Neuburg (ed.), *Literacy and Society* (1971).

of Seale over at least fourteen years and three changes of the printer's premises, and also by Francis Place having approached Seale's wife, in St Pancras Workhouse in her old age, for information about Spence.[8]

Other evidence suggests that Spence was more than just a passive observer of the growth in millenarian prophecy. For example, it is most interesting that among Spence's works at this time was a new edition of a phonetic Bible, proof-sheets of which were acquired by Place. This is the first indication of Spence's renewed interest in printing the Scriptures since the abortive proposal he made in 1782.[9] In 1795 he also published his only tract to denounce the city in moralistic terms, the usually overlooked *Letter from Ralph Hodge, to his Cousin Thomas Bull.* The latter, a village blacksmith, is rewarded by the village squire with a position in London for having informed on an enclosure riot. The moral judgements are implicit rather than explicit and the letter features a specific commentary on the state of the English countryside, unique for its author and strongly reminiscent of the later writings of Cobbett. While the pamphlet is free of any millenarian overtones, it is interesting that only in the mid-1790s was Spence moved to make any kind of denunciation of the metropolis: an echo, maybe, of Brothers's identification of London with Babylon. No less suggestive is Spence's choice of material to publish with the letter: Volney's *Ruins of Empires.* This free-thinking, deistical work was profoundly influential on English radicalism, and is evidence of Spence's burgeoning interest in religious matters. The equation it makes between the rise of despotism and the history of priestcraft is also of significance for Spence's millenarianism.[10]

8 *Restorer* (1801), 'printed by A. Seale, Fitzroy Place, New Road'; *Spence's Songs*, part ii (n.d., but part iii of the Goldsmiths' Collection's copy is watermarked 1811), 'printed by A. Seale, 16 Little Brook Street, New Road'; 'Seale and Bates, Tottenham Court Road' printed all the Society of Spencean Philanthropists' publications, Seale being a member of the group. BL Add. MS 27808, fo. 139, list of authorities consulted by Place for the proposed biography of Spence. Seale printed *Copy of a letter from Mr Brothers ... to Dr Samuel Foart Simmons, MD* (1802): see J. A. Hone, 'The Ways and Means of London Radicalism, 1796-1821', Oxford University D.Phil. thesis (1975), 73. Spence's association with Seale was probably established in the 1790s, for copies of *Pigs' Meat* (1793) were found in Seale's workshop in 1804, TS 11/939/3362.

9 BL Add. MS 27808, fo. 429. O. D. Rudkin, *Thomas Spence and his Connections* (1927; repr. 1966), 222, deduces that this was published in 1795. The printer was J. Cooke of Paternoster Row, who had first employed Spence when he arrived in London, so the phonetic Bible might in fact be earlier, for John Cooke appears to have passed the business on to his son Charles by 1790; see Ian Maxted, *The London Book Trades, 1775-1800* (1977), 50-1.

10 T. Spence, *A Letter from Ralph Hodge, to his Cousin Thomas Bull* [1795]; the pamphlet is one of the genre of rural letters favoured by radicals and their opponents. Spence had first reprinted extracts from Volney's *Ruins of Empires* in the 1793 volume of *Pigs' Meat*, which places him among the earliest popularizers of the work in England. For a brief assessment of Volney's importance for English radicalism see E. P. Thompson, *The Making of the English Working Class* (2nd edn., 1968), 107-8, 815-16, and I. Prothero, 'William Benbow and the Concept of the "General Strike"', *Past and Present*, 63 (1974), 161-2.

The extent to which millenarianism dominates Spence's thought can be, and has been, exaggerated. We have seen that his earlier Newcastle works were entirely free of it. It is tempting to conflate metaphor with method; but, on the other hand, it is all too easy to dismiss millenarian overtones in radical politics as rhetorical dressing. This broadly is the interpretation of T. M. Parssinen: 'The cry of revolution entailed a new rhetoric. Although Spence denounced religion as a "delusion", he found in his fundamentalist religious background a ready source of language to suit his purpose.' One suspects, however, that Spence's millenarianism went deeper than this: the sequence of external events and of his publications, the renewed interest in making the Scriptures easily accessible to the poor and illiterate, the insistent and even obsessive note which some of his later writings, especially the songs, reveal — all these add up to reveal a man to whom religious terminology meant more than a cynical means of self-promotion. A tendency to see Spence within the context of the development of socialist theory, as a far-sighted 'pioneer' and 'forerunner', has encouraged in historians an anachronistic disbelief that he actually *meant* what he wrote. There are, it must be conceded, some grounds for interpreting Spence's millenarianism as metaphor:

> I have all my life thought the State of Society was capable of much Amendment and hope by the Progress of Reason aided by the Art of Printing that such a State of Justice and Felicity would at length take place in the Earth as in some measure to answer the figurative descriptions of the Millenium, New Jerusalem, or future Golden Age.[11]

This was part of Spence's defence speech at his trial in 1801. In making it he may have remembered that Richard Brothers's espousal of millenarianism before the Privy Council six years previously had been rewarded with eleven years in a lunatic asylum. Spence was not afraid to be blunt about his politics even when he knew that he risked dire consequences; and he may have made a conscious decision not to appear to hide behind the character of a religious seeker. Most important of all, however, for any interpretation we might lay on this passage is the fact that among Christians and millenarians the Apocalyptic Scriptures had always been regarded as figurative to some degree. Therefore, the emphasis he placed upon human agency in securing the millennium was not incompatible with some type of millenarian belief in the divine. In his last published work, the periodical *Giant Killer*, Spence drew an important distinction. The millennium, he wrote, 'solely applies to the temporal punishment of the nations, great and small, leagued with Anti-Christ … and to the restoration of the New Jerusalem state of happiness on earth;

11 T. M. Parssinen, 'Thomas Spence and the Origins of English Land Nationalisation', *Journal of the History of Ideas*, 34 (1973), p. 139; Spence, *Important Trial*, p. 35.

and not in heaven'. But it was a time, he claimed, 'of the restoration of the Jews in common with the Christians: in the enjoyment of the *new heaven*, and the new, or renovated earth, wherein *dwelleth righteousness*, in contradistinction to the former *unrighteous* state'. In no way, he emphasized, was this interpretation a negation of the truth of 'the particular judgement of individuals', from which he was careful to distinguish it. It is pertinent at this point to draw attention to the congruence between Spencean eschatology and the views of the Philadelphian universalist Elhanan Winchester, resident in Britain from 1787 until 1794. Though, unlike Spence, he inclined heavily towards belief in Christ's preternatural intervention as securing the millennium, Winchester was insistent in distinguishing it as 'a kind of Middle State, between this present, and the final condition of the earth'. For Winchester, as for Spence, the millennium is not 'the final judgement of men'.[12]

In effect Spence was not a millenarian at all, but a millennialist and more specifically a post-millennialist. In post-millennialist eschatology the Second Coming is preceded by the millennium: this is itself the penultimate step in the culmination of God's providential plan, but one achieved through progressive human action. Pre-millennialists, on the other hand, believed the millennium was to be established by cataclysmic divine intervention. This, the millenarian position, was the dominant form of apocalyptic belief among contemporary labouring people. His belief, however, in Christ's purely spiritual millennial reign was more akin to that of 'respectable' divines, for example Joseph Priestley in his early phase of francophile millennialism and before, under the shock of French Jacobinism, he shifted to a pre-millennialist stance of passive resignation. The lack of discrimination between the various millennial themes has led to confusion over Spence's religious position. He exhibited the tone and temper of popular millenarianism certainly, but adhered to a theology that was post-millennial in character.[13]

As a post-millennialist Spence was in a position easily to equate the expected millennium with the growth of equality, a widespread idea that we have encountered in James Murray and examples of which could be duplicated from outside Spence's experience. For instance, 'A Dissenting County Attorney' wrote to Edmund Burke:

> As I am a believer in Revelation, I, of course, live in the hope of better things; a millennium (not a fifth monarchy, Sir, of enthusiasts and fanatics), but a new heaven and a new earth in which dwelleth

12 *Giant Killer*, no. 1 (6 Aug. 1814), 3-4 — copy in Place Papers, BL Add. MS 27808, fos. 287-94; E. Winchester, *A Course of Lectures in the Prophecies that Remain to be Fulfilled*, 4 vols. (1790), ii. 285.

13 This consideration of Spence's millennialism follows the distinctions suggested by Harrison, *Second Coming*, pp. 3-10, E. L. Tuveson, *Redeemer Nation* (1968), esp. pp. 32-5, and R. H. Bloch, *Visionary Republic* (1985), *passim*.

> righteousness; or, to drop the eastern figure and use a more philosophical language, a state of equal liberty and equal justice for all men.[14]

Or to take a second example, presumably known to Spence since he sold the author's works: Richard Price in his sermon on *The Evidence for a Future Period of Improvement in the State of Mankind*:

> A tide has set in. A favourable gale has sprung up. ... We see the clouds scattering. We live in happier times than our forefathers. The shades of night are departing. The day dawns; and the Sun of righteousness will soon rise with healing in his wings.[15]

In equating the millennium with the advent of liberty and equality Spence resembled respectable intellectual millennialists, but he had drunk deep at the well of popular culture, and absorbed from it much of the tone and temper of the radical millenarian tradition (the essence of which was derived from the popular sects of the English Revolution). He prefaced the 1807 edition of his *Important Trial* with verses from Isaiah 29, beginning 'And the Vision of all is become unto you as the Words of a Book that is sealed', recalling (deliberately?) the sealed prophecies of Joanna Southcott.[16] His later writings contain numerous quotations from the Old Testament, particularly descriptions of the Mosaic agrarian polity which, with their pastoral freshness, must have conveyed a far more immediate reality for Spence's contemporaries than they do now. Spence had always adhered to the historical veracity of the state of nature, and in the Hebrews under the early years of Mosaic law he believed that he had an irrefutable record of this. The Apocalyptic Scriptures now seemed to presage a no less tangible reality. Spence did not give up his vocation as 'The Restorer of Society to its Natural State', but he now added to it a compatible 'Receipt' to make a 'MILLENIUM OR HAPPY WORLD'.[17]

Of course in practice the distinction here applied to types of apocalyptic belief was not absolute. 'The insistent literalism of the pre-millennialists', Ruth Bloch has pointed out, 'constituted only an extreme version of a more general interpretative development.' Pre- and post-millennialism were not

14 *A Letter to the Right Hon. Edmund Burke, Esq., from a Dissenting County Attorney* (1791), p. 141 cited by P. H. Marshall, 'William Godwin: A Study of the Origins, Development and Influence of his Philosophy', Sussex University D.Phil. thesis (1976), 28.

15 R. Price, *The Evidence for a Future Period of Improvement in the State of Mankind* (1787), 3, 53. It is not known whether Spence sold this sermon, but he did sell the same author's *Observations on the Nature of Civil Liberty ... With the Declaration of Principles, and Regulations of the Friends of Liberty* [?1794] (Spence is one of a number of radical booksellers listed on the cover: copy in Sussex University Library).

16 *Important Trial* (1807 edn.), title-page. The verses are Isaiah 29: 11, 12, 18.

17 Spence, *A Receipt to Make a Millenium or Happy World. Being Extracts from the Constitution of Spensonia* (2nd and 4th edns., [1803]).

inflexible categories (as Priestley's case indicates); moreover, neither were contemporary terms. Spence himself demonstrates that this is a distinction that can be made absolute only in theory. Davidson has suggested that 'The boundaries of millennial thought are certainly more complicated than the traditional pre- and post-millennial classifications indicate.' Bloch's more recent study of American millennialism, however, suggests that the quickening of millennial interest across the Atlantic was followed by a division from the 1790s onwards into 'pre-' and 'post-' currents. This was for social and political reasons as much as for theological ones, as Spence and Priestley in their different ways demonstrate.[18]

It is possible to arrive at a more exact understanding of Spence's eschatological leanings by considering the place in his thought of jubilee. This Mosaic institution, referred to briefly at the close of the previous chapter, was part of the popular radical inheritance; it was especially apparent in the thought of Spence, those known to have influenced him, and in turn those influenced by him. In Spence's usage jubilee and revolution are virtually synonymous: in the 1793 edition of the original Newcastle lecture, for example, the remedy for securing the rights of man of the title is brisk and pointed: 'one hearty revolution and one jubilee will do the business for ever: for we find societies once possessed of the land do not easily give it up, but are very tenacious of their property ...'.[19] The use of jubilee and revolution as synonyms is a Spencean innovation, but the incorporation of the Levitical institution into the vocabulary of politics is not. Interestingly, it extends back beyond Spence's mentor, James Murray, to Harrington, who used it as an example of an agrarian law fixing 'the balance of the commonwealth of Israel'. Harrington's focus upon jubilee was shared by the eighteenth-century nonconformist theologian Moses Lowman, whose *Dissertation on the Civil Government of the Hebrews* (1740) analysed Mosaic Israel in the light of seventeenth-century political ideas — specifically of the civic-humanist variety. Lowman, like Harrington, characterized the jubilee as an agrarian law which, in providing for the periodic redistribution of property, ensured the equitable balance of state by preventing the concentration of property in too few hands.[20]

Occasional references to jubilee in contemporary sources indicate that it was part of the radical vocabulary;[21] but only in Spence is the term used in

18 Bloch, *Visionary Republic*, pp. 131 and 144; J. W. Davidson, *The Logic of Millennial Thought* (1977), 75.

19 Spence, *Rights Of Man* (1793), 26.

20 Harrington, *The Art of Lawgiving* (1659), bk. iii, ch. 1, in *Political Works*, ed. J. G. A. Pocock (1977), 665; M. Lowman, *Dissertation on the Civil Government of the Hebrews* (1740), esp. pp. 46-50.

21 e.g. 'Freedom's Jubilee, July 14th', untitled list of toasts (c. 1797), BL 648.C.26; 'We groan, being burdened, waiting to be delivered, but we rejoice in hopes of a Jubilee', Halifax banner inscription (1819), quoted in Thompson, *Making*, p. 760.

the sense which Harrington gave to it, a sense derived very closely from the biblical original. To Spence, however, belongs the distinction of first deploying jubilee as a synonym for revolution, often preferring the one to the other. Doubtless its very specific agrarian connotations recommended it to him; but in addition it clarified his call for the restoration of society to its natural state. By this he did not mean a return to noble savagery. The natural state of society, in Spencean theory, is any condition in which the natural right of property is upheld and guaranteed. Thus Spence pointed to the early Hebrew republic, with the Levitical law of jubilee on which its equitable functioning depended, as an example of society in a natural state: not the anarchy of Hobbes's *Leviathan*, but a self-regulating association of equals. Nor was it the Arcadian wilderness of Locke, but a constitutional republic in which an active civic life was the right, indeed obligation, of all.

Though divinely ordained, the revolutionary mechanism of jubilee is dependent entirely upon human agency. This further underlines Spence's essentially post-millennialist stance, in which a millennium secured by human action precedes the Second Coming. Thus in the 'Jubilee Hymn' (sung, with delicious irony, to the tune of 'God Save the King'):

> Hark! how the Trumpets sound,
> Proclaims the Land around,
> the Jubilee!
>
> Welcome the Day is come,
> Blessed Millenium,
> That gives to all their Sum,
> of Property![22]

The title Spence gave to the 1795 printing of this hymn makes it clear that he believed the jubilee to prefigure or commence the millennium: 'A SONG, to be sung at the End of Oppression, or the commencement of the political MILENNIUM [*sic*], when there shall be neither Lords nor Landlords, but God and Man will be all in all.'[23] Spence's concept of jubilee illuminates his notions of both millennium and revolution, emphasizing the role of human agency in securing the former, the redistribution of property necessary to the latter, and the emancipation and regeneration of society made possible through both. Spence nowhere refers to Christ's Second Coming, except, as we have seen, by implication in distinguishing carefully the millennium from 'the particular judgement of individuals'.

22 'A Dream', in *Spence's Songs*, iii; Supplement (1787), 11; *Jubilee Hymn* (broadside, n.d.). The Jubilee Hymn was reprinted several times; an alternative, non-millennial version of this verse is; 'Hark! How the Trumpet's Sound / Proclaims the Land around / The Jubilee! / Tells all the Poor oppress'd, / No more they shall be cess'd; / Nor Landlords more molest / Their Property', *Songs*, i.

23 Spence, *End of Oppression*, p. 11.

The Second Coming, it is implied, will be contingent upon humanity securing balanced democratic government, an obligation divinely ordained. Just as this itself will be the culmination of enlightened educational processes, so will it form the basis for the mind's further development, necessary preparation for the truths to be revealed at the Second Coming.

Among the consequences of enlightened education Spence included fundamental improvements in the rights of women. His own position reveals a progressive change in this respect. In his original lecture of 1775 'the whole people' would seem implicitly to exclude women, while the remaining publications of his Newcastle and early London years certainly disregard any need to make an explicit case for the rights of women. However, in a striking parallel to the development of his millennial interests, his *Rights of Infants* of 1797 contains a sustained argument in favour of allowing women full political rights. In an imagined dialogue 'woman' declares:

> Our sex were defenders of rights from the beginning. And though men, like other he-brutes, sink calmly into apathy respecting their offspring, you shall find nature, as it never was, so it never shall be[,] extinguished in us. You shall find that we not only know our rights, but have spirit to assert them.

Here is the germ of a concept of male oppression, and an admission that masculine brutishness and turpitude lay at the root of inequality. Spence saw women organizing for themselves as paralleling, and even superseding, the male-dominated organizations he had earlier proposed. Furthermore, the Spencean polity affirmed the right of swift and easy divorce for all desirous of it: '… the chains of Hymen would be among the first that would be broken, in case of a Revolution, and the family business of life turned over to Cupid: who though he maybe a little whimsical is not so stern, and Jailor-like, a Deity.'[24] This conception of the ideal relationship between the sexes is strongly reminiscent of the beliefs of some seventeenth-century radicals. It is possible that these, like the belief in imminent apocalypse, were nurtured in the underground of popular culture in the eighteenth century. If so, they were powerfully and decisively reinforced by more contemporary developments: 'The transmission of feminist ideas into the radical working class was part of a wider process which might best be described as the proletarianization of the Enlightenment.'[25]

To this process Spence himself made a significant contribution, but if it is to be fully appreciated, it is necessary to consider in some detail the

24 Spence, *The Rights of Infants* (1797), 9; *Restorer*, pp. 14-15.

25 B. Taylor, *Eve and the New Jerusalem* (1983), 306. On the seventeenth-century 'sexual revolution' see C. Hill, *The World Turned Upside Down* (1975 edn.), 306-23.

manner in which others came to be influenced by him. For the greater part of his life there was no identifiable Spencean group or party. Spence was first and foremost a publicist and educator, and rejected the need to form any particular caucus to introduce into society the changes he envisaged. Drawing on his experiences as a self-taught schoolteacher, and as a member of Newcastle's artisan intelligentsia, Spence put his faith in the efficiency of educated public opinion to secure radical change. His case for the overthrow of private property in land, as we have seen, rested on sophisticated philosophy rather than upon crude iconoclasm, and it was as an educator, rather than as a leader or founder of a society, that Spence saw his function. This is clear from the very outset of his career, when he resolved to publish the lecture of 1775 beyond the small society to whom he had given it, and was promptly expelled 'not for printing it only, but for printing it in the manner of a half-penny ballad, and having it hawked about the streets'.[26] He next chose to promote his ideas in the popular style of a Utopian travelogue, in chapbook form, based on *Robinson Crusoe* and *Gulliver's Travels*, two 'best-sellers' of the day. His first political action, once he had settled in London, was the countermarking of currency with radical slogans: 'War or Land', 'Spence's Plan Full Bellies and Fat Bairns' — the very terminology is indicative of the audience he sought to reach. He was among the most enterprising of all issuers of token coinage, drawing from one expert the unintended compliment 'that he alone has done more harm to the coinage than other persons in the aggregate'. It was said that he flung handfuls of them, from the thousands piled up in his Oxford Street premises, to the crowds passing on the way to executions at Tyburn.[27] He also published broadsides, songs, and an allegorical map, and employed placards and chalk graffiti. It may well be that the *Rights of Infants* (1797) represents a conscious attempt to widen the constituency of radicalism by an explicit appeal to women. Finally, and of particular significance as evidence of Spence's chosen role as an educator, there is his phonetic alphabet, so designed 'that I cannot but think it possible such a method of spelling may take place, especially among the laborious part of the people, who generally cannot afford much time or expence in the educating of their children'.[28]

There were additional personal considerations suggesting that Spence's contribution to politics was better made as an educator through the printed word than from the platform as a leader. To quote Francis Place:

---

26 E. Mackenzie, *Memoir of T. Spence* (1826), 5.

27 Waters, *Notes*, pp. 50-2; C. Sh., 'The History of the Modern Provincial Half-pennies', *Gentleman's Magazine*, Feb. 1798, p. 122; R. Y., 'Remarks on Provincial Tokens and their Arrangement', ibid., Apr, 1797, p. 269; Mackenzie, *Memoir*, p. 8.

28 T. Spence, *Grand Repository*, conclusion to preface. Cf. Olivia Smith's recent evaluation of Spence in *The Politics of Language* (1984), 96-109.

> In person he was short, not more than 5 feet high he was small and had the appearance of feebleness at an age when men still retain their vigour, this was however partly occasioned by a stroke of palsy from which he never entirely recovered … he had a strong northern 'burr in his throat' and a slight impediment in his speech.

Place goes on to make a more impressionistic judgement:

> He was as thoroughly satisfied of the truth, the goodness, of the system he endeavoured to promulgate as any man ever was of any matter of faith or discipline … he held those who disputed his doctrines in the utmost contempt, and his words as well as his manner were frequently expressive of the contempt he felt. He was above either concealment or disguise, and could not in any way compromise his opinions. He spoke his thoughts freely without regard to the words he used or the person to whom he addressed them, and notwithstanding he was seldom intentionally uncivil he was frequently when opposed not a little offensive. His system was so good — so plain — so excellent indeed beyond any thing ever before propounded for the advantage of mankind that he could scarcely conceive it was possible that anyone [might] conscientiously dissent, and he was therefore too apt to persuade himself this dissent was dishonesty.[29]

The scarcely veiled self-righteousness of the above is arguably as revealing of its author as it is of its subject, yet Place's overall portrait of Spence is warmly admiring, and consistent with the experience of another contemporary and friend, Thomas Bewick.[30]

It seems clear, however, that Spence was not greatly disposed to be a political leader even had the opportunity presented itself. He was a 'grass-roots' activist in the London Corresponding Society, member no. 1 of the 30th, and host to the meetings of the 12th Division. In addition Spence was a member of the General Committee, and of the Committee of Constitution. Meanwhile he continued to promote his own ideas with the quiet confidence of a believer. During his early years in the capital Spence derived more from London radicalism than he contributed to it, particularly imbibing through it the influence of the French Revolution. Significantly, he did not resume publishing until 1792, when he had set himself up as a bookseller, and joined the newly formed Corresponding Society; before the year was out he had been arrested for selling Paine's *Rights of Man*. He was one of a select group of signatories to the first *Address* of the Friends of the Liberty of the Press. The following year Spence began publishing for the Corresponding Society, issued the most substantial text of his

29 Francis Place, BL Add. MS 27808, fos. 152-4.

30 Bewick, *Memoir*, pp. 52-3.

original 1775 lecture, and commenced his weekly *One Pennyworth of Pigs' Meat*. The latter ran for three years and was reprinted in book form at least twice.[31]

Throughout the 1790s Spence crops up frequently in records of metropolitan radical activity. He was several times arrested but not charged — four times in 1794, he claimed, quite apart from seven months spent in prison that year. His son, aged 12, was also arrested and imprisoned until Spence paid a fine. He was an important vendor of London Corresponding Society publications, and in June 1794 acted as publisher on the Society's behalf of *The Report of the Committee of Constitution*, the most explicit statement of its principles. His wife received a total of 3 guineas in 1794 from a relief fund for political prisoners run by the Society. Spence also sold tickets for Society suppers, and received subscriptions and the signatures of petitioners. He did not, however, neglect his own publications. In 1797 he was employing two boys to sell his broadside *The Rights of Man in Verse*, and distributed perhaps over 3,000 copies per week this way.[32]

His unique periodical *One Pennyworth of Pigs' Meat* reveals a new facet of Spence's politics, one which emerged apparently in response to metropolitan stimuli. The very title, subheaded *Lessons for the Swinish Multitude*, locates him at the centre of the radical defence against the reaction to the French Revolution. However, the magazine was not the vehicle for the kind of knock-about satire its title might imply, nor does its substantially contain Spence's own works. Instead, the compiler avowedly espouses the 'good old cause', giving extracts from Cromwell, Harrington, Sydney, and a *Modest Plea for an Equal Commonwealth* (1659), by William Sprigge, a follower of Harrington. He also places himself in the intellectual, dissenting tradition of the eighteenth century by the inclusion of passages from Berkeley and Lyttelton as well as John Locke. Finally, there are the passages which reveal an acute awareness of contemporary politics; Thomas Cooper's reply to Burke, Joseph Priestley on government, Richard Price on civil liberty, Volney's *Ruins of Empires*, the French Constitution of 1793, the 'Marseillaise', and poems by his fellow radical bookseller, 'Citizen' Lee.[33]

31 *Proceedings of the Friends of the Liberty of the Press* (1793); *Rights of Man* (1793); *Pigs' Meat* (first pub. 1793-5; 2nd edn. 1795; 3rd edn. 1796). Copies were seized from Seale's shop in 1803, so there may have been a further edition, TS 11/939/3362. On Spence's activism within the LCS see especially TS 11/951/3494, 21 Feb. 1794; TS 11/955/3499, 8 Apr. 1794; TS 11/958/3503, 12 Nov. 1793.

32 *Morning Chronicle*, 3 Jan. 1795; TS 11/959/3505(2); Price, *Observations; Report of the Committee of Constitution of the London Corresponding Society* (Spence, 1794), cf. report of Groves, 26 June 1794, TS 11/965/3510A; *The London Corresponding Society Addresses the Friends of Peace and Parliamentary Reform* (1793); HO 119/1, fos. 39, 41; M. Thale (ed.), *Selections from the Papers of the London Corresponding Society* (1983), 199-200.

33 *Pigs' Meat*: Cromwell, 'Speech at the Dissolution of the Long Parliament' (i. 100); Harrington, extracts

Pigs' Meat is another aspect of Spence's clearly felt mission as an educator, making available cheaply political writings that were otherwise expensive and inaccessible. It also contains an indication of its compiler's changing stance on the use of force, which it is important to note in connection with any consideration of his relationship with other radicals. Arising, presumably, from the combination of an awareness of the seventeenth-century inheritance, events in France, and exposure to London radicalism, Spence was moved to endorse explicitly the right of just resistance, and this is reflected in certain passages he chose to insert in *Pigs' Meat* — for example Godwin 'On Kings', Sydney's 'Character of an Evil Magistrate', and Murray's *Fast Day Sermons*. It also reflects the mood of some of his token coinage of about the same time, for example the depiction of a pig trampling a crozier and emblems of monarchy on the reverse of a representation of armed citizens and the inscription 'WHO KNOW THEIR RIGHTS AND KNOWING DARE MAINTAIN' or a farthing bearing the impression of a man hanging from a gibbet, endorsed 'END OF P—T'.[34]

It was against this background that Spence became involved with the Lambeth Loyalist Association. It was certainly not a 'Spencean' organization; it is not clear if Spence was even a member, but he did permit the Association to meet twice weekly for armed drilling in a large room above his bookshop. The Association comprised a dozen or so London radicals, including two tailors, a miller, a hatter, an apprentice gun engraver, and a spy, one Frederick Polydore Nodder, 'Botanic Painter to Her Majesty'. Considered in isolation, it is difficult to take the group seriously. It was small, poorly equipped (broomsticks were used to supplement the small supply of muskets), and almost studiously informal. In one sense, however, it was that studied informality that constituted the gravest threat. If the Association is viewed in the context of other armed initiatives, some of them no less elusive (and the evidence for which is too complex to consider here), it appears that the informal and shadowy nature of the underground was its greatest strength. The underground did not need to be a mass movement, as Spence clearly comprehended, as long as the popular will for reform was strong: 'In a country so prepared, let us suppose a few Thousands of hearty determined Fellows well-armed and appointed with Officers, and having a Committee of honest, firm, and intelligent Men to direct their Actions to the proper object.'

---

from *Oceana* (i. 79-81 and vols. i-iii *passim*; Sydney, 'Character of an Evil Magistrate' (ii. 16-19); Sprigge, *Modest Plea* (i. 44-9, 74-8); Berkeley, extract from *The Querist* (ii. 72-4); Lyttelton, 'From the Persian Letters' (i. 78-9 and vol. ii passim); Locke, 'On Civil Government' (i. 42 and vols. i-iii passim); Cooper, 'Utility of Political Societies' (ii. 129-31); Priestley (i. 92 ff.); Price (i. 205 ff.); Volney (i. 69-73); 'The French Constitution at August 1793' (i. 176 ff.); 'Marseillaise' (i. 67-8); Lee (ii. 97 ff., 176-7, 284).

34 *Pigs' Meat*: Godwin (i. 200-1); Sydney (ii. 16-19); Murray (i. 165-7, ii. 19-22). J. Atkins, *The Tradesmen's Tokens of the Eighteenth Century* (1892), types 655, 798.

The Privy Council, examining Spence, were met by a refusal to answer any questions, but he did make a statement: 'Spence said the Plot for the Reform of Parliament will go on, notwithstanding all the Examination of persons and seizing of persons. He said, if the Burthens and Grievances were not attended to, they must look to the Consequences.'[35] Once released from custody Spence was by no means cowed into submission; indeed, it is significant that he stepped up his own radical campaign just as government suppression apparently began to take effect. The tokens continued to flow, while his activities as a 'patriotic bookseller' increased: 1795 was one of his busiest years, *Pigs' Meat* was completed, and all three volumes reissued in a second edition; the *Letter from Ralph Hodge, to his Cousin Thomas Bull* was published, along with two editions of *The End of Oppression* and, very shortly afterwards, a so-called 'recantation'. In *The End of Oppression* Spence suggested that the mere appearance of 'a few Thousands of hearty determined Fellows well-armed' might suffice to secure the land, 'but if the Aristocracy arose to contend the matter, let the People be firm and desperate, destroying them Root and Branch, and strengthening their Hands by the rich Confiscations'. This pamphlet marks the irrevocable change in his views on the use of force, and gives the lie to the conclusion that Spence 'stopped short of violent and conspiratorial revolution'.[36] It also contains interesting strictures, however, on his fellow radicals, opening with the statement '… there is another RIGHTS OF MAN by Spence, that goes farther than Paine's: It is amazing that Paine and the other Democrats should level all their Artillery at Kings, without striking like Spence at this root of every abuse and grievance.'[37]

It was a controversial claim: not only did Spence explicitly endorse the use of force, if needed, to secure radical objectives, but he was also emphasizing that chief among those objectives should be the destruction of the economic basis of that political power and social control which made the need for physical force likely. This permissive, though (it ought to be emphasized) carefully qualified, attitude to the use of violence was not something his followers subsequently grafted on to Spenceanism. It was developed precisely in response to his increasing awareness of the economic realities of political power based on land; Spence commenced the harnessing of physical-force radicalism to nascent class consciousness. It was not an act calculated to endear him to certain elements within the

35 *End of Oppression*, p. 6-7; 'Treason: Examination of Thomas Spence', 23 May 1794, Privy Council Register, PC 2/140, p. 177. The Register is the principal source of information about the Lambeth Loyalist Association; see PC 2/140, pp. 169-70, 173-4, 252, 316-18; see also TS 11/951, printed indictment for high treason against Spence; cf. *The Trial of Thomas Hardy* (1794-5), ii. 305-37; TS 11/953/3497, 28 April and 2 June 1794 (reports of Nodder).

36 *End of Oppression*, pp. 5-6; T. R. Knox, 'Thomas Spence: The Trumpet of Jubilee', *Past and Present*, 76 (1977), 75.

37 *End Of Oppression*, p. 5.

London radical movement, uncomfortably conscious as it was of the barb 'Leveller', and supported by some substantially propertied patrons. A pamphlet which expounded such a theory, invoked the probability of physical conflict, and criticized Thomas Paine, could only meet with a dominantly hostile reception from within radicalism. Hence the publication shortly afterwards of *Spence's Recantation of the End of Oppression*, a mock-serious satire the flavour of which is difficult to convey in short quotation:

> Whereas I, T. Spence, by publishing a small Pamphlet, entitled 'The End of Oppression', have given great cause of uneasiness and alarm to many well-meaning Democrats and Friends of Reform, I hope by this public retracting, denying, and recanting, of all those doctrines of an offensive nature propogated by me, to regain the good-will and applause of my fellow-citizens, … I have *foolishly* laid it down as fundamental, that the Earth belongs at all times to the living inhabitants … to the great alarming of the landed interest, I being deeply concerned for the peace of every gentleman and lady, whether Aristocrat or Democrat, do, most solemnly for myself and for the whole plebeian race of mankind, renounce and give up all claim to this world, to its soil, and every product thereof for the time present and for ever … Avaunt Rights of Man! I am henceforth a Democrat, but no Leveller.[38]

The nature of Spence's theoretical and practical position is further underlined in the *Rights Of Infants*, published in 1797. This was not only the vehicle of his advocacy of the rights of women, it was also a sustained critique of Paine, and particularly of the latter's *Agrarian Justice*. Spence's admiration of Paine had always been tinged with a trace of envy, along with — as we have seen — an acute sense that republicanism was not in itself enough to secure real justice. The very name of its author guaranteed for *Agrarian Justice* an audience and influence far beyond Spence's vainest hopes; one can sense the latter's indignation that Paine should now venture on agrarian reforms entirely without regard to his extensive writings on the subject. Spence had spent time in prison and risked the collapse of his business for selling Paine's publications. It is, of course, unlikely that *Agrarian Justice* (published initially in Paris) was written with any knowledge of Spence's work, but the exaggerated deference paid to Paine, then and now, has meant that the proposals in *Agrarian Justice* have gone largely uncriticized, while it has been the misfortune of Spence usually to be dismissed as 'a tender-hearted crank', and 'outside the mainstream of modern British radicalism'.[39]

38 *Spence's Recantation of the End of Oppression* (1796), 3, 4, 7.

39 Rudkin, *Spence*, p. 53; T. M. Parssinen, 'Thomas Spence', in J. O. Baylen and N. J. Gossman (eds.), *Biographical Dictionary of Modern British Radicals* (1979), i. 458.

Like Spence, Thomas Paine postulated the historical reality of the state of nature, in which the right of every individual to an equitable share of the land was absolute; and Paine, too, believed that such a situation still obtained among the North American Indians. In such a state, he claimed, there were none 'of those spectacles of human misery which poverty and want present to our eyes in all the towns and streets of Europe. Poverty, therefore, is a thing created by that which is called civilised life. It exists not in the natural state.' The two shared, then, their primary supposition, but thenceforward their proposals diverged. Paine did not countenance the kind of figurative natural state that Spence proposed to 'restore'. He held that 'it is never possible to go from the civilised to the natural state', in which latter condition the land was incapable of supporting the level of population which — with the assistance of arts, manufactures, and agriculture — it could in civilization. The problem as Paine conceived it, therefore, was not really agrarian at all: it was one of poverty, and he proposed that all landowners pay 'to the community a ground-rent', to be accumulated in a national fund. From this fund every person reaching the age of 21 would receive a bounty of 'Fifteen Pounds Sterling to enable him, or her, to begin in the World'; and all persons aged 50 or above receive an annuity of £10 'to enable them to live in Old Age without Wretchedness, and go decently out of the world'. This established, the bulk of the pamphlet is given over to the arithmetic of the plan, calculations no more or less spurious than those which distinguish other social reformers — Owen, say, on spade husbandry, or O'Connor on the Chartist land scheme.[40]

Paine's proposals had sufficient in common with Spence's, especially the payment by landowners of a rent to the community, for the latter to feel with good reason that his own ideas might be eclipsed. It is worthy of note, in considering the common ground between them, that both assumed nil population growth. Spence was primarily irked, however, by Paine's refusal to return to first principles. *Agrarian Justice* extended no democratic control over the land, no opportunity for the landless to return to it should they so wish; in short it did not alter the distribution of ownership in any respect. In Spence's opinion, Paine's plan would effectively reinforce the landed interest by incorporating it into the state-centralized machinery of benefits:

> Under the system of Agrarian Justice, the people will, as it were, sell their birthright for a mess of porridge, by accepting of a paltry consideration in lieu of their rights. ... the people will become supine and careless in respect of public affairs, knowing the utmost they can receive of the public money.

40 T. Paine, *Agrarian Justice* (1797; new edn. 1840), 5-6, title-page.

By contrast, in Spence's view his own plan was an incentive for vigilance over public expenditure, for democratic government, and for the education of all its participants. His greatest fear was that the Paineite system would become a placebo, masking the continuation of oppression. 'The toil of the labouring classes first produces provisions, and then the demand of their families creates a market for them', therefore all increase in the value of land derives from labour, which should benefit accordingly.[41]

Great as Paine's reputation as a democrat and polemicist was, his proposed agrarian reforms were markedly less democratic, and less precise in identifying the roots of injustice, than those of Spence, without the compensation of being more plausible or practicable. They reveal also an estrangement between their author and English popular radical feeling, perhaps the product of Paine's years of exile. A so-called agrarian reform which did nothing to reduce the power of the landed interest would surely have attracted little attention, were it not for the fame of its proposer. Spence was quick to point out that Paine's scheme would give rise to 'the sneaking unmanly spirit of conscious dependence'.[42] Not the least persuasive factor behind the continuing appeal of agrarian ideas in the nineteenth century was the apparent opportunity they advanced for the restoration and maintenance of labour's independence. Although Paine's posthumous reputation ensured successive editions of *Agrarian Justice*, it was Spencean agrarianism that was to inform theory and practice in the labour movement wherever gradualism was rejected. The first hints of this become apparent in the early years of the new century.

By 1797 Thomas Spence had effectively become one of the most sophisticated theoreticians of revolutionary radicalism in the capital. The substance of his thought is a clear indication that the insurrectionary contingents within popular radicalism were not crude iconoclasts, but can firmly be located within the context of the evolution of class consciousness. It is within this broad context that the gradual emergence of organized Spenceanism has to be seen. Only towards the end of his life did Spence attract admirers who can properly be referred to as Spenceans. It is evident that he regarded his function as one of supplying a theoretical basis for insurrection, rather than active participation or leadership, for there was no Spencean group during the 1790s. Nor is there evidence to implicate him in the United Englishmen: it may be that memories of 1794 made him circumspect, or that poor health disqualified him, or even, as Edward Thompson suggests, that 'he did not have the discretion, nor the practical application for a serious conspirator'. Whatever the reason, Spence entered the nineteenth century as one who theorized upon, rather than actively

41 Spence, *Rights of Infants*, pp. 11, 16.

42 Ibid. 12.

organized, the redress of political grievance by force.[43]

However, throughout the first two decades of the nineteenth century the names of active conspirators in the capital are consistently associated with Spence — evidence that he was at last beginning to be taken seriously as a theorist of revolutionary politics. It has never attracted comment that the first recorded meeting of any Spencean group took place in 1801, a year of renewed United Irish activity, and preceding that in which the so-called 'Despard conspiracy' was exposed. There is no evidence to link them, but it is not unreasonable to suggest that the formation of a Spencean group at this critical juncture derived impetus from the renewed interest in the strategy of insurrection which, as is now generally recognized, extended far beyond the activities brought to light at the trial of Colonel Despard. The earliest Spencean gatherings also took place against a background of widespread food riots.[44] This doubtless underlined the economic, and especially agrarian, roots of contemporary grievances and hence contributed to increased interest in Thomas Spence's ideas. He cited this context of 'unprecedented dearness of Provisions' several times in the course of a publication which, significantly, unequivocally invoked the right and probable necessity of applying force to secure reform. The most extensive development of Spence's political philosophy, *The Restorer of Society to its Natural State*, published in 1801, earned for its author in June of that year twelve months' imprisonment on a charge of seditious libel. Referring to food shortages in the offending pamphlet, Spence criticized the oft-proposed panacea of small farms as impractical, since this would have to be introduced through the goodwill of the landowners, who are guided entirely by profit motives and therefore prefer to rent to richer tenants in larger units; their interests they then secure in Parliament through the corn laws. 'It is childish therefore to expect ever to see small Farms again; or even to see anything else than the utmost screwing and grinding of the Poor, till you quite overturn the present system of Landed Property.' The reader is left in no doubt as to Spence's preferred method for accomplishing this:

> How lately have we seen unions of the People sufficiently grand, and well conducted, to give sure hopes of success Abroad and at Home; in America, France, and in our own Fleets, we have seen enough of public spirit and extensive unanimity in the present generation, to accomplish schemes of infinitely greater difficulty than a thing that may be done in

43 Thompson, *Making*, p. 543.

44 M. Elliott, 'The "Despard Conspiracy" Reconsidered', *Past and Present*, 75 (1977), 46-61; R. A. E. Wells, *Insurrection: The British Experience, 1795-1803* (1983), chs. 9-11; Thompson, *Making*, pp. 515-28; J. Baxter and F, Donnelly, 'The "Revolutionary Underground" in the West Riding: Myth or Reality?', *Past and Present*, 64 (1975), 124-32; and J. Dinwiddy, 'The Black Lamp in Yorkshire, 1801-2', ibid. 113-23.

> a day, when once the public mind is duly prepared. ... For who, pray, are to hinder the people of any Nation from doing so when they are inclined? Are the Landlords in the Parishes more numerous and powerful in proportion to the People, than the brave warlike Officers in our mutinous Fleets were to their Crews? Certainly not.[45]

With these remarks in mind, the resolutions passed at the first Spencean meeting, on 18 March 1801, assume particular significance through their dual emphasis on the preparation of 'the public mind' and the mode of organization:

> AT A MEETING OF *Real Friends To Truth, Justice*, and HUMAN HAPPINESS, IT WAS RESOLVED. That the Principles of CITIZEN SPENCE'S THEORIES OF SOCIETY, are immutable and unchangeable as Truth and Nature on which they are built, and therefore only require universal investigation to be universally acknowledged. RESOLVED — therefore, that it be recommended to all the Well-wishers to that System, to meet frequently, though in ever so small Numbers, in their respective Neighbourhoods, after a Free and Easy manner, without encumbering themselves with Rules, to converse on the Subject, provoke investigation, and answer such objections as may be started, and to promote the circulation of *Citizen Spence's Pamphlets*.[46]

Citizen Spence's pamphlets were indeed circulated: an informer's report to the Home Office mentions one 'which explains the way of dividing the Land and property after a Revolution is gained', in almost the same breath as the United Irish revival. It is possible that the circulation of such pamphlets contributed to the proposed reward for troops participating in the 1802 insurrection: 'if the Point be carried [they] shall be at Liberty to retire and to have 10 acres of Land with a proportion of money to cultivate it with'.[47]

It is impossible to verify how successful gatherings 'after a Free and Easy manner' were — or even the frequency with which they took place. This extremely decentralized initiative mirrored Spence's antipathy to centralization in government: it reflected his determination to promote his ideas in ways which maximized their exposure among 'my Friends, the industrious Part of Mankind', and it was scrupulously within the definition of lawful assembly. Although the proposal met with the hostile scrutiny of the Parliamentary Committee of Secrecy of the same year, there is no evidence of the business transacted at these early Spencean meetings: it is likely they followed the tradition of earlier 'free-and-easies' patronized by London radicals, as Lord Cloncurry remembered those of the 1790s: 'if the

45 Spence, *Restorer*, p. 16-17. On the contemporary food riots see Wells, *Insurrection*, ch. 9.

46 Broadside, London School of Economics, pressmark R(SR)422.

47 HO 42/61, 8 Apr. 1801; HO 42/65, information of Fletcher, 7 July 1802.

business transacted was treason, it was carefully wrapped up in the jokes and ribaldry said or sung in such places'. Spence told William Hone 'they were very merry with a little social drinking and singing songs written by himself'. Participation doubtless increased the conviction and resolve of those who were also involved in the underground movement.[48] Several of those who later became avowed Spenceans, and who were probably associated with this initial venture, were implicated in conspiracies about this time. The leader of the Spencean Philanthropists after their founder's death, Thomas Evans, was the most prominent of them; Alexander Galloway was another. Both men were involved in the United English movement of 1798. A year earlier Evans, while secretary of the London Corresponding Society, had sought to set up an umbrella organization of insurgents, the United Britons. He was deeply implicated in Arthur O'Connor and James O'Coighley's abortive trip abroad in 1798 to secure assistance from the French, and his home appears to have been a house of call for senior United Irishmen. Following three years of imprisonment Evans appears a few days after the first Spencean meeting, castigating the remnants of the United English in London for 'their Supineness and inactivity' during his absence. Galloway had similarly been imprisoned; both men were released a couple of weeks before the first Spencean meeting.[49] Two others, the boot-closer Thomas Pemberton and the cobbler Charles Pendrill, subsequently Spenceans, were also 'deeply in the business' of 'Despard's Conspiracy'. Both were arrested in 1801 on suspicion of contact with United Irish emissaries. For Pendrill this was the second time, as he had also been seized in 1798. 'It appeared to me as though Penderill was one of the *Executive*', thought a key prosecution witness at Despard's trial; some years later the spy Oliver uncovered something of the function of Pendrill, in the events of 1801-2, as an important contact between London and the provinces. The evidence only came to light because Oliver used Pendrill's influence to secure

48 Spence, *Supplement*, preface to the phonetic alphabet edn., p. iii; V. B. Lawless, *Personal Recollections of the Life and Times, with Extracts from the Correspondence, of Valentine Lord Cloncurry* (1849), 64; W. Hone to F. Place, 6 Nov. 1830, bound in a volume of Spencean tracts, London School of Economics, pressmark R(SR) 422; the second report of the House of Lords Committee of Secrecy, 15 May 1801, imputed conspiratorial intentions to the free-and-easies, see *Parliamentary History of England from the Earliest Period to the Year 1803* (1819 edn.), xxxv., 1307.

49 HO 42/42, 12 Mar. 1798, information of Powell identifying Evans and Galloway as the two principal members of the United Englishmen; ibid., 14 Mar. 1798; HO 42/61, fos. 187-8, 2 Mar. [1801], re-release of prisoners; HO 42/65, 7 July 1802; HO 100/75/110-12, Portland to Camden, 23 Feb. 1798; PC 1/3526, information of Thomas, 4 Apr. 1801; PC 1/3535; TS 11/122, abstract of information concerning Despard, O'Coighley, and others; TS 11/689, 14 Mar. 1798, examination of Evans; *Trial of James O'Coighley* (1798), 83; F. Place, *The Autobiography of Francis Place*, ed. M. Thale (1972), 177-9. Galloway was also a linkman between London radicals and the Nore mutineers in 1797, see Wells, *Insurrection*, p. 95.

introduction to the provincial underground movement.[50]

The imprisonment of Spence himself in June 1801, to say nothing of the traumas of the following year, possibly interrupted the projected free-and-easy meetings, but a small circle, at the very least, formed round Spence on his release. Besides Evans, Galloway, Pendrill, and Pemberton, it is likely to have included the three Corresponding Society veterans Arthur Seale, Jonathan Panther, and George Cullen, and the lame street-entertainer William Tilly. Seale had been printing Spence's works since at least the *Restorer* (1801), possibly before, because copies of Spence's periodical *Pigs' Meat* were found on his premises when they were raided in October 1803. The latter event points to concerted activity in the Spencean group: Seale was successfully prosecuted for publishing a seditious libel defending Despard that had been commissioned by Galloway for delivery to Evans. Panther was implicated in the affair by an informer, but his friendship with John Horne Tooke and the latter's Wimbledon circle perhaps made him more circumspect of openly defending Despard. He was, however, tried the same day as Seale (22 February 1804) on an unconnected charge of refusing to name the residents at his address for the militia list. His reply was a vigorous defence of 'the Genuine Constitution of 1688', and an attack on the Government and the 'War of the Rich Men, against the most sober, Honest and Industrious part of the people'; it earned him an exemplary three months in Newgate and a £100 fine.[51] Cullen and Tilly were more fortunate, or maybe just more cautious. Cullen, an early member of the London Corresponding Society and friend of Thelwall and Hardy, had stood bail for Spence in 1801. His annotated copy of the trial proceedings reveals an enthusiastic admiration of Spence. Tilly, a lame ballad-singer, was altogether different from Panther and Cullen, his song 'The Spencean Jubilee' appearing on the reverse of advertisements for the *Restorer*. The latter circulated widely in its trial proceedings edition, the author himself hawking it round workshops in the capital saying it 'ought to be in the hands of every Englishman in the country'. It is likely, too, that the Deptford shipwrights' leader John Gast was also an associate of Spence

50 PC 1/3117, Ford to 'Notary', Monday, [28] Nov. 1802 — mentions Pemberton and Pendrill; PC 1/3526, J. Thomas, 4 Apr. 1801; HO 42/61, to. 4845, 8 Apr, 1801; HO 40/9(2), narrative of Oliver, esp. fos, 82-6; *Trial of Edward Marcus Despard* (1803), evidence of Blades, p. 99. See also BL Add. MS 27816, fo. 575 (Place Papers) — copy of Pelham's charge to the keeper of Newgate, handing over Pendrill, 1 Dec. 1802; ibid., fos. 576-7, Pendrill to the Committee for the Relief of Prisoners in the Late State Trials (1802). For a fuller reconstruction of Pendrill's activities in these years see Wells, *Insurrection*, pp. 127, 205-7, 213-15, 245-7.

51 TS 11/939/3362 R. v. Seale, 22 Feb. 1804; TS 11/939/3361, R. v. Panther, 22 Feb. 1804; HO 42/78, 23 Feb. 1804 — information of 'Notary'. Panther's early association with Spence is clear from the latter's letter to him from Shrewsbury Gaol, BL Add. MS 27808, fo. 22, 20 Nov. 1801. Another London Corresponding Society veteran associated with Spence about this time was the printer Smith — see J. A. Hone, *For the Cause of Truth: Radicalism in London, 1796-1821* (1982), 56, 119, 201.

at this time. His pamphlet of 1802, *Calumny Defeated*, closely parallels Spence's thought on property and labour.[52]

Sometime about 1807 a further attempt was made to place Spenceanism on a more permanent footing. William Cobbett recalled having first become acquainted with Spence and his ideas about this time. So did William Hone, who bought a copy of the *Important Trial* from Spence's 'vehicle ... in Parliament Street, near the Duke of Richmond's'. Shortly afterwards Spence purchased one of Burdett's speeches from Hone and, lingering in the shop,

> ... talked about his Plan and the Landlords against whom he was inveterate. On leaving he gave me a card (long since lost) admitting the bearer to a meeting at the something and Lamb in or near Windmill Street, where he said he met his friends to talk over and co-operate towards his 'Plan'.

Besides the two editions of the *Important Trial* of this year, further Spencean broadsides were issued, one of which refers to weekly meetings at the Swan public house, New Street Square (between Fleet Street and Holborn). So there may have been two regular free-and-easies: at the Swan in the City on Mondays, and later in the week at the public house Hone remembered. The ranks of professional Spencean songsters, meanwhile, swelled as Tilly was joined by Thomas Porter, an unemployed stonecutter who, a Home Office informer noted ruefully, 'sings loud'.[53]

A formally constituted Spencean society was set up in 1811 or 1812. They still met in the form of a free-and-easy, at 'the sign of the Fleece' in Little Windmill Street, perhaps the same premises whose title Hone could only partially recall. It was in 1811 that Thomas Preston began his association with the Spenceans, and annual meetings commemorating Spence's birthday were instituted the following year. Evans was now playing a leading part in the group and was instrumental in its publication of Spencean songbooks.[54] Among those almost certainly associating with Spence at this time was Maurice Margarot, the veteran London

52 Spence, *Important Trial* (2nd edn., 1807), BL pressmark 900.H.24(1); J. A. Hone, *For the Cause of Truth*, p. 228; W. Tilly, *The Spencean Jubilee* (broadside, [?1801]; A. Davenport, *Life and Literary Pursuits* (1845), 41; J. Gast, *Calumny Defeated: Or, a Compleat Vindication of the Conduct of the Working Shipwrights, During the Late Disputes with their Employers* [1802], 9.

53 *Cobbett's Weekly Political Register*, 14 Dec. 1816, 1 Mar. 1817; BL Add. MS 27808, fos, 314-15, Hone to Place, 23 Sept. 1830; Spence, *Important Trial* (12mo and 8vo edns., 1807, in Goldsmiths' Library); T. Porter, *Spence's Plan* (undated broadside inserted in the Goldsmiths' Library's copy of *Important Trial*); HO 42/172, [1817], copy of *A Humourous Catalogue of Spence's Songs* [?1811].

54 'At the sign of the Fleece, little Windmill-street, the Free and Easy meets every Tuesday at 8 o'clock', *Humourous Catalogue*; *Spence's Songs*, i-iii [?1811]; T. Preston, *The Life and Opinions of Thomas Preston* (1817), 22; HO 42/178, 30 June 1819, enclosing admission ticket to the 'Eighth Fraternal Anniversary', 14 July 1819; BL Add. MS 27808, fo. 227, T. J. Evans to Place. n.d.

Corresponding Society activist, who had returned in 1810 from Australia (whither he had been transported in 1793 for his participation in the Edinburgh Convention). Curiously, Margarot's biographer observes of his return 'His attitude to English politics had changed hardly at all'; yet Margarot reveals the influence of Spence in the very title of his 1812 pamphlet *Proposal for a Grand National Jubilee: Restoring to Every Man his Own and Thereby Extinguishing both Want and War*. In it the author deplores the divorce from the land of the vast majority of the population, praises 'the Mosaic Law', and proposes local meetings to consider a plan whereby a progressive tax will be applied to land with the aim of eventually breaking it up into small lots. Envisaging the imminent failure of commerce, Margarot advanced, as the people's only effective remedy, 'a resumption, and repartition of the soil of their forefathers by A GRAND NATIONAL JUBILEE'.[55] Evidence that Margarot associated with the Spencean group was uncovered by a Home Office informer in the following year, 1813. The same informer was able to provide the names of 'the persons who have lately chalked the walls in and about London with "Spence's plan", "Spence's System etc"'. Acting as a delegate of a shadowy conspiratorial group, 'The Patriots', Margarot proposed a clandestine trip to France in order to urge Napoleon to invade Britain and restore the Saxon constitution in its original purity. The anticipated consequence of this clearly reflected a firm agrarian basis:

> The revival of the old Saxon laws — The Confiscation and Sale of all the great estates; the abolition and destruction of those damned Nobles and Clergy. I shall prove to you at another opportunity that the great principle of our party, that everybody should have a bit of land, is perfectly practicable — only compare the population of England with the number of Acres and you would see that every individual should then have 4 or 5 acres — You see then what a hold we shall have upon the common people.[56]

Other known Patriots included the veteran Thomas Hardy and a recent recruit to metropolitan radicalism, Arthur Thistlewood. This association is instructive: throughout his meteoric rise and fall Thistlewood was closely associated with the Spenceans. The spy Edwards (of Cato Street notoriety) claimed to have met Thistlewood through Spence about this time; it is therefore likely that Thistlewood's introduction to the Patriots as a potential financier was through Spence also.[57] The implication of Hardy is

55 M. Margarot, *Proposal for a Grand National Jubilee* [1812], 14-15, 38. There is a full biographical article on the author's career by M. Roe, 'Maurice Margarot: A Radical in Two Hemispheres, 1792-1815', *Bulletin of the Institute of Historical Research*, 31 (1958), 73.

56 HO 42/136, 'Information Monday morning'. There are a number of reports on the Patriots in this file.

57 HO 42/136; HO 40/8(4), fo. 168 (31 Jan. 1818), information of W——r (i.e. Edwards, alias 'Windsor'). Thistlewood was rumoured to have been in France during the Revolution 'and engaged in Despard's

interesting, not only because it indicates the frailty of any distinction between respectable and conspiratorial radicalism, but also because of Hardy's avowed support of Napoleon. Admiration of Bonaparte was common among the Spenceans: Jonathan Panther was notable for his continuing warm support of the Emperor; Evans deplored Napoleon's defeat in 1815, believing him to be the only effective obstacle to the spread of Russian autocracy; Preston's Spencean group condemned his incarceration on St Helena; Davenport criticized him only for being too soft on monarchical tyranny; while for John George, Bonaparte was quite simply 'the greatest friend of humanity that ever lived'.[58]

As Dr Hone has recently pointed out, it is extremely difficult to assess the importance of events in the winter of 1812-13, but again we have the spectacle of an increase in conspiratorial activity closely associated with renewed interest in Spence, and strong personal and ideological connections apparent between them. There is also the familiar national context of insurrectionary plans (quite apart from Luddism). It is not being suggested here that, as in 1801-2, all this was the consequence, or ultimate responsibility, of the Spencean meetings. Clearly, Spenceanism and insurrection responded to a common stimulus, but in view of the personalities and ideas involved some more direct connection between them can be justifiably supposed.[59]

Margarot's proposed French trip did not materialize. Despite his rumoured windfall of £10,000 in a Chancery suit, Thistlewood could find no one to discount the bill from which he proposed to pay Margarot. It was an ignominious introduction to metropolitan ultra-radicalism, yet already a Home Office informer could presciently observe that 'from his past life, his present pursuits, principles and low connections etc he seems to be a second edition of Colonel Despard'. Margarot, meanwhile, was despairing, believing that 'all hope is now over and possibly for ever; that the great Bonaparte whom he had hailed as the Salvator of the World and of England is stopped in his career of glory'.[60] Spence, however, was resilient

---

business': the first is unlikely and the second unsubstantiated. The only authority for either claim is John Castles, chief prosecution witness at the Spa Fields trial, HO 44/4, fo. 362. Thistlewood was barely 15 in 1789, and in 1795 'Arthur Thistlewood of Tupholme, grazier', appears as surety for a marriage bond now in the Lincoln Diocesan Record Office. See A. Smith, 'Arthur Thistlewood', *History Today*, 3 (1953), 846-52.

58 HO 42/78, 'Notary', 19 Jan. 1804; T. Evans, letter to the editor, *Independent Whig*, 27 Aug. 1815; HO 42/181, anonymous information, n.d. [Oct. 1818]; A. Davenport, *The Kings, or Legitimacy Unmasked* (1819), 10; *PMG* 47 (5 May 1832), 380. See also E. T. Lean, *The Napoleonists* (1970), for a detailed consideration of non-plebeian supporters.

59 J. A. Hone, *For the Cause of Truth*, pp. 233-4. When Margarot died in 1815 the Spenceans Galloway and Pendrill were among the chief mourners at the funeral, BL Add. MS 27816, fos. 89, 91; Galloway also undertook to write, with Thomas Hardy (a close friend), to the Duke of Portland, explaining Margarot's visits to France, ibid. fos, 231-3, cf. BL Add. MS 27818, fo. 186.

60 HO 42/136, 8 Feb. 1813, Smith to Home Office, and ibid., n.d. The Home Office took the activities of

and in 1814 he commenced a new periodical along the lines of *Pigs' Meat*, entitled *The Giant Killer, or Anti-landlord*. It maintained the apocalyptic tone of Spence's later writings, but also clarified his figurative interpretation of Revelation ('the restoration of the New Jerusalem state of happiness on earth, and not in heaven'), while not denying the particular judgement of the individual. *Giant Killer* also included extracts from a further Spencean travelogue, *The Marine Republic*; material provided by Evans on the American community of Harmony; and a spirited defence of 'the true and genuine Leveller'.[61] However, only two issues of *Giant Killer* appeared before Spence died on 1 September 1814 from a bowel complaint. His funeral brought for the first time the Society he had founded into the public eye. The cortège was followed 'by a numerous throng of political admirers. Appropriate medallions were distributed, and a pair of scales preceded his corpse, indicative of his views.'[62] William Snow, one of the most readily disposed of the Spenceans towards violence in the years that followed, was the orator at the graveside. In spite of this, it was the Corresponding Society and United English veteran Thomas Evans who emerged as the unchallenged leader of the Spencean Philanthropists after their founder's death.

Margarot and the Patriots seriously enough to offer Smith £100 for his anticipated services in Jan. 1813, but he declined, ibid., 11 Jan. 1813, Smith to Beckett.

61 *Giant Killer*, 1, 2 (6, 13 Aug. 1814).

62 Obituaries: *Morning Post*, 10 Sept. 1814; *Courier*, 12 Sept. 1814; *Gentleman's Magazine*, Sept. 1814, p. 30. HO 42/168, T. Evans to T. J. Evans, 18 Sept. 1814.

4

Agrarians and Revolutionaries: Spencean Philanthropy, 1814-1820

> Are you then of the opinion, that the land or territory of a nation is by nature the people's farm, in which all persons as equal partners, might receive their just share of the rents? Are you of the opinion, that this principle is founded in divine justice, and that its adoption would tend to extinguish war, poverty, oppression and misery, and restore peace, liberty, security and happiness to society?
>
> Are you then willing to become a true Spencean Philanthropist, by endeavouring to extend a knowledge of these natural rights of mankind?[1]

This was the catechism faced by those applying to join the Society of Spencean Philanthropists. 'Weavers, shoemakers and the like' all lived in the capital and none moved in its respectable circles. Alexander Galloway, alone among Spence's associates in achieving significant upward social mobility, kept a discreet distance, occasionally funding the Society's publications. The rest, variously described as 'low Tradesmen', 'the dregs of the late Corresponding Society', and 'next to nobody and nothing',[2] were a typical cross-section of London workers: shoemakers, boot-closers and translators, tailors, printers, bakers, carpenters, 'surgeons', coachmakers, a butcher, 'Smithfield cutter', whitesmith, trimming weaver, brace-maker, paper-hanger, stonecutter, wireworker, window-blind-maker, City policeman, labourer, child's chairmaker, cooper, beershop keeper, 'servant out of place', and so on. Among them were recent arrivals from every corner of Britain; two were mulattoes, one of them of slave parentage (Davison and Wedderburn, respectively). Many were ex-sailors or ex-

1 'Of the Admittance and State of Members', *Address and Regulations of the Society of Spencean Philanthropists* (1815), 7.

2 These four contemporary descriptions of the Spenceans are from: HO 42/136, J. Smith, 'Information', n.d. [1812/13]; editorial, *New Times*, 29 Apr. 1818; HO 42/155, J. Hanley, undated report [Nov. 1816]; BL Add. MS 27809, fo. 100, Francis Place.

soldiers. Two at least (Preston and Tilly) were quite severely disabled. John Hooper, a labourer, lived with a prostitute. Porter was a pickpocket. Thomas Evans had been a member of a blackmail syndicate.[3] A few Spenceans were, or had been, licensed as dissenting preachers: several more spoke with authority and feeling on religious issues in public. This introduces a further motif into the picture of working-class life which a description of the Society's membership gives. An important feature of the development by this group of Spence's ideas was an even greater emphasis on religious elements and parallels. It found expression in behaviour which was greeted by the archly rational Francis Place, for one, with a mixture of mild amusement and contempt:

> Evans as other fanatics before him had done attempted to found a society which was to unmake the world, and produce a millenium. He most sincerely believed that the well being of mankind depended solely upon the system he borrowed from Thomas Spence. Evans was a devout Christian in the sense in which multitudes are Christians, departing in some particulars from the discipline of the Church of England. Like many other half crazy people in all times and in every country he found the principles of his system in the bible. He used to march from his house to the public houses where he says the meetings of the society were held with an old bible under his arm, from it he preached to whoever would hear him.

Intent on exposing the nefarious conduct of Lord Liverpool's administration, Place argued in writing the above that 'the plain truth is, there was nothing which could fairly be called a society'.[4] This mistaken belief, combined with an understandably ingrained suspicion of Evans, as well as contempt for his conduct, prompted Place to devalue the Spenceans at almost every turn. Although considerable interest adheres to his description, his conclusion is of dubious validity. Something more than accusations of mental deficiency and religious fanaticism are needed if we are to understand the Spenceans.

The context of Spence's own millenarian development was one which his followers shared: poverty, metropolitan sectarianism, the French Revolution's powerful impulse to millennial speculation, and the cross-fertilization of popular religious and radical movements. With the post-war

3 Occupations drawn from various spies' reports in Home Office papers. On criminality in this radical underworld, see the two illuminating studies by I. D. McCalman, 'Unrespectable Radicalism: Infidels and Pornography in Early 19th Century London', *Past and Present*, 104 (Aug. 1984), 74-110, and 'A Radical Underworld in Early 19th Century London: Thomas Evans, Robert Wedderburn, George Cannon and Their Circle, 1800-1835', Monash University Ph.D. thesis (1984).

4 BL Add. MS 27809, fo. 99. Evans had been one of a group which had earlier tried to blackmail Place over his conduct as foreman of the coroner's jury in the notorious Sellis affair; see BL Add. MS 27851, fos. 6-7, and McCalman, 'Unrespectable Radicalism,' p. 82.

depression millennial speculation renewed, along with political agitation. In the face of repression there arose a popular faith in the rectitude of the radicals' cause. Successive editions of the *Address and Regulations of the Society of Spencean Philanthropists* emphasized with increasing sense of urgency 'the calamitous condition of the great majority of mankind'. The tailor Robert Wedderburn spoke of 'impending ruin', and declared, 'Fly ye borough mongers, or perish in the flames, your day of retribution is at hand.' In 1816 the brace-maker Thomas Evans saw 'a dread crisis ... a whole people paralysed and in danger':

> These nations are arrived at a crisis the most tremendously awful to contemplate, brought upon us by the mistaken policy of our rulers, the avarice of our landholders and merchants, the influence of a corrupted press, ... the great body of the people ... drained by taxation, of their rightful share of national property the only source of power.

The language was apocalyptic, but the essence of the argument secular even when bolstered by scriptural reference:

> The sacred records declare, that such establishments shall not endure in peace, and the awful visitations arising therefrom in our own days are evidence, that till we put away the abomination of desolation, paganism; and return to a just admiration of that property which is equally the natural right of all, by abolishing lordship in the soil, the earth will be filled with violence, will continue to be deluged with blood. Christian policy would make the world a paradise, the prevailing pagan system constitutes a hell: both are now fairly and truly before you, reader, choose for yourself.[5]

Like Spence's, their argument for universal ownership of the land rested on natural rights; but, unlike Spence, they made no great emphasis of the issue. Natural right to the land is axiomatic; and *nature* is a keyword that indicates an underlying affirmation of a neo-Lockian natural rights argument, without any extensive discussion or development of it. Arguably, it would be unfair to expect otherwise; the purposes of Spence differed from those of his followers, as did the character of their written pronouncements. Though he sometimes wrote verse, for example, this was only to substantiate and supplement his serious prose, but for those of his followers who left written record of their opinions, verse is often the only form they used; accordingly ideas tended to be asserted rather than argued. Take for example the Hackney hairdresser Edward James Blandford:

5 *Address of the Society of Spencean Philanthropists* (1817), 1, and *Address of the Society of Christian Philanthropists* [1819], 1. Cf. *Address* (1815), 'the time is arriving when men will feel it in their interest to be just'. R. Wedderburn in *Axe Laid to the Root*, 3 (1817), col. 44, and ibid. 5 (1817), 76; T. Evans, *Christian Policy the Salvation of the Empire* (1816), pp, iii, 1, 15.

When Nature her pure artless reign began,
She gave in entail all her stores to man;
The earth, the waters, eke the air and light,
And mines, and springs, man held in equal right
For ever; the probate of her will declares,
Her boundless bounty fram'd in equal shares.[6]

By contrast the scriptural element in the Spenceans' ideas was greater than in Spence. This probably reflects, as well as their religious faith, a desire to buttress opinion by recourse to widely recognized authority, but the recurring theme of 'Christian Policy' was also developed in answer to official repression following the Spa Fields meeting of 2 December 1816.[7] Such a concept reaffirmed the probity of Spenceanism, and its insistent condemnation of all outside it as pagan, or even 'Antichrist', can be construed as both the sustenance of faith and an attempt to embarrass opposition. Spence had made little reference to Christ or the New Testament generally, preferring the Old Testament for inspiration, support, and analogy, in keeping with his Calvinistic background. Under Evans's influence, however, the Spenceans placed great emphasis on their status as Christians, though in a manner consistent with the overall tenor of deism inherited from their founder. By 1819 he had even come to prefer the sobriquet 'Christian Philanthropist'; divisions among followers of Spence and explicit references to the Spencean Philanthropists in the Seditious Meetings Act of 1817 provided additional reason for this.[8]

Evans denied the divinity of Christ while emphatically affirming his historicity. In the Spenceans' eyes Christ was a reformer, dedicated to restoring Mosaic law and the rule of jubilee in particular. As Wedderburn preached:

> God gave land to the Children of men; then why should we suffer it to be taken from us, then Jesus Christ come; he says call no man Master,

6 E. J. B[landford], 'Nature's First, Last, and Only Will! Or a Hint to Mr Bull', *Medusa*, 8 (10 Apr. 1819), 60.

7 (First) Report of the Committee of Secrecy on papers which were presented to the House by Viscount Castlereagh on 4 Feb., *PP* 1817.

8 Evans should probably be credited with the development of the idea of Christian Philanthropy though it was never his exclusively. In an article in *Independent Whig*, 27 Aug. 1815, he praised the revolutionary 'Atheists of France' as 'practical Christians'; about this time the first *Address* of the Society was published. Surviving copies of Evans's *Christian Policy* were designated the second edition, so the first may have appeared the previous year too. Wedderburn and Jennison make use of the concept in their periodicals of 1817, *Axe Laid to the Root* and *The Forlorn Hope*. Evans published *Christian Policy in Full Practice among the People of Harmony*, and Wedderburn his anonymous *Christian Policy; or Spence's Plan, in Prose and Verse. By a Spencean Philanthropist*, in 1818. The *Address of the Society of Christian Philanthropists* appeared shortly before Peterloo. An aspect of Evans's thinking at this time is noted by G. Claeys, 'Documents; Thomas Evans and the Development of Spenceanism, 1815-16: Some Neglected Correspondence', *Bulletin of the Society for the Study of Labour History*, 48 (1984), 24-30.

there's a reformer for you: there's a leveller for you: be your own masters and take your own portion of the Land for God gave it you.[9]

The true essence of Christ's teaching was subverted first by Paul, then by 'the pagan Greeks, that made this man a divinity' (Evans), and finally by 'the clergy of every description, they are bound by law and interest, in all countries, to preach agreeable to the will of the governor under whom they live'. For doing this, of course, they fatten and prosper, to quote notes of a speech by the shoemaker Allen Davenport, '... robbing the Lower Class of people and not only them but the poor Farmers where [*sic*] even eaten up with them. Tythes and Taxation all owing to them by their Extravagance and Luxury.'[10] It follows then that the true Christian denies Christ's divinity. Christ himself, claimed Wedderburn, was 'an *Unitarian*, a true DEIST!' Further to this, the true Christian upholds those laws of God and Nature which Christ held, and in particular that agrarian law currently flouted so conspicuously. Only agrarianism on the Spencean model, therefore, is truly Christian; 'If any thing can discover the finger of God, delineating rules of conduct for man to be guided by in his passage through life, it is this system, and this system only'. Consequently Antichrist is the embodiment of all who oppose Spencean Philanthropy. 'There is no other salvation for the sons and daughters of Adam under heaven.'[11]

These claims were further refined in two ways: first, by drawing parallels between the Spenceans and early Christians; second, and more crucially, by pointing to similarities between Spencean Philanthropy and what were held to be residual elements of true Christianity in the organization of the Church. Essentially, this was to demonstrate the veracity and viability of the joint stock principle, whereby the members of a community could hold a property jointly and in perpetuity, unaffected by deaths or fluctuations in numbers. For all its faults the Church provided in the management of its property a paradigm for organizing public ownership. By analogy the institution of private property is 'pagan'.[12]

At this juncture the Spenceans wove a second, secularized, line of argument into their advocacy of Christian Policy: the Norman Yoke. It is an argument almost ignored by Spence, who had been inclined to dismiss

9 HO 42/197, 27 Oct. 1819, report of constables Plush and Mathewson. A substantial body of material concerning Wedderburn's religious views was gathered together for his prosecution for blasphemy in Feb. 1820, and is preserved in TS 11/45/167. See also *The Trial of Robert Wedderburn (a Dissenting Minister of the Unitarian Persuasion) for Blasphemy*, ed. Erasmus Perkins [i.e. George Cannon] (2 edns., both 1820).

10 TS 11/45/167, fo. 20; Evans, *Christian Policy*, p. 10; *Axe Laid to the Root*, 1 (1817), 7; HO 42/198, 8 Nov, 1819, report of Dalton.

11 R. W[edderburn], in *Theological Comet*, 16 (6 Nov. 1819); *Address* (1817), 6, 8; *Christian Policy, or Spence's Plan*, p. 5.

12 *Axe Laid to the Root*, 3 (1817), 47-8; Evans, *Christian Policy*, *passim*.

it, arguing that 'William the Conqueror and his Normans were fools', compared to modern landlords, 'in the Arts of Fleecing'. The adoption of this popular belief was perhaps the most obviously populist manifestation in Spencean Philanthropy. To the enduring popular idea of a happy and prospering Saxon democracy forcibly subverted by an alien Norman aristocracy, the Spenceans added the weight of religious arguments. The apothecary-surgeon Dr Watson, in a private letter to his brother, sketched out a typical interpretation: Britain is ruled by 'vain and monstrous justice dealt out by a set of Norman Oligarchs, so partially [and] in scraps scarce sufficient to supply the calls of nature to the poor Plebeians'. It is easy, argued Watson, to trace

> ... the primary and immediate cause of the Calamities of the Country ... to a source, continuance and effect, worse and longer than the Egyptian Bondage, to the eruption 1800 years' [*sic*] ago of a Norman Tyrant, who destroy[ed] the most just and equal Laws, ever possessed by any Country, and established on the ruins the monstrous ones invented by heathens.[13]

The keyword here is the last: heathens. It is not mere invective, but derives from the Spenceans' particular amalgam of scriptural and popular historical ideas. In their view, the Saxon polity was a purely Christian one, its system of property-holding broadly in accordance with Mosaic law. Evans even went so far as to hail Alfred the Great as 'the third saviour of the world', following Moses and Jesus Christ: 'He was a philosopher, a philanthropist and law-giver, who guided by justice, again established in this island the agrarian commonwealth, rooting out that enemy of mankind — paganism.' The feudal system replacing the Saxon polity was therefore a reversion to paganism. Thus Spenceanism condemned the Normans and their heirs, perpetrators of the feudal system of private property, as at best 'heathens' and at worst 'servants of Anti-Christ'. Thus was Spence's thought reinforced by arguments drawn from both popular historical ideas and biblical analogy.[14] The sense of mission so apparent in Spence was further reinforced by republican biblical exegesis. Pre-monarchical Hebrew history exhibits republican liberties and political forms: the embodiment of Antichrist is not the Pope of Rome, but government based on a system of private property. This eschatology was a subject of peculiar urgency to the Spenceans and goes some way towards explaining their adoption of

13 Spence, *Restorer* (1801), 11; J. Watson, copy of undated letter (?Nov. 1816) in TS 11/199/868, pt. 1.

14 Evans, *Christian Policy*, pp. 12-13; Watson, TS 11/199/868, pt. 1; *Address* (1817), 8. Evans's writing on the subject is placed in the broader context of ideas about Saxon constitutionalism in Christopher Hill, 'The Norman Yoke', in J. Saville (ed.), *Democracy and the Labour Movement* (1954), reprinted in C. Hill, *Puritanism and Revolution* (1958), 110-11, 119-20. So idiosyncratic were Evans's views of the issue that not all the Spenceans agreed with them: in 1819, for example, Allen Davenport scorned even Alfred in his satirical poem *The Kings, or, Legitimacy Unmasked*, p. 4.

precipitate political strategies[15] — for their biblicalism did not lead them to adopt a quietist posture, waiting upon divine intervention to expedite reform. On the contrary, the vigorous historicity of their view of Moses, Christ, and Alfred — coupled with a starkly materialist social philosophy — led them to affirm strongly the role of human agency in securing the rule of God and nature. They were also resolutely opposed to gradualist approaches to reform. The solution was to be sought neither in 'political expedients, or particular modes or forms of government', nor in superficial modifications of property law, 'but by a radical adjustment of the social system on the broad basis of individual justice, and the securing to every member of the community his indefeasible right to an equal share of the profit of the land and its appurtenances.' This 'public farm of the people' would embrace 'houses, mines, fisheries, canals, bridges and all permanent property of whatever description', a significant development of their founder's own views and further evidence that the flow of ideas among the Spenceans was not all one way. Spence's only explicit references to property in 'other Great Concerns' had, of course, been made in one of the earliest publications of the Society; it is to the latter, rather than to Spence, that the credit perhaps belongs of first developing a theory of public ownership of non-landed property. Nevertheless, it was not accorded great emphasis, and it was left to Davenport and the tailor George Petrie to make an explicit extension of Spencean arguments to machinery some years later. By then such an idea, though no less revolutionary, had lost something of its novelty. The reasons for this ostensible want of emphasis lay first in the experience of metropolitan labour, with little appreciation of the nature of factory production, but an acute awareness of property in skill (symbolized for many in their owning the tools of their trade); the Spenceans emphatically excluded moveable property from the public domain. That housing or collieries were not excluded, however, underlines their perception of the iniquities of landed property. 'The Land is the strength of the Country':

> Things will continue as at present under any form of government, if whole parishes and towns — nay, whole counties are monopolised by individuals, whilst the great mass of the people are dispossessed. Landlords, and landlords only, are the oppressors of the people.[16]

Yet the conception of social struggle expressed in this quotation was capable of certain refinement. At its most basic it was expressed in the

15 American, rather than English, eschatology of this kind has received most attention. See N. O. Hatch, *The Sacred Cause of Liberty* (1977), esp. pp. 153-63.

16 *Address* (1815), 10; *Address* (1817), 4-5; *Christian Policy, or Spence's Plan*, p. 3; A. Davenport, *The Life, Writings, and Principles of Thomas Spence* (1836), 23-4, and *The Life and Literary Pursuits of Allen Davenport* (1845), 11; G. Petrie, *Man*, 25 Aug. 1833. HO 42/198, 3 Nov. 1819, anonymous report of Wedderburn's sermon; *Address* (1815), 3-4.

terminology of Christian versus pagan, people versus Norman oligarchy, landless versus landed; but the conviction (first encountered in Spence's own writing) that 'it is property alone, that gives power and influence' was pregnant with important implications. Robert Wedderburn saw no essential difference between colonial slaves and factory labour. Dr Watson described how 'Tradesmen employing Great Capitals' extracted from labour its surplus value, which he estimated at three-fifths of 'the profits arising from the labour of the journeyman'. Hence the Spenceans naturally suspected the motives of gentry and middle-class reformers, and were concerned more to promote co-operation between the traditionally divided skilled artisans and unskilled workers. By the autumn of 1818 Watson was confident that 'the working People are become fully competent to manage for themselves', and advised against any alliance with 'Persons of Property'.[17]

At the same time the Spenceans adhered to a conception of social hierarchy based on a precise view of relative utility. A speaker at Evans's Archer Street Chapel, sketching post-revolutionary society, opined:

> He would have Mechanics put in the first list, that he was one himself and that they were the most useful Persons to Society making Ploughs and Harrows for the Husbandman, and all the Implements for the labouring people to work with; the second Class, he said should be the working people, labourers etc., the third Class should be the Merchants who were very good in their places; the fourth class should be the Borough Mongers, great Lords etc., they clean Knives and Shoes and Sweep Streets, the fifth Class should be the Kings and Princes but, said he, I must not say much about these kind of people, as for the Prince he would put them with the King and Royal Family on board Ship and send them to the deserts of Arabia.[18]

Whatever the extent of public ownership, therefore, society as the Spenceans envisaged it would be one of small, self-employed producers, buttressed by the land, which would eliminate poverty and provide equality of opportunity. It was quintessentially an artisan's view of society, and this was doubtless partly responsible for the coolness with which Robert Owen's proposals were greeted by the Spenceans, who formally condemned them 'as destructive of social happiness'. Wedderburn and Jennison went further:

> The Spencean doctrine is truth and must be adopted. As for Mr Owen attempting to make the people out fools, he will find that the lower classes are pretty well convinced that he is a tool to the landholders and Ministers to divert the attention of the public from contemplating on the

17 Evans, *Christian Policy*, p. 31; HO 42/195, 18 Sept. 1819; 42/192, 14 Aug. 1819; 42/181, 12 Oct. 1818.

18 Stafford's report, quoting an anonymous speaker, HO 42/181, 22 Oct. 1818.

obstinacy and ignorance of their governors.[19]

Spenceanism was essentially an ideology of small producers: it is revealing that in explaining his theories of surplus value Watson should seize on the example of master and journeyman. Spence's advocacy of the right to the whole product of labour, arising from his endorsing moveable property, was reaffirmed by his disciples:

> The property of everyone, obtained by means of industry, ingenuity, carefulness, or decency, [should] be held sacred by all who have regard for justice. If those who have a sufficient competency to live comfortable should from covetousness, endeavour to obtain by unfair means the property of others, what can we call it but indirect robbery ... All such proceedings are contrary to true religion, morality, or honest policy.[20]

This view was typical of a far wider constituency than the Spenceans: it was by combining it with the 'People's Farm' policy that they sought to breach the divide between skilled and unskilled workers. While affirming an artisan social philosophy, the Spenceans attempted to broaden their appeal and embrace unskilled lumpen labour. The division between the latter and skilled labour was perhaps the most vitiating weakness of metropolitan radicalism. Arguably the Spenceans came close to fusing the two in December 1816.

This was a tribute to their style of agitation as much as to its content. Tavern radicalism was a keynote of Spencean tactics and it was to this area that much energy was directed. The Spenceans reached out towards an overtly populist style of politics: this can be seen as a direct continuation of some of Spence's own initiatives, such as token coins, the free-and-easy, songs, and graffiti. Burlesque, ribaldry, and rhetorical bombast were all facets of this style. In this context Thistlewood's melodramatic challenge of Sidmouth to a duel is intelligible; so too is Preston's conspicuous suit of red, white, blue, and green specially made for his mission to the provinces; or there is the proposal made 'by the Lower Class of Preston's party' to raise a subscription to present the Prince Regent with 'an elegant Snuff box ... decorated, with various Revolutionary emblems, particularly the head of Charles 1st, and an Axe'. Spencean meetings included 'obscene parody' of the Scriptures, and frequent imprecations upon 'that Great Fat Boobey in Pall Mall'. Wedderburn and Davenport's oratory could reach heights so

19 HO 40/7(4), fo. 2076, 7 Dec. 1817; *Forlorn Hope*, 1 (4 Oct. 1817), 15-16. It is interesting to note that Thomas Wooler, by contrast, believed Owen's proposals merely 'The SPENCEAN PLAN writ large': *Black Dwarf*, 20 Aug. 1817, col. 468,

20 Wedderburn, *Sherwin's Weekly Political Register*, 5/3 (22 May 1819), 40-1. Like much else published over Wedderburn's name, the actual author of this was Cannon; see McCalman, 'Unrespectable Radicalism', p. 94.

fiery that even some fellow Spenceans expressed unease.[21] The Norman Yoke, anti-clericalism, and anti-monarchism were all important factors of this rhetoric. So too were a number of other elements, for example a fierce patriotic pride in

> This nation, to whom the modern world owes so many, and such great obligations — the parent and nurse of liberty, civil and religious — the radiance of whose brightness has pierced all comers of the earth, extending a knowledge of the blessings of freedom; all the present enlightenment of mankind emanates from this small spot, this England, as from a divinity.

Or a mistily-perceived 'Golden Age' in the recent past that owed more to Cobbett than to Spence: 'Before the inclosure Bill passed, every Poor Person … had a little Garden and Cottage and Orchard.' And there was a tendency to outright infidelity that Davenport and Wedderburn especially exhibited from 1818: 'They tell us to be quiet like that *bloody spooney Jesus Christ* who like a *Bloody Fool* tells us when we get a slap on one side of the face turn gently round and ask them to swack the other.'[22]

Thus the tone and temper of the Spenceans was very different from that of Spence himself — as close to the radicalism of the streets as he had been to the tenets of the Enlightenment — but still they called themselves Spenceans, and shared with him the critical perception that the ownership of property was the key to reform:

> The Mammonites have swayed us too long we must have no property mongering jugglers, they have always entailed misery on the most industrious and useful people in every nation. I scarcely ever knew a man of property sound to the core — I have mostly found them proud and intolerant towards all whom they considered below them. Surely such a perversion of reason will in some age have an end.[23]

This private letter was written to Arthur Thistlewood by Watson in July 1818 when the fortunes of the Spencean circle seemed at a low ebb: successive attempts to force reform had conspicuously failed, the anticipated breakthrough in metropolitan radicalism had not been achieved. Earlier pronouncements exhibit far greater faith in the imminence of real progress. Faith is indeed apposite in this context, for the Spenceans were moved by a singular confidence in their ideas, as will by now have become

21 Preston's clothes — HO 47/171, 26 Nov. 1817; snuff-box — HO 42/194, 15 Sept. 1819; obscene parodies — HO 42/158, 9 Jan. 1817; 'Fat boobey' — HO 40/3(3), fo. 875; oratory — 42/182, 2 Nov. 1818, 42/191, 10 Aug. 1819. For an illuminating analysis of tavern radicalism, see I. McCalman, 'Ultra-radicalism and Convivial Debating-clubs in London, 1795-1838', *English Historical Review*, 102 (Apr. 1987), 309-33.

22 Evans, *Christian Policy*, pp. 7-8; HO 42/181, 22 Oct. 1818; TS 11/45/167, fo. 58.

23 Watson to Thistlewood (copy), HO 42/178, 24 July 1818.

clear. Reading Thomas Spence's *Restorer of Society to its Natural State*, Allen Davenport was moved to something akin to religious conversion; Wedderburn hailed 'the Kingdom of Christ forwarded by Spence', anticipating the 'experience of the new birth, for a nation shall be born that day'.[24] This confidence derived in no small measure from the sense of religious rectitude which is never far from the surface in Spence's later pronouncements and those of his followers. It was, however, no mystical faith, and the Society of Spencean Philanthropists can in no realistic sense be deemed millenarian. Although an occasional intelligence report linked the Spenceans with the Southcottians, it was rather with the materialistic Freethinking Christians that the Society had its closest connections and affinities. The probable outcome of the Spencean system, thought Evans, would be that everyone would be left 'to the reflection of their own minds, reason, and enquiry ... taught to do the will of God by following that policy in which it consists'.[25]

The central thrust of the Spenceans' unwavering confidence was consequent rather upon their faith in the 'Progress of Reason, aided by the Art of Printing'. In the catechism that admitted them to the Society each member pledged 'to become a true Spencean Philanthropist, by endeavouring to extend a knowledge of these natural rights of mankind'. Declared Davenport:

> 'Tis reason's light, — an intellectual sun,
> Whose influence, none but fools and tyrants shun:
> 'Tis human knowledge, and a sense of right,
> That burst upon us like a flood of light.[26]

Making due allowance for the flights of rhetoric, it seems clear that the Spenceans were animated by a sense of mission unusual even in the reformers of their age. It was this that impelled them in successive attempts to force the pace of reform, literally to seek something like the jubilee so long heralded by Spence. In 1819, just as the specifically Spencean thrust to their activities seemed to be diminishing, Peterloo served to galvanize them once more. 'Are not the recent transactions at Manchester the commencement of a Revolution irresistible', pondered the congregation at Hopkins Street. 'High Treason was committed against the people', declared Thistlewood. Allen Davenport was yet more specific: the people had for

24 Davenport, *Life and Literary Pursuits* pp. 41-2; *Axe Laid to the Root*, 1 (1817), 17.

25 HO 40/15, fo. 1, 8 Jan. 1820, report of Shegoe: 'A few fanatics are endeavouring to alarm the weak and credulous by Preaching and pronouncing Judgements: they are mostly the followers of Joanna Southcott and Thomas Spence and Preach to a few in Lambeth, St. Lukes, and the Borough'; Evans, *Christian Policy*, p. 42.

26 Spence, *Important Trial*, p. 35; 'Spencean Philanthropists', *Essay on Printing* [1816], 1; *Address* (1815), 7; Davenport, *Kings*, p. 12.

too long been bought and sold as 'living stock … I compare the present time to the crisis of the French Revolution, we must arm ourselves as they did'.[27]

The Spenceans figure significantly in a number of illuminating studies of early nineteenth-century radicalism.[28] Yet the broader character of their beliefs has usually been obscured by their involvement in revolutionary conspiracy — and even this involvement has still to be understood. The Cato Street conspiracy of 1820, customarily regarded as a somewhat bizarre episode in English radical history, is intelligible only in the light of the Spencean experience — the failure of mass meetings and attempted *coups d'état*, and the final adoption of the assassination tactic in the light of the 'revolution begun in blood' at Peterloo.[29] Just as Spence himself passed from pacific rebellion to the endorsement of force, so the Spenceans moved from his mature stance to conspiracy and violence.

In the late summer of 1814, as the members of the Society which had taken his name attended the funeral of Thomas Spence, Evans's son was entrusted with the revival of personal links between Spenceans and British radical émigrés in Paris. In the company of Thistlewood (whose business there, it has to be said, was apparently gambling), Thomas John Evans sailed, armed with a parcel of Spence's works to distribute and a strict paternal injunction 'that I consider you the agent of mankind and that no opportunities are to be lost of propagating the true Philosophy of Nature'. His uncle, Alexander Galloway, provided a letter of introduction to Richard Hodgson, and he was also to seek out a former neighbour, Benjamin Binns, a 'Doctor Hall', and William Putnam McCabe. Evans senior, Galloway, Hodgson, and Binns had been linked in underground activities in the late 1790s, and all four were imprisoned in the years 1797-1801. Dr Hall may have been George Cullen's friend, the agrarian theorist who had corresponded with Spence back in 1807, though this cannot be verified. McCabe had been prominent as a United Irishman and linkman with the United English: but it was the erstwhile United Irishman Binns who seems to have been regarded by his former Corresponding Society colleague as the most important contact, and Evans wrote to his son in terms clearly implying that the exile had known Spence well. It is also clear that the son's letters home were read out to meetings of the Spencean Philanthropists. The trip, however, was ill starred. Thistlewood

27 HO 42/195, 29 Sept. 1819; TS 11/202, fo. 872, HO 42/197, 18 Oct. 1819.

28 T. M. Parssinen, 'The Revolutionary Party in London, 1816-1820', *Bulletin of the Institute of Historical Research*, 45 (1972), 266-82; J. D. Belchem, 'Henry Hunt and the Evolution of the Mass Platform', *English Historical Review*, 93 (1978), 739-73; id. *'Orator' Hunt: Henry Hunt and English Working-class Radicalism* (1985); I. J. Prothero, *Artisans and Politics in Early Nineteenth Century London* (1979); J. A. Hone, *For the Cause of Truth* (1982); McCalman, 'Radical Underworld'.

29 TS 11/45/167.

antagonized Hodgson, apparently over his handling of the latter's property in England. T. J. Evans returned to England ahead of him, and there is no record of how the exiled radicals reacted to 'the true Philosophy of Nature'.[30]

At home, however, the Society was quietly expanding. It issued copies of an *Address and Regulations ... with an Abstract of Spence's Plan* in 1815, printed by Arthur Seale. The regulations are detailed: admission cost a shilling, and a further shilling's subscription was payable quarterly; however, the weekly meetings, 'for Lectures, Readings, Free-Debate, or Conviviality', were 'free of admission to all persons of decent demeanour'. The Spenceans paid dear for this arrangement, which reflected Spence's original concern with the promotion of educated public opinion, but which considerably facilitated the infiltration of the Society by informers. The emphatic educational objectives inherited from its founder were also to be furthered by the Society's 'library of useful books for the instruction of members', presided over by its chief officer, the Librarian, and backed by a purchasing fund. About the same time Seale produced an *Essay on Printing*, which underlined the importance of the printed word: 'Printing is the best gift that Nature, in its clemency has granted man. It will ere long change the face of the universe.' A *Journal of the Proceedings of the Spensonians, or Sons of Philanthropy* was also issued, but no copy survives.[31]

Rapid expansion in the ensuing months necessitated organizational changes. The Society divided into four sections meeting at public houses in Soho, Carnaby Market, Moorfields, and the Borough. A 'Conservative Committee', comprising two delegates from each section, plus the Librarian, treasurer, and secretary, was formed. The chair of a section was taken by rotation. The usual format of meetings was a debate on a political question, for example, 'Is Spence's plan for parochial partnership in Land consistent with the principles of Nature?' This would then be followed by singing, recitations, drinking, and toasts, and often the reading aloud of the

30 HO 42/141, 4 Nov. 1814 — Evans Jun. to Thistlewood Jun.; HO 42/168, 18 Sept. 1814 — Evans sen. to his son; on Hodgson, Binns, and McCabe, see J. A. Hone, *For the Cause of Truth*, and R. A. E. Wells, *Insurrection: The British Experience, 1795-1803* (1983), *passim*; J. R. Dinwiddy, 'Charles Hall, Early English Socialist', *International Review of Social History*, 21 (1976), 256-76, does not record any French visit by Hall, who was, by 1816, imprisoned for debt; C. Hall, *Effects of Civilisation* (first pub. 1805); Hall-Spence correspondence, BL Add. MS 27808, fos. 280 ff., repr. in G. Claeys (ed.), 'Four Letters between Thomas Spence and Charles Hall', *Notes and Queries*, 28/4 (Aug. 1981), 317-21; Thistlewood and Hodgson, BL Add. MS 27818, fo. 164; Hardy to O'Connor, 13 Oct. 1814, and Hardy to Hodgson, 2 Mar. 1815, fo. 186; HO 42/172, 'A Statement of the grounds on which the several Persons apprehended under Lord Sidmouth's Warrants ... were so arrested and detained' (1817).

31 *Address* (1815), 7, 8, 10; *Address* (1817), 20; *Essay on Printing*, p. 1; HO 42/168, 'Schedule of papers laid before the Committee of Secrecy', lists the *Journal*.

latest newspapers and radical journals.[32] At first the Spencean Philanthropists appear to have been content to follow this pattern of activities, and the first break in the routine occurred only in July 1816 when they met at The Cock, Grafton Street, Soho, for the annual supper in honour of Spence and his plan.[33] The post-war depression, however, exacerbated by the Corn Laws of 1815 and the presence in the capital of large numbers of discharged sailors, provided an obvious context for the revival of reform and the reactivation of the underground. Moreover, the Society numbered among its members many whose experience of attempted insurrection encompassed every major underground movement since the formation of the United Irishmen. It was therefore both appropriate and likely that the resurgence of underground activity in the capital would begin with the Society of Spencean Philanthropists, equipped as it was with the experience, contacts, and ideology for the task. The initiative behind many key events in metropolitan radicalism in the years 1816-20 derived from members of the Society acting in pursuit of objectives that were clearly Spencean in character.

It would, however, be erroneous to seek a rigid dichotomy between underground and public political activity, or between Spenceanism and other forms of radical politics. Not only was 1816 a time of acute social unrest, it was also one of growing disquiet at the domination by the Westminster Committee of London radicalism, and at the way attitudes and aspirations had atrophied around the personality of Sir Francis Burdett, whose radicalism was arguably diminishing. A local Spencean objective was therefore to outmanoeuvre the Westminster Committee, and to build a more broadly based movement than Francis Place's eminently respectable associates, dedicated to more drastic change than Westminster gradualism. This meant bridging the divide between artisans and the unskilled, between the East and West Ends, between those skilled workmen who had the vote and those lumpen elements who did not; this of course provided another element in Place's animosity towards the Spenceans.[34] The Society constituted a definite threat to the Westminster Committee's predominance. They received warm support from disenchanted elements within the committee itself: from Finnerty and Sparks, who spoke at the first Spa Fields meeting; from William Parr, a Strand silversmith; and from Giles and West, two of Henry Hunt's warmest supporters within the borough of Westminster. Effectively it was the Society of Spencean Philanthropists who did most to establish Hunt in metropolitan radical circles.

32 TS 11/204, report of Mulberry Tree section, 26 Dec. 1816.

33 TS 11/201, ticket of admission, 1 July 1816.

34 Add. MS 27809, fos. 94-101, esp. fo. 100. Place was conspicuous by his absence from the committee formed to collect subscriptions for the defence of the Cato Street prisoners, the members of which included Hone, Wooler, Harmer, and Sir Richard Phillips — see J. A. Hone, *For the Cause of Truth*, p. 347.

Towards the end of 1816 the Conservative Committee of the Society thus began to expand its activities and a primary objective was the creation of a public broadly in sympathy with an agrarian platform. Two strategies were pursued; firstly Preston, who had involved himself in an anti-machine committee composed of trades delegates, succeeded in being elected its secretary. He called on its behalf a 'Meeting of the Distressed Manufacturers, Mariners, Artisans, and others', from both sides of the river, at Spa Fields on 15 November 1816. Arthur Seale printed the publicity material, which was distributed in such copious quantities that the Trades Committee, sensing matters had passed beyond its control, expelled Preston; but it was too late for it to cancel the meeting, billed 'to petition the Prince to put down Machines in Factories'.[35]

The second objective was to secure for Spa Fields a speaker likely to attract a capacity crowd: accordingly, Preston and Thistlewood wrote to Henry Hunt inviting him to attend, enclosing the motion on which they desired him to speak. However, at a preliminary meeting in Preston's home in October, the Spenceans were dismayed to hear Hunt decline to endorse the motion they had prepared. Hunt's subsequent account of the Spa Fields meetings, written in Ilchester gaol after Peterloo, is unreliable, being primarily an attempt to exonerate the author from all blame for subsequent events. But his account of this first encounter rings true:

> I found, in fact, that the whole affair was made up of Spencean principles, relating to the holding of all the land in the kingdom as one great farm belonging to the people, or something of that sort. I told them my ideas upon the subject, which were, that the first thing the people had to do, in order to recover their rights, was to obtain a Reform of the Commons' House of Parliament. When once the people were fairly and equally represented in that House, such propositions as were contained in their memorial might then be considered.

Hunt's account is consistent with Cobbett's claim to have advised him, prior to the meeting, to attend but not permit the 'cause of reform to be mixed up with what was called the Spencean Project'.[36]

It was at this point that serious divisions within the Society first appeared. Preston, Watson, and Thistlewood accepted Hunt's more anodyne memorial for use at Spa Fields, seeing their main objective as securing the largest possible attendance. Evans, however, dissented and withdrew from further involvement, though he had been fully active until

35 HO 42/155, 15 Nov. 1816, Shadwell JP's report on the Trades Committee; ibid., 13 Nov. 1816, handbill advertising meeting; ibid., 14 Nov. 1816, Wright to Lord Mayor, disavowing both Preston and the meeting. These corroborate Preston's account in his *Life and Opinions* (1817), 28.

36 H. Hunt, *Memoirs* (1820), iii. 333; *Cobbett's Weekly Political Register*, 14 Dec. 1816, p. 650. Cobbett had declined an invitation to speak, as had Burdett and Waithman.

this point: in the months leading up to Spa Fields the Conservative Committee had published two editions of his *Christian Policy the Salvation of the Empire*. This, and a further broadside, were part of the educational programme intended to precede the meeting which would expedite reform in the manner Spence had proposed: 'after much reasoning and deliberation ... a day [is] appointed on which the inhabitants of each parish meet, in their respective parishes, to take their long lost rights into possession'. The Committee cast itself in the role of the 'hearty determined Fellows well-armed', to whom Spence had alluded in his *End of Oppression*.[37] Of necessity this action was covert, but official intelligence gleaned reports of Spencean evangelizing in London public houses: selling tracts, creating discussion, winning over waverers with bread, cheese, and ale. At Newton's beer shop in Long Acre, Watson's son (a discharged naval rating) was reported saying that 'the Earth and the produce thereof was ordained for the use and support of all Mankind but was solely enjoyed by the few Rich'. Wise after the event, a Holborn copperplate printer told the Lord Mayor how at the beginning of October Preston began to frequent his regular pub,

> ... offering for Sale a Book edited by one Evans, entitled 'Spence's Plan'; accompanying the same with observations that the present Calamities arose entirely from the Monopoly of the Land and the Fund Owners; that it was a system pernicious to any Country whatever, and ought to be pulled down.[38]

In order to reinforce the anticipated effect of Hunt's presence on the platform, and in accordance with the objective of outflanking Place and his circle, Thistlewood arranged for supporting speeches from two prominent Westminster Committee men, W. Sparks and Peter Finnerty — the latter formerly printer to the United Irish Society in Dublin. It was anticipated that their contributions would supply the agrarian perspective lacking in Hunt's oration: but the latter was so lengthy, and incidentally insulting to Finnerty and Sparks, that the two were left with little time and less inclination to make their speeches. An embarrassingly public quarrel between the three men ensued. Despite this inauspicious beginning, however, the main purpose of this first Spa Fields gathering on 15 November, to arouse interest in the more ambitious second meeting, was resoundingly achieved. Although Hunt defused a proposal to march on Carlton House to present the petition to the Regent in person, a group of

37 *Spence's plan for parochial partnership in land is the only effectual remedy for the distress and oppression of the people* (broadside, Seale, 1816); Spence, 'Lecture' (1775), in M. Beer (ed.), *The Pioneers of Land Reform* (1920), 10; Spence, *End of Oppression* (1795), 7-8.

38 TS 11/197/863, p. 72, prosecution brief — statement of Hillingsworth; HO 40/3(3), fo. 180, deposition of Higgins.

youths and 'poor-looking men' detached themselves from the crowd and ran riot through Westminster, attacking bread shops. One contemporary spectator was particularly unnerved by the encouragement the rioters received from women, especially those in St Martin's workhouse. As an indication of the mood among certain sectors of the city's populace, the riot gave promise of a lively meeting on 2 December.[39]

Expectations for the second meeting ran high, both in London and the provinces. It is clear that the Spencean Conservative Committee reactivated provincial connections and that the Spa Fields meeting on 2 December was intended, like the 'Despard conspiracy' before it, to act as a signal for a general rising; this was Major General Byng's assessment in a letter to the Home Office from army headquarters, Pontefract. Thomas Preston predicted 'that a Riot was concerted for Monday at Nottingham at the same time'. In Sheffield the Riot Act was read after a mob had paraded the streets shouting 'Bread or Blood'; as the crowd dispersed a ringleader exclaimed 'never mind, my lads, tomorrow shall be our day'. In Norwich the London mail coach was greeted by a crowd that had thronged the main streets since dawn shouting 'Bread or Blood' and 'Burdett forever'; in Towcester, to quote the High Constable, 'the principal people Dare not go to Bed. A mob gets together and threatens the Bakers houses and a Large Mill with Destruction.' Suffolk and Essex sources reported men on the move towards London, disturbingly not destitute but in employment and 'avowedly for the purpose of attending the Meeting on Spa Fields'. In Ely paupers receiving the weekly parish dole remarked with alarming candour to the Overseer: 'it will depend upon what passes on Monday night in London whether we shall trouble *you* any more or not'.[40] But it was in Lancashire that the greatest ferment was recorded:

> All the Country in a Bustle about the News from London. The public mind in the highest agitation and ferment. The Road crowded with Groups of disaffected. About Midnight Delegates from all the adjoining Townships began to flock to Manchester ... When the Mail Coach drove up they ran towards the Bridgewater from all Sides ... In the course of the Day it had been reported that the Tower in London was taken by the Rioters ... all agree in expressing the fullest determination

39 HO 42/155, 15 Nov. 1816, information of Hanley; on Finnerty, see William Hone's *Reformist's Register*, 19 July 1817. Finnerty was an important figure in Anglo-Irish radicalism, of whom a study is wanting — see though, the cumulative portrait in J. A. Hone, For the *Cause of Truth*, *passim*; on Sparks, see ibid. 218, 408. Thistlewood had himself served on the Westminster Committee in 1812, BL Add. MS 27840, fo. 3; *London Chronicle*, 16 Nov. 1816; the original petition of the first meeting, sent by Hunt to Sidmouth, is filed in HO 42/155, 19 Nov.1816.

40 HO 40/3(1), fo. 64, Byng, 7 Dec.; Nottingham, HO 42/155, 28 Nov.; Sheffield, HO 42/156, 3 Dec.; Norwich, HO 40/3(6), fo. 958, and Devon CRO, Sidmouth Papers, 152/M C1817/OH, Firth to Sidmouth, 13 June 1817; Towcester, HO 42/156, 2 Dec.; Suffolk, HO 42/155, 30 Nov.; Romford, Essex, HO 42/156, 1 Dec.; Ely, Sidmouth Papers, 1817/OH, 9 Jan. 1817.

> to have mustered and armed immediately, in case the Disturbance in London had been attended with Success.[41]

From the rumours concerning the Tower, and others about the Bank of England, that circulated in the north ahead of the arrival of any official news from the capital, it can only be concluded that the evidence advanced by the prosecution at the subsequent trial of Dr Watson, of plans to storm prisons, the Bank, and the Tower, had a strong basis in fact. It is furthermore clear that the planned insurrection was developed within the Spencean group as a refinement of Spence's proposals and members' past experience: the role of the government agent John Castles was that only of an informer, not of an *agent provocateur*. It has been said that 'the origin and significance of these riots remains obscure'; and not a few historians have taken their cue from Francis Place's assessments of 'the poor harmless Spenceans'.[42] But a careful reconsideration of the issue in the context of organized Spenceanism does reveal origins, logic, and significance: this was an attempted *coup d'état* and its ideology was essentially agrarian. Nowhere is this more apparent than in the speech made by Dr Watson at the Spa Fields meeting, minutes before rioting commenced:

> We have been truly told that Trade and Commerce are at an end — but we still have the Earth — which Nature designed for the support of mankind — The Earth is capable of affording us all the means of allaying our wants and of placing Man in a Comfortable situation — If a Man has but a Spade, a Hoe, and a Rake and turns up his Mother Earth — He will be sure to find the means of averting Starvation … must we not then act for ourselves (yes! yes!). Ever since the Norman Conquest Kings have deluded you and in many instances converted you to their own wicked purposes (Cheers), This must not last any longer (Shouts and cries of No, No).[43]

Watson's place on the wagon which formed the platform was taken by his son: 'If they will not give us what we want, shall we not take it?' On receiving shouts in the affirmative he leapt from the wagon and, seizing a red, white, and green tricolour, led a substantial crowd off the fields. Although the greater part of the audience remained behind to await Henry Hunt, it was still possible for the throng led by the younger Watson to divide into several groups and still not be contained. One body, led by

41 HO 40/4/1(2), fo. 42, Chippendale to Fletcher, 3 Dec, 1816; see also HO 40/3(1), fo. 62, Chippendale to Byng: 'When the news was not confirmed their Disappointment was extreme.'

42 E. P. Thompson, *The Making of the English Working Class* (2nd edn., 1968), 691; BL Add. MS 27809, fos. 43, 100.

43 HO 40/3(3), fos. 895-9, speech as minuted by Home Office note taker. A slightly variant transcription is given in W. Hone, *The Riots in London. Hone's Full and Authentic Account* (1816).

Preston, headed for the Tower; another ran riot in the city, looting particularly gunsmiths' premises. At one of them, Beckwith's in Skinner Street, a customer was shot — possibly by Watson junior — but 'the Villain was rescued by the Mob'. Only at nightfall was order restored.[44]

Frustrated as the Spenceans were by the inconclusive manner in which events on 2 December turned out, the meeting had the compensatory effect of widely publicizing their existence, ideas, and founder. The significance of the latter for the episode was quickly appreciated by William Hone, who swiftly followed his initial 'full and authentic' accounts with a third, including details of Spence's life and plan. In the opinion of one Home Office correspondent the Spa Fields meeting served only to increase the popularity of Spenceanism. Attendance at one Mulberry Tree meeting in early February topped 130. New sections were opened in Bethnal Green and Shoreditch, reflecting the growing support of Spitalfields silk-weavers who had been among the most prominent protesters at Spa Fields. The very entry of Watson senior and Preston into a room could transform a radical meeting, as Samuel Bamford vividly recalled. Seale rushed through his press a new *Address of the Society of Spencean Philanthropists to All Mankind, on the Means of Promoting Liberty and Happiness*. Their general mood is conveyed in one of the toasts popular at this time: 'May the Spencean Hogs never cease grunting until they have got their rights.'[45]

Although the younger Watson was forced into hiding, and in spite of the arrest, trial, and hanging of an Irish sailor for his part in the gunshops raid, there was initially little adverse effect on the Spencean group. As section meetings continued, the leadership perforce keeping a low profile, further members rose to prominence. Among them were Thomas Pemberton, a boot-closer and veteran of both the London Corresponding Society and the 1801 conspiracy; Charles Jennison, a newcomer to metropolitan radicalism, later an influential co-operator, Owenite, and Chartist; and the 54-year-old tailor and 'Unitarian preacher', Robert Wedderburn. Thomas Evans 'expressed a perfect confidence that the Spencean System would sooner or later prevail', and Jennison spoke of sending 'Delegates to go in the Country and promulgate the system more widely.' Already there were rumours of provincial Spencean groups in Bath, Richmond, and Birmingham. Whether there was any substance in

44 W. Hone, *The Meeting in Spa-Fields. Hone's Authentic and Correct Account* (1816); Devon CRO, Sidmouth Papers, C1816/OH, deposition of 'Richard Platt, shot at Beckwith's'. There are numerous accounts of events on 2 Dec.: William Hone's *Meeting in Spa-Fields, Riots*, and *Hone's Riots in London, Part II. With Most Important and Full Particulars* (1816) together form the best, but see also the *London Chronicle*, 3 Dec. 1816. Also Thompson, *Making*, pp. 693-6; J. A. Hone, *For the Cause of Truth*, pp. 263-4; J. Stevenson, *Popular Disturbances in England, 1700-1870* (1979), 193ff.

45 W. Hone, Meeting in *Spa-Fields, Riots*, and *Riots, Part II*; HO 40/3(4), fo. 926; HO 42/160, 17 Feb. 1817; TS 11/202, 13 and 17 Feb. 1817: HO 42/158, 16 Jan. 1817; S. Bamford, *Passages in the Life of a Radical* (1984; 2nd edn. 1844), 25; *Address* (1817), copy in TS 24/3/100 endorsed 12 Feb. 1817.

these rumours it is impossible to determine, but probably they formed the basis for remarks made by the Parliamentary Committee of Secrecy:

> Your Committee find, from ... undoubted information, that the doctrines of the Spencean clubs have been widely diffused through the country, either by the extension of similar societies, or more frequently by the intervention of missionaries or delegates, whose business it is to propagate these doctrines.[46]

Presumably such intelligence motivated the otherwise surprising offer of bail to the Spa Fields leaders, in the hope that their subsequent activity would reveal more of radical underground networks. Occasional reports do suggest a degree of Spencean involvement with the provinces that went beyond merely keeping contacts alive. From Bristol the Home Office received news of 'a Sett of Villains who Stile themselves Spencean or Hampton Club Men and who ... have the impudence Still to circulate their Damnible Doctrines of Levelling'. At a crowded Manchester meeting in mid-February a collection was made for the Spa Fields defence fund following a powerful speech by one of the Bradbury brothers on agrarian reform. Some knowledge of Spenceanism among Wiltshire textile workers around the same time may be deduced from the publication in Salisbury of a pamphlet attacking Spence and all his works.[47] A number of provincial delegates had attended Spa Fields in order to secure 'the earliest Intelligence of the Success that attended the Attempt'. Among them were John Kay from Royton and Joseph Mitchell from Middleton. Before the year passed Mitchell and William Benbow (a shadowy figure at this time who may well have belonged to the Society) had been deputed to tour the country 'where the nature and cause of our distress had not been publicly asserted and its remedy insisted upon'. Sidmouth was told 'the people of Leicester are all for the Spencean plan', and that a thousand addresses had been printed for circulation there; this may well have contained a kernel of truth since the report specified Seale as the printer. This was on 29 January, shortly after Spencean leaders had entertained delegates to the Hampden Club convention. There were persistent rumours that the Spenceans 'cherished some desperate project which they intended to attempt carrying into execution' at a further Spa Fields meeting in early February. The possibility of this seemed to increase when they met 'county delegates' for over two hours on 6 February; but the third Spa Fields meeting, which took place four days later, passed off peaceably. One clue

---

46 HO 42/161, 10 Mar. 1817, information of Meredith; TS 11/204; HO 40/3(3), fo. 877, Conant quoting information of Gypson; *Hansard's Parliamentary Debates* (17), xxv. 445.

47 HO 42/161, 12 Mar. 1817, Davison (Bristol) to Sidmouth; HO 42/163, 19 Feb. 1817, report of I. K. Manchester; W. Rose, *A Letter to the Rev. Wm. Douglas ... Containing a Review of the Spencean Philosophy* (Salisbury, n.d., copy 'written last assizes' in HO 42/165, 15 May 1817).

why this was so may be found in Bamford's retrospective claim that the abortive Blanketeers' March the following month was 'one of the bad schemes which accompanied us from London', foisted on the movement by the Spenceans. Though implausible in itself, this does imply that the Spenceans had been persuaded to support the new tactics at these meetings: on 2 February Preston referred to the proposed march urging united action 'to divest all Landholders and Stockholders of their present possessions'. To explain the conduct of the February Spa Fields meeting entirely on this supposition is, however, to credit the radical underground with an unlikely degree of self-discipline. No less influential was the increased official surveillance which followed an alleged attempt on the Regent's life, amidst rioting at the opening of Parliament on 28 January. Hunt reflected the mood of a considerable majority when, from the platform on 10 February, he pointedly dissociated himself from the Spenceans and the events of 16 December. In any case, the Evanses had been arrested the previous evening. Events were beginning to take their toll of the Spenceans.[48]

In arresting the elder Evans the Home Office, seemingly haunted still by spectres from the 1790s, acted in the mistaken belief that he was still a pivotal figure in the radical underground. The actual impression given was of an apparently arbitrary action which deterred attendance at Spencean meetings, even before the suspension of habeas corpus on 3 March. Customers at the Mulberry Tree in Moorfields (always a popular local for the Spenceans) dwindled to the point where the landlord Johnson began glumly to contemplate the workhouse: Savidge, for example, the undertaker and window-blind maker prominent in the section, had switched to the less obtrusive Bethnal Green group. Meetings were actually abandoned at the end of February, but resumed as free-and-easies when, after examining the habeas corpus and seditious meetings legislation at the suggestion of a staunch member, the veteran radical John Baxter, it was concluded that informal meetings of less than fifty were legal. Only the central, core of the Society appear to have attended though.[49]

Covert activity continued, however: the younger Watson was still hiding in London and efforts had to be made to secure his escape abroad; and there were the links with the increasingly restless provinces to be kept alive. Critical for both these areas of activity was the involvement of the cobbler Charles Pendrill, the Corresponding Society and United Irish veteran whose involvement with the 'executive' of the so-called 'Despard

---

48 HO 40/4/1(2), fo. 1156; H. W. C. Davis, 'Lancashire Reformers, 1816-7'. *Bulletin of the John Rylands Library*, 10 (1926), 36; HO 42/158, 27 and 29 Jan., 7 Feb, 1817); HO 42/168, deposition of 'N.N.'; W. Hone, *Full Account of the Third Spa-Fields Meeting* (1817). Belchem, *'Orator' Hunt*, pp. 63-9; S. Bamford, *Passages* p. 30; HO 40/3(3), fo. 908.

49 HO 42/160, 17 Feb.; HO 42/162-9.

conspiracy' has already been noted. Watson junior had been hiding in Pendrill's home at the very moment when the latter spoke at the third Spa Fields meeting. Pendrill made the arrangements for Watson's departure from Gravesend to America and shortly afterwards followed himself;[50] but he did so only after he had unwittingly made a disastrous contribution to the unhappy events of the year 1817. It was he who introduced the notorious spy Oliver into the restless midst of northern radicalism. Oliver first made the acquaintance of the Lancashire organizer-in-chief Joseph Mitchell at Pendrill's home in mid-April. Later that month he and Mitchell left together for a provincial tour; not the least of the factors assisting Oliver's progress was the memory of Pendrill's name from the Despard business.[51]

The Pentrich tragedy had an incidental and happy consequence for the Spenceans, however. The exposure of Oliver's part in it occurred at just the right moment to reinforce powerfully the defence case at Dr Watson's trial in June, on charges of high treason arising from Spa Fields. The exposure of the crown's chief witness John Castles as a pimp, perjurer, and plausible *provocateur*, backed by the parallel example of Oliver, resulted in the acquittal of Watson and hence Hooper, Preston, and Thistlewood as well. Both affairs seemed triumphantly to vindicate Cobbett's assessment of the situation in the week following Spa Fields, imputing the entire affair to government machinations: 'They sigh for a PLOT, oh, how they sigh! They are working and slaving and fretting and stewing; they are sweating all over; they are absolutely pining and dying for a plot.'[52] Spencean moves for renewed insurrectionary activity resumed almost at once. The moment was judged right for a revival of 'Spencean Principles', reported an informer who noted in an aside that the assassination of a government minister was one strategy mooted. This sounded ominous, but at this stage was only loose talk in the atmosphere of euphoria that followed the acquittal of Watson. It suggests, though, a growing awareness among those who had been disciples of Thomas Spence that the jubilee he had desired was unlikely ever to be secured by the growth of informed public opinion alone. As the informer John Shegoe bluntly put it: 'They intend inculcating the Principles of the Luddites instead of the Spenceans, as some of the

---

50 W. Hone, *Full Account*; HO 42/169, 7 Aug. 1817; HO 40/8(2), fo. 49; HO 40/6(7), 'VGD'.

51 HO 40/5(6), fo. 1626: HO 40/9, narrative of Oliver. On the latter's career see Thompson, *Making*, pp. 711-34; J. Stevens, *England's Last Revolution* (1977), *passim*; and A. F. Freemantle, 'The Truth about Oliver the Spy', *English Historical Review*, 47 (1932), 601-16.

52 *The Trial of James Watson* (Gurney, 1817); *Cobbett's Weekly Political Register*, 14 Dec. 1816. The acquittal generated much useful propaganda for the radical cause, e.g. 'Peter Pindar', *Bubbles of Treason* (1817); W. Hone, *Another Ministerial Defeat!* and *Official Account of the Noble Lord's Bite* (both 1817); Cobbett, 'A History of the Last Hundred Days of English Freedom', *Cobbett's Weekly Political Register*, 18 Oct. 1817. A pamphlet entitled *Spencea, or the State Papers of Spa Fields* was also published, according to an advertisement in the *New Times*, 1 May 1818.

most vindictive of them say the Philanthropy and Benevolence of Spencean Principles will never effect any Change, and that Luddism is best calculated for the times.' Not surprisingly, Thistlewood was one of those specified by Shegoe as holding this opinion; but lest it be thought that Thistlewood was an atypical psychotic uninterested in Spenceanism as such, it is useful to note that among those sharing this view were several avowed disciples of Spence whose attachment to his principles was unquestionable, for example Hooper, Jennison, the veteran John George, and Spence's close friend and funeral orator, William Snow.[53]

Immediate activity, however, conformed to the familiar pattern. The customary July celebration of Spence's birthday was combined with the Spa Fields acquittals, the event being organized by William West and the indefatigable Arthur Seale. A committee was formed to publicize the trial verdicts, the membership of which reveals something of the complexion of grass-roots Spenceanism: Savidge, Seale, Shegoe, and a Society member more usually noticed as a Westminster man, the Wych Street baker William Giles (who had stood bail for Preston before the trial). Two other members had spoken at the third Spa Fields meeting: W. Green and William Clark, who had formerly been an associate of Spence himself, and was like Savidge a regular at the radical Clerkenwell Green public house the Northumberland Arms.[54] Among the non-Spenceans involved were another Westminster activist, the silversmith William Parr, and as the committee's figure-head, Henry Hunt. His evidence at Watson's trial had proved crucial, emphatic as it was that Castles had deliberately provoked insurgency during the last weeks of 1816. Hunt's renewed involvement with the group won him Watson's allegiance once more, and henceforward the latter's White Lion group took a leading role in the metropolitan management of the 'mass platform', as Hunt's biographer has recognized. Yet Watson was hardly quick 'to quash any plans for insurrection by members of the revolutionary party'. He played, rather, a dual role, one which emphasizes the extent to which the 'open constitutionalism' of the period still cloaked potential insurgency.[55]

During July and August fresh plans were devised for the seizure of power in the capital. Their precise germination is unclear, since government intelligence was at a low ebb: the reliable Castles naturally

53 HO 40/7(1), fo. 1929, 30 June; HO 40/8(1), fo. 5, 30 June, 7 July; ibid., fo. 11, 8 July 1817.

54 HO 40/8(1), fo. 5, 30 June, 7 July; ibid., fo. 11, 8, 12, and 20 July; HO 47/168, n.d., Watson et al., defence fund cash-book. From the latter it seems Galloway was the greatest donor (2 guineas). Other contributors included the London Corresponding Society veteran and Westminster man John Ridley and the printer John McCreery, publisher to the Hampden Club, associate of Hone, and, like Evans and Thistlewood, a former member of the West London Lancasterian Association. For details of Giles, Ridley, and McCreery see J. A. Hone, *For the Cause of Truth, passim.* Clark claimed that 'he and Spence Rote Hogs Meat', but that subsequently they fell out, HO 42/162, 1 Mar. 1817.

55 Belchem, *'Orator' Hunt*, p. 77.

had withdrawn; and Shegoe, an erratic and excitable informer, had somewhat discredited himself among the Spenceans by his proposal to become an itinerant Christian evangelist. So it was that the Home Office learnt at only the last moment of plans to ferment a riot at Bartholomew Fair on 6 September. The annual Smithfield Fair was notorious for its mob violence, and major rioting had occurred on several occasions earlier in the century, so the possibilities of disturbance were great. Lord Sidmouth compared the plan directly to the Despard conspiracy. Spencean emissaries, among them William Snow, were reported going into the country; plans were laid to seize arms from the Honourable Artillery Company's ground, and from the Volunteer Cavalry headquarters in Gray's Inn Lane; the Bank was to be stormed and 'all the Books' destroyed. Among the ancillary objectives, Preston and Thistlewood planned to release the Evanses from Horsemonger Lane Gaol. Pike-heads, abandoned after Spa Fields, were apparently dredged up from the Thames. A supper at the Piebald Horse in Chiswell Street, Finsbury Square, was to be the occasion of the rising.[56]

Nothing happened. The plot was real enough, but it was defeated by a combination of last-minute official precautions and the all-too-familiar optimism of the protagonists:

> Preston declared he was so disappointed, that if he had had a Pistol by him, he thinks he should have blown out his brains. He took leave of his Family on Friday night, thinking he might never see them again. As nothing had been done he wishes to encourage the idea that nothing was intended.

Preston's wish was readily granted, for the Government were reluctant to become involved in further invidious controversy over the use of spies. Seale issued handbills denying that any kind of disturbance had been contemplated, while Hone made it the occasion for one of his brightest anti-Government satires.[57]

The frustration of Bartholomew Fair prompted further discussion of the assassination strategy. Almost at once Thistlewood aired the idea of an attack on the Privy Council 'in the manner of Despard', whose example was also invoked by Preston. John George, a paper-hanger from the Surrey side, also endorsed the assassination idea, 'the best signal … that would set

56 H. Pellew, *The Life and Correspondence of the Rt. Hon. Henry Addington*, iii (1847), 200; HO 40/8(1), fos. 6-3O; HO 42/170, 5 and 9 Sept. 1817; HO 42/172, *'Statement of the grounds …'*; *Sherwin's Weekly Political Register*, 1/24 (13 Sept. 1817). For examples of the frequently riotous nature of Bartholomew Fair see H. Morley, *Memoirs of Bartholomew Fair* (1858; 2nd edn. 1874), *passim*; *Independent Whig*, 7 Sept. 1817.

57 HO 40/8(1), fo. 30, information of spy 'A' (i.e. Hanley), 9 Sept.; HO 40/8(2), fo. 83, notice (printed by Seale) denying all allegations that a plot was contemplated; TS 11/197/859; W. Hone, *Official account: Bartholomew Fair Insurrection and the Pie-bald Poney Plot!* (1817).

all going'. The company had not lost sight, though, of political principles in the midst of conspiratorial excitement. Their objectives, as discussed at Preston's home on 20 September, were clear: 'Monopoly is to be declared at an end, the Land is said to belong to the People, and everyone has an equal right to it.' Some days later Watson and Preston were reported as follows: 'It was a shame that the High Men should have so much of the Poor Man's Labour, that it were better to die, than to live in such Slavery; they added "Let us follow King Charles' rule".'[58] Plans were then laid to lead an attack on the Tower and Bank on the night of 11 October; but on the evening only eighty men turned up, plus an unspecified number at Bethnal Green under Preston's command: another proposed insurrection thus dissolved away, this time under circumstances approaching farce, and the attraction of an attack on the Privy Council or Cabinet correspondingly increased. Thistlewood briefly contemplated fomenting another riot on Guy Fawkes night, but was persuaded against it when Savidge pointed out the probable extent of police surveillance. So a policy was adopted of public-house agitation, 'upon the Spencean Principles', seizing upon the issues of the day — for example the trial and execution of Brandeth, and the death of Princess Charlotte. The latter was a popular talking-point; the death of the Regent's daughter was variously held to be a sign of divine disapproval of the Derby trials, or of her father's attempt to divorce her mother. The Spenceans were not above a populist cause of this kind: Thistlewood wanted to chalk graffiti to the effect that the Regent had actually poisoned his daughter; and during the Queen Caroline agitation three years later, Allen Davenport's eulogy to the deceased princess, containing caustic comments on her father's marital life, was published by the prodigious ballad-printer John Pitts.[59]

It may be that this interest in Princess Charlotte reflected a realization of the need to build up popular support for, and awareness of, Spencean Philanthropy. It certainly marked a re-entry into the tavern radicalism to which Spenceans had made a most significant contribution, but from which they appear largely to have been absent after March 1817. Formal meetings recommenced at the Mulberry Tree about this time, with Wedderburn playing a leading role. This was the direct successor of the old Society of Spencean Philanthropists, now meeting as 'The Polemic Society'. It also revealed that the rift which had opened during preparations for the first Spa Fields meeting had not resolved itself. Led in Evans's absence by Wedderburn, the Polemic Society still adhered to the ideal of reform

58 HO 42/170, 18 Sept., 9 Oct. 1817; HO 40/7(1), fo. 1961, 20 Sept.; ibid., fo. 1967, 30 Sept. 1817.

59 Public-house agitations, e.g. HO 40/8(3), fo. 101, 29 Oct.; HO 40/7(3), fo. 2024, 29 Oct.; ibid., fos. 2032-4, 10 Nov.; police surveillance, ibid., fo. 2029; Guy Fawkes night, HO 42/170, 30 Oct.; Princess Charlotte, HO 40/7(3), fos. 2034 and 2045, 20 Nov.; E. J. Blandford, *Prince Cobourg's Lamentation for the Loss of Princess Charlotte* [1817], A. Davenport, *Claremont, or the Sorrows of a Prince* [1820].

through the growth of knowledge, and were unwilling to compromise Spencean principles for short-term pragmatic considerations. Watson's circle, while still Spencean in outlook, was more flexible and fully reconciled to the extensive application of force. Several Spenceans, notably Preston, moved happily in both camps, and relations between them were not as sour as has sometimes been supposed; nevertheless a polarity of opinion, purist and pragmatic, did exist.[60]

The 'purist' Spenceans especially renewed the policy of agitation through the press at this time. It is quite probable that the impetus for the revival arose out of a desire to counteract the influence of Robert Owen, whose much-publicized August meetings at the City of London Tavern had been attended by (among others) Preston, Thistlewood, and Watson. By December the Mulberry Tree society had condemned 'Mr Owen's Plan … as destructive of social Happiness'. Watson launched a new journal, *Political Disquisitions*, which ignominiously folded after one issue. It was rather Wedderburn's group that did most to publicize Spencean ideas: in collaboration with his *éminence grise*, Erasmus Perkins, their leader had been among the earliest contributors to the young W. T. Sherwin's *Weekly Political Register*: Blandford was another, so too was Davenport. More significant, Wedderburn and Jennison launched two new journals, both printed, of course, by Seale.[61]

The spy Shegoe implied that Alexander Galloway was the financier of these small, short-lived journals; this seems plausible. Less so, however, were his claims that Wooler, Hone, and Sherwin were warmly encouraging, though the latter did influence Davenport decisively in his development as a writer. Preston, meanwhile, travelled north to address the Birmingham Hampden Club and raise funds for further ventures in the capital. After just four days he returned, 'complaining heavily of the lukewarmness of *their* people'. Despite this the final months of 1817 did see some revival of fortunes; and it was with evident satisfaction that a speaker at a dinner held on 5 November in aid of the Evanses boasted: 'The Government had been more annoyed by individuals belonging to them than by any other body and strongly recommended the adoption of similar Societies in Town and Country.'[62]

However, a new group formed about this time revealed the widening division between the circles led by Evans and Watson, and along with it the increasingly sectarian tone of 'purist' Spenceanism. Subscriptions

60 HO 40/7(3), fos. 2036-7, 13 Nov.; HO 40/8(3), fo. 115, 13 Nov.; HO 42/171, 7 Nov. 1817.

61 *The Times*, 15 Aug. 1817; HO 40/7(4), fo. 2076, 7 Dec.; HO 42/172, 2 Dec. 1817; *Sherwin's Weekly Political Register*, 1/15 (12 July 1817), 2/11 (13 Dec. 1817); *Forlorn Hope*, 1 (4 Oct.)-3 (18 Oct. 1817); *Axe Laid to the Root*, 1 (Oct.)-6 (Dec. 1817).

62 HO 42/172, 2 Dec. 1817; HO 40/7(4), fos. 2065-6; HO 42/171, 22, 24-6, and 28 Nov. 1817 — reports of Preston's Birmingham visit; HO 40/8(3), fos. 114-15, 13 Nov. 1817.

raised at the Mulberry Tree were used to lease a chapel in Worship Street, Shoreditch, in the name of Thomas Evans. Regular Sunday meetings commenced in October, some months before he and his son were released from prison. There was a sizeable overlap of membership between Worship Street and the Polemic Society, and meetings at the former frequently adjourned to the Mulberry Tree. Meetings at 'Evans Chapel' (as it was commonly called) were chaired by the Camden Spencean Faux (or Fox). It was patronized by several Unitarian businessmen from the City, and there is evidence of close links with the Jewin Street 'Church of God', or 'Freethinking Christians'. The Holborn Hill wine dealer Coates, co-founder of the latter congregation, was a regular patron; his partner, and editor of the *Freethinking Christians' Magazine*, Samuel Thompson (a prominent City liveryman and radical), was also rumoured to have 'encouraged' Spencean activity about this time.

The Church of God had its origins in the universalist congregation established by Elhanan Winchester when living in London, 1787-94. Similarities between his and Spence's views of the millennium were noted in the previous chapter, so it may be that the association between Freethinking Christians and Spenceanism was a long-established one. How long joint meetings continued is unclear. Intelligence surveillance was focused upon Watson's group rather than Evans's, which in the absence of its leader seemed to constitute little threat to security.[63] The soundness of official policy in this respect was evident at the funeral of John Hooper, who died on 5 January 1818 after a lengthy illness. With Savidge acting as undertaker, it was proposed to turn the funeral into a mass demonstration following Hooper's interment at Stepney alongside Cashman, the Irish sailor hanged for his part in the Spa Fields riots. 'The Friends of Patriotism' were invited to view the body where it lay at Savidge's Southwark premises, and contribute towards the expenses of the funeral; meanwhile rumours grew that an attempt would afterwards be made to storm the Bunhill Road Artillery ground. According to the spy Williamson, the project was abandoned only on the morning of the funeral when the Spenceans realized the extent of police activity in the area. The frustration of yet another attempt to ignite popular grievances through a rising in the capital served only to fuel the view that 'some other method must be found out to get at the Root of the Evil', as Savidge exclaimed that same

63 HO 40/7(3), fos. 2043-4; HO 40/8(3), fo. 121; HO 42/171, 18 Nov. 1817; HO 42/172, 3 and 16 Dec. 1817; HO 40/8(4), fo. 146, The Freethinking Christians, who included several important radicals, deserve more attention: but see Prothero, *Artisans*, pp. 259-60, 273, 276, 386; *Freethinking Christians' Magazine*, 1/1 (Jan. 1811)-4/47 (Nov. 1814); *A Brief Account of the Church of God, known as Freethinking Christians: Also, an Abstract of the Principles which they Believe, and the Laws of Church Fellowship they have Adopted* (1841). Subsequent members included Henry Hetherington; see his *Principles and Practice Contrasted* (1828).

evening.[64]

A strategy of assassination might well have emerged at once, for the idea had been canvassed since the Spa Fields trials. However, while some of Watson's group inclined to support it, only Arthur Thistlewood actively promoted it. Following his imprisonment for rashly challenging the Home Secretary to a duel (on the matter of property confiscated in December 1816 and not returned to him), talk of assassination subsided. Freed of Thistlewood's baneful influence, Watson and his circle proceeded to build up a nation-wide movement for reform that was only incidentally Spencean. Tempering idealism with pragmatism, they tried to rebuild bridges broken in 1817, succeeding perhaps to a greater extent than historians have acknowledged. Not the least of Watson's tasks was to complete the reconciliation with the London trades that had become necessary since Preston's manipulation of events in the autumn of 1816. That Watson succeeded in attracting into his circle so crucial a figure as John Gast underlines the extent of the relationships built up. By July strong contacts with the North-west had been secured, besides the warm support of William Washington, a Lancashire Luddite of 1812 now resident in London, who acted as secretary to the group. Provincial links may have been reactivated with the return from America of Charles Pendrill, though he himself kept a low profile. Albeit short-lived, Watson's new journal *Shamrock, Thistle and Rose, or the Focus of Freedom* enjoyed wider circulation and success than the Spencean periodicals of the previous year, and his *Rights of the People* had passed quickly through three editions by the following February, largely because of demand from the North-west.[65] As the meticulous reconstructions of the period by Belchem and Prothero show, Watson and his circle agitated for a straightforward programme of parliamentary reform to be achieved through a radical national convention. But they did not abdicate their interest in Spencean ideas. As Watson wrote to Thistlewood in Horsham Gaol:

> The Mammonites have swayed us too long — we must have no property mongering jugglers, they have always entailed misery on the most industrious and useful people in every nation. I scarcely ever knew a man of property sound to the core — I have mostly found them proud and intolerant towards all whom they considered below them.

64 HO 40/7(4), fo. 2079; HO 40/8(4), fos. 154-9; HO 42/173.

65 HO 42/177, 26 June 1818 (Pendrill's return); there are extensive intelligence reports on Watson's White Lion group in 1818 in HO 42/177-82, and a good secondary account in Prothero, *Artisans*, pp. 99-110; *Shamrock, Thistle and Rose*, 1 (Aug. 1818) and 2 (Sept. 1818); J. Watson, *The Rights of the People: Unity or Slavery* (1st edn. in HO 42/180, Sept. 1818; 2nd edn. in HO 42/182, Dec. 1818; 3rd edn. in HO 42/184, Feb. 1819 — this edition was printed by James Wroe on the presses of the *Manchester Observer*).

> Surely such a perversion of reason will in some age have an end.[66]

Besides Watson and Washington, the other key member of the White Lion group was a hairdresser, Edward Blandford, whose poetic contributions to *Medusa* and to *Sherwin's Political Register* reveal him to have been a thoroughgoing Spencean. Other avowed Spenceans who took a close hand in the affairs of the circle included the Irishman Phillips and the tireless John George. It is likely that Davenport too was involved, for certain of his contributions to *Sherwin's Political Register* mirror the Watsonite strategy of seeking Hunt's election and the disavowal of Sir Francis Burdett.[67] In respect of Hunt's candidacy, however, 1818 was a frustrating year. He was defeated at the poll in June in spite of his acclamation at the hustings, and he declined to pursue the nomination later the same year following the suicide of Sir Samuel Romilly, Burdett's fellow member. Hopes of wresting the initiative from Place and his circle faded further, and it was impossible for Watson's group effectively to organize on Hunt's behalf. Observing the 'character of the meeting' to nominate Romilly's successor, a government observer noted:

> The revolutionary Advocates were also strong in muster, but evinced a degree of caution and quietude seemed evidently to be the effect of previous concert. All the old friends of Mr Hunt were mixed in the multitude, they appear to have gained prudence from defeat and apparently wished to gain Strength by a subtle moderation.[68]

More generally, 'subtle moderation' was enforced by the financial problems which dogged the Watsonites. Their style of organization had changed, though, towards a cellular structure in both capital and provinces; each section met for fund-raising and discussion rather than any covert activity. Exchange of delegates was frequent, and the policy avowedly one of parliamentary reform. This was a very different political animal from the Society of Spencean Philanthropists.

It was different, too, from the activities of Evans's group, now meeting at a chapel in Archer Street, Soho. Informal free-and-easies meanwhile continued at the Mulberry Tree. At Archer Street meetings followed the debating format first favoured by the Society of Spencean Philanthropists. The chapel was licensed for worship, and in addition to two Sunday 'services' there was an evening meeting as well. Thomas Evans usually chaired proceedings, but Wedderburn increasingly took a leading role.

66 Belchem, *'Orator' Hunt*, *passim*: Prothero, *Artisans*, p. 103; see also T. Parssinen, 'Association, Convention, and Anti-Parliament in British Radical Politics, 1771-1848', *English Historical Review*, 87 (1973), 5116; Watson to Thistlewood, 24 July 1818, in HO 42/178.

67 *Sherwin's Weekly Political Register*, 3/6 (13 June 1818), 78-9, 3/12 (25 July 1818), 191-2; for Phillips see HO 42/162, Mar. 1817; HO 42/179, Aug. 1818; For George see HO 42/178, 7 July 1818.

68 HO 42/182, 17 Nov. 1818; J. A. Hone, *For the Cause of Truth*, pp. 286-9.

Other notable participants included John Gast; John Wright, an orator much admired by radical contemporaries; the group's secretary James Mee, a young carpenter whose political career was to extend well into Chartism; and Allen Davenport: 'I seized the first opportunity, to deliver myself of the mass of thoughts, and Spencean ideas … with all the warmth and zeal of an enthusiast … my maiden speech consisted of fiery and ungovernable declarations, and invectives against the present administration of landed property in England, and all the other nations of the civilised world.'[69]

Divisions among the Spenceans, however, had yet to be reconciled. Preston, George, and Wedderburn moved within the ambit of both Evans and Watson. Evans tried to dissuade them from participating in any way in Watson's activities. Preston doubtless knew his own mind too well to take any notice, but Wedderburn resigned from the White Lion group in consequence, while George, though continuing his association with Watson, was dissuaded from establishing his own independent Spencean meeting in the Borough.[70] One reason for this antagonism, suggested already, lay in the rift between purists and pragmatists that opened over the original Spa Fields petition; but there were more personal reasons why it continued in an atmosphere of increasing acrimony. The two Evanses, imprisoned without trial for nearly a year, resented the adulation received by the Spa Fields four on their acquittal, not least because each had actually been bailed shortly after arrest. Matters deteriorated further when a prisoners' relief committee, chaired by Galloway (Evans's brother-in-law), was accused of partiality in its distribution of relief. In May 1818 Evans made the rift more public in a letter to the *New Times*, attacking Watson and his circle as renegades who courted government repression of all radicals. In reply Watson accused Evans of 'putting forward misstatements with a view of obtaining a little popularity'. Stressing the need for 'the most determined co-operation … to overthrow a system destructive to the people's freedom and happiness', Watson attacked Evans for creating precisely the opposite, not least through presuming to monopolize the title 'Spencean Philanthropists' now that the Society had folded. Spencean Philanthropy, declared Watson, was a general creed, 'founded in truths unanswerable but by acts contrary to natural justice'.[71]

The fragile remnants of organized Spenceanism were further undermined the following March when a squalid dispute arose between Evans and Wedderburn over the ownership of furniture and effects in the

69 There are intelligence reports on Archer Street throughout HO 42/177-82; Davenport, *Life and Literary Pursuits*, pp. 47-8; for Mee see HO 42/190, 15 Apr. 1819; Gast's participation can reliably be inferred from HO 42/182, 15 Dec. 1818, which notes a speech by the author of an article in the *Gorgon*, 5 Dec. 1818, identified as Gast in Prothero, *Artisans*, p. 86.

70 HO 42/182, 11 Nov. 1818.

71 Evans, *New Times*, 1 May 1818; Watson, *Shamrock, Thistle and Rose*, 1 (Aug. 1818).

Archer Street Chapel, Evans having decided to close it when Wedderburn wished to continue. As in the dispute with Watson the mantle of true Spenceanism was disputed, with Evans branded an 'apostate' by his erstwhile associate. Wedderburn carried the majority of the congregation with him, first at Archer Street and then from August 1819 at larger premises in Hopkins Street. Evans briefly led a splinter group to a chapel in Wood Street, Cripplegate, and then finally contented himself with attending the old haunt in Long Alley, Moorfields — the Mulberry Tree, where free-and-easies of a Spencean character were still held weekly. At Hopkins Street Wedderburn was joined in preaching virulently anti-religious sermons by Allen Davenport, now confident enough to drop his alias of Ferguson and writing regularly in the radical press.[72]

With Evans effectively peripheralized, Davenport and Wedderburn reached something of a *rapprochement* with Watson. Besides Spenceanism, they shared a common ground of infidelism. Watson's *Shamrock* had commented on the mortality of the soul, and its author had taken a close interest in the trial of Richard Carlile, even claiming to be helping in the preparation of the defence case. According to the informer John Williamson, Watson's group meant to attend the trial armed. Now Wedderburn and the group's treasurer, Blandford, pledged themselves to take up publishing Paine should Carlile be convicted.[73] There was much overlap between membership of Hopkins Street and Watson's committee: most notably Preston, Blandford, and the Lambeth Irish leader Dennis Shaw (formerly a United Irishman). Meetings of Watson's committee were sometimes held at Wedderburn's, and chaired by him. When covert arming commenced following Peterloo, the Hopkins Street Chapel section was among the most effective: 'Thislewood [*sic*] says he depends more on Wedderburn's division for being armed than all the rest.'[74] The stature of Watson was meanwhile increasing, partly because of his continuing and mutually profitable association with Hunt, but partly also because he was an energetic reformer of some flair in his own right. In resuming the convention strategy, dormant since the 1790s, Watson shared in reviving an idea of considerable significance: to him, perhaps more than any other, should go the credit for restoring confidence in the radical underground network following the Oliver affair. An indication of this is to be seen in Evans and Pendrill's swiftly frustrated attempt 'to take the London County correspondence' out of Watson's hands. These contacts did not collapse in

72 HO 42/190, 8 Mar.; Davenport, *Life and Literary Pursuits*, p. 48; [R. Wedderburn], *A Few Plain Questions for an Apostate* [1819]; HO 42/191, 3 and 4 Aug. On Davenport's Hopkins Street preaching see HO 42/197, 19 and 27 Oct.; HO 42/198,1 Nov.; TS 11/45/167, fo. 56.

73 Watson, *Shamrock, Thistle and Rose*, 1 (Aug. 1818), 13; HO 42/190, 29 Apr. 1819; HO 42/191, 4 Aug. 1819.

74 HO 42/191, 1 and 8 Aug. 1819; HO 42/197, 18 Oct.; E. Blandford, 'Satan's will ...', *Medusa*, 22 May 1819, 108.

1818 along with his embryonic 'Union of Non-represented People'. Interception of letters by the Post Office had certainly caused problems, but the underground had long since ceased to rely on this medium. In July 1819, according to George Edwards, the most reliable government informer, the correspondence was directed through the paper-hanger John George 'by means of a *Roll* of Paper directed to him as if in the course of his trade'.[75]

This has a particular significance: in all that has been written on the subject of Peterloo the extent to which the underground remained active, and elements within it committed to revolution, has gone unnoticed. The extent of 'open constitutionalism' in 1819 can be exaggerated. Spenceans at least expected the Manchester meeting of 16 August to succeed where Spa Fields had failed: 'They look with great Anxiety to the Manchr. Meeting, on Monday, where they expect the Row to begin, and this they look upon as the Signal to begin. They will be much disappointed, if that Meeting goes off quietly.'[76]

The tide of fortune seemed to be turning in reform's favour. In common with radicals nationwide, there had been a flurry of activity among the Spenceans in the months leading up to 16 August. In June George Petrie appeared in Leeds to make two major speeches at mass rallies. Preston and Thistlewood reactivated contacts with workers willing to lend military assistance, and the unemployed servant John Hartley prepared to travel north to Manchester to secure accurate information about events there. A few weeks before, he had been glimpsed ordering pikes for the use of 'old George's section'.[77]

Particularly interesting at this time is the extent of Spencean participation in the press. In the spring and summer of 1819 there appeared a new *Address of the Society of Christian Philanthropists to All Mankind, on the Means of Promoting Liberty and Happiness*; Wedderburn's broadside songs 'for the New Dispensation'; and Dr Watson's *More Plots, More Treason, More Green Bags*. All of these reiterate the Spencean case: to quote Watson, 'I am dissatisfied with the exclusive privileges a few persons are invested with, to make laws to suit their own selfish purposes

75 HO 42/191, 1 Aug. 1819, report of W——r; HO 42/189, 14 July 1819. See also Belchem, 'Henry Hunt', pp. 751-8.

76 HO 42/191, 6 Aug. 1819, report of W——r. This raises a question as to whether the Home Office authorized the forcible repression of the Peterloo meeting. D. Read, after an exhaustive search, concluded it did not, *Peterloo: The 'Massacre' and its Background* (1958); however, Thompson, *Making*, p. 750, points to lacunae in Home Office files implying the opposite. The apparent existence of a threat to security in the capital, contingent on events in Manchester, might well have persuaded Sidmouth quietly to withdraw an earlier instruction to Manchester justices to employ no force (an instruction on which Read lays great emphasis, *Peterloo*, p. 120).

77 *Leeds Mercury*, 19 and 26 June, 1819; HO 42/188, 26 June 1819; Belchem, *'Orator' Hunt*, pp. 100-1; HO 42/189, 14 July 1819, report of W——r; HO 42/191, 6 Aug. 1819; HO 42/188, 30 June 1819.

... they retain the national property from the People.' Further to these publications were frequent articles in the radical press on agrarian themes, with Davenport and Blandford responsible for many. Those pieces appearing in the *Medusa* particularly might be interpreted as an attempt at popular education, at urging Spencean policies to be implemented: 'On the Blowing Up of the Present System, and Breaking Up of the Regiment', 'The Day of Reckoning', 'the day of disorganization must be the day of justice and retribution'.

> Thus all the world BELONGS TO MAN,
> But NOT to Kings and lords;
> A country's land's the people's farm,
> And all that it affords:
> For why? divide it how you will
> 'Tis all the people's still:
> The people's country, parish, town;
> They build, defend and till.[78]

Even before Peterloo, then, the London Spenceans had renewed speculation upon the likelihood and consequences of a mass rising triggered off by some violent incident. In the Manchester meeting itself they had invested considerable hope, and its outcome galvanized them to renewed conspiratorial activity. This was 'the revolution begun in blood', 'High treason committed against the people'. In one of his angriest speeches Davenport declaimed: 'War ... has already been declared against us why then should we hesitate, for my own part I am ready now ... I compare the present time to the crisis of the French Revolution, we must arm ourselves as they did.'[79] Davenport in fact was one of the handful eager to take precipitate action at the Clerkenwell Green meeting on 1 November, shortly after active preparations were put in hand by Watson, Thistlewood, and Preston. The failure of subsequent attempts to rouse a mass response at public meetings confirmed the group in their decision to pursue a clandestine strategy. Their mood was hardened by a final rift with Hunt. His conceit and hauteur during the demonstrations they had organized in his honour offended many. His apparent failure to capitalize on the popular indignation Peterloo had caused was more offensive still.

The maturation and exposure of the Cato Street conspiracy are reasonably well known.[80] It is necessary, however, to emphasize the

78 Address [1819]; A. Davenport, *Kings; Song for the New Dispensation and Britannia's Command to the Universe* (published by Wedderburn, copies in HO 42/190); [J. Watson], *More Plots, More Treason, More Green Bags* (1819), 3; *Medusa*, 4 (20 Mar. 1819), 10 (24 Apr. 1819), 11 (1 May 1819). Pieces by Spencean authors appear throughout this journal.

79 TS 11/202, fo. 872; HO 42/195, 29 Sept. 1819; HO 42/197, 18 Oct. 1819.

80 Prothero, *Artisans*, pp. 116-31, contains a detailed and intelligible account of the evolution of the

'Spencean dimension' to the episode, sometimes lost sight of in secondary works. While it is unlikely that the full history of the conspiracy can ever be discovered, what comes to light in official papers conforms to a pattern familiar from Spa Fields, Bartholomew Fair, and, to no little extent, the Despard affair. Tavern evangelizing was resumed with renewed vigour. Preston was observed at the Hope, Clare Market, in mid-January, 'speaking on the subject [of] the Spencean Plan and the division of Land saying it was the Property of the people'. Of Thistlewood at this time one Crown witness recalled, 'the whole drift of his Conversation was to make every person of property appear contemptible'. All concerned cultivated their workmates and trade societies, and special efforts were made to gain the confidence of 'the Navigators' from Ireland. The full extent of provincial correspondence on the subject is conjectural, but it is certain that Thistlewood toured the provinces in mid-October.[81]

Of the five executed for their part in Cato Street, Thistlewood alone had been a member of the Society of Spencean Philanthropists; however, the extent of Spencean involvement was far greater than this might suggest. One reason why the duplicity of the spy Edwards was never guessed at was because he had been first introduced to the circle by Thomas Spence himself. Edwards's brother William was a Spencean activist and one-time secretary of the Mulberry Tree section, so the circumstances of George Edwards's return to the capital from Windsor were never suspected.[82] Richard Tidd, another of the executed conspirators, had been attending radical meetings since at least 1818, but was said to have been involved in the Despard affair. Thomas Preston was on his way to the Cato Street loft when the group there were disturbed. The two conspirators who were persuaded to turn King's evidence, Robert Adams and John Harrison, had stewarded Spence memorial dinners and frequented Evans's Archer Street Chapel, respectively. Waiting elsewhere in the capital, ready to act, were Hartley and George; at the home of the latter a substantial arms cache was rumoured to be hidden. George's son Robert, another memorial dinner steward, was arrested but not charged.[83] Given his eagerness to rise the

conspiracy. Belchem's study of *'Orator' Hunt* is indispensable for understanding the deteriorating relationship with Hunt. See also Thompson, *Making*, pp. 769-79: these are to be preferred to the bright but shallow accounts by J. Stanhope, *The Cato Street Conspiracy* (1962), and D. Johnson, *Regency Revolution* (1974). There were several editions of the subsequent trial proceedings: G. Wilkinson, *An Authentic History of the Cato-Street Conspiracy* (1820) is the best and contains a substantial, if uneven, sketch of the background.

81 HO 44/4, fo. 342; TS 11/205/877; HO 44/1, fo. 185; HO 42/196, 13 Oct. 1819.

82 HO 40/3(4), fo. 926; HO 40/8(4). fos. 167-8; TS 24/3/99/1. The Home Office recruited Edwards in 1817 to replace Castles, and financed his move to premises adjoining Carlile's from Windsor — hence his code name W[indso]r: regular reports filed in HO 42/173-201.

83 Wilkinson, *Authentic History*, p. 398; Prothero, *Artisans*, p. 127; HO 42/182, 5 Nov. 1818; HO 42/188, 30 June; HO 42/190, 21 June 1819; HO 44/4, fo. 3, 10 Jan.; ibid., fo. 5, 25 Jan. 1820.

previous November, it is not unlikely that Davenport, too, was implicated. Had they not been imprisoned on a miscellany of charges, Blandford and Wedderburn might well have become involved, less so perhaps Watson.

The web of those implicated in Cato Street will never be fully clear. Coachmakers, navvies, tailors, typefounders, and shoemakers are among the occupational groups who apparently lent large-scale support. That of the shoemakers was especially notable. Decades later three cobblers surfaced independently, each revealing substantial knowledge of the conspiracy, yet whose names appear nowhere in official records. Like a number of their trade fellows who had known of the plans afoot in February 1820, two had gone on the tramp: one ended up in Leigh, Essex, the other in Northamptonshire. The third, less centrally involved, remained a further two years in London before moving to Cambridge. It is unlikely their experiences were unique.[84] The final strands of this web of conspiracy may eventually be traced in the provinces. Though apparently no longer acting in direct concert with any national network, the Cato Street conspirators firmly believed in the readiness of the country to take up their signal. 'When the account of the fate of Thistlewood and his party at last reached them, they were staggered and confounded', wrote one observer about the North. It was a view firmly shared within the Government. It is unlikely that Sidmouth was moved by hazy presentiment alone when he wrote to Wellington 'A simultaneous explosion appears to be meditated at an early period'; nor even that Castlereagh was indulgently melodramatic when alarmed house-guests found him sporting a brace of loaded pistols about his home.[85]

Cato Street is fully intelligible only within the Spencean context. The popular interpretation (a melodramatic confection of grinding poverty, espionage, and a hint of psychosis) fails to lay open the logic of the conspirators' actions. That logic derived firstly from the events of 1819; secondly, and at root, it was born of the idealism and frustration of adherents to Spenceanism.

In the wake of Cato Street, Spenceanism in any organized form dissolved, but as a distinctive constituent to radical thought it did not disappear, as has been supposed, 'until H. M. Hyndman rediscovered it'.

84 Prothero, *Artisans*, p. 129; HO 42/191, 6 Aug. 1819; HO 42/196, 13 Oct. 1819; P. Benton, *The History of Rochford Hundred* (1867), 343; 'A Master Shoemaker', 'My Life and Adventures', *Boot and Shoemaker*, 14 June-6 Sept. 1879 (the issues between 14 June and 9 Aug. are particularly pertinent to Cato Street); J. Brown, *Sixty Years' Gleanings from Life's Harvest* (1858), 278. See also N. Mansfield, 'John Brown: A Shoemaker in Place's London', *HWJ* 8 (Autumn 1979), 134.

85 A. B. Richmond, *Narrative of the Condition of the Manufacturing Population* (2nd edn., 1825), 184 ff.; Devon CRO, Sidmouth Papers, 152/M C182/OH, Sidmouth to Wellington, 21 Mar. 1820; W. Hinde, *Castlereagh* (1981), 255. F. K. Donnelly, 'The General Rising of 1820: A Study of Social Conflict in the Industrial Revolution', Sheffield University Ph.D. thesis (1975) details the main incidents of unrest during 1820, though the overall concept of a general rising is somewhat strained.

The Spenceans were propelled backwards along the trajectory Spence had followed, no longer casting themselves as the 'Officers' of 'a few Thousands of hearty determined Fellows well-armed', but focusing their energies once more on 'the Progress of Reason aided by the Art of Printing'. The 'Propagation of Spensonianism' anticipated by Spence while gaoled in 1801 was only beginning.[86]

86 W. H. G. Armytage, *Heavens Below* (1961), 72; Spence, *End of Oppression*, p. 7, *Important Trial*, p. 35; 'The Propagation of Spensonianism', quoted in *Spence's Songs*, ii.

5

Agrarian Ideas in Radical Politics: The 1820s and 1830s

'The writings of Thomas Spence', wrote G. D. H. Cole, 'make an interesting study in British Socialist origins, but they had little practical bearing on the contemporary development of British Radical or working class thought.'[1] It is necessary to extend the study of Spenceanism beyond Cato Street to establish the truth or falsity of Cole's view. Posthumously, through former Spencean Philanthropists and their associates, Spence contributed much to English radical thought. The extent to which they successfully imparted a distinctively Spencean twist to radical thinking about land becomes apparent in the 1820s and 1830s, both in the development of agrarian ideas and in the application of those precepts in practice. This and the ensuing chapter do not focus exclusively on Spenceanism: however, it will be suggested that the continuing vitality of Spenceanism was an important factor in ensuring that agrarian issues remained high on the radical political agenda. Many of the theories of land and fiscal reform discussed in these decades were derivatives of Spenceanism; and its adherents were prominent in those forums where such theories received a public airing.

The immediate consequence of the events of late 1819 and early 1820 was that radicalism somewhat withdrew in on itself. As Raphael West, son of the second president of the Royal Academy, told his father's close friend Joseph Farrington in December 1820:

> He spoke of the disturbed state of the country. He said Parliamentary Reform is the change called for, not Revolution; that the Spencean Plan of dividing the National Property is not now spoken of; the Queen is used by the Radicals to suit their purpose in keeping up discontent.[2]

That Spenceanism should have been touched on at all in the table talk of Royal Academicians is itself noteworthy, and an indication of the extent to

1 G. D. H. Cole, *History Of Socialist Thought*, i (1953; new edn. 1977), 25.

2 K. Cave (ed.), *The Diary of Joseph Farrington*, xvi (1985), 5595 (18 Dec. 1820).

which Spence's ideas had made a mark beyond revolutionary, and even general radical, circles.[3] However, the association between the Spenceans and revolutionary politics could scarcely have been closer and of all radicals they particularly lay low in the early 1820s. Preston disappeared into the opaque society of tavern radicalism for virtually the entire decade. On his return from Manchester, where he had published a studiously innocent *Brief Sketch of the Life of Mr Thomas Spence* in 1821, Evans involved himself in the early moves to found a London Mechanics' Institute. Allen Davenport made some spirited contributions to the literature of the Queen Caroline affair, an unimpeachable opportunity for agitation, but was otherwise absent from the radical press for nearly three years.[4] The extent to which the Queen Caroline campaign filled both the street and the popular prints can obscure how far radicalism had to undergo a period of reassessment and renewal. During this phase the burden of sustaining detailed popular political discussion rested particularly on infidelism. It is both appropriate and necessary, therefore, to begin an examination of the 1820s by looking closely at the most important infidel journal of the day, Richard Carlile's *Republican*.

The extent to which radical debate was permeated by agrarianism is strongly evident in the *Republican*. Although its editor's reputation rested largely on his trial and conviction for blasphemy in October 1819, the paper nevertheless reflected those views which had first drawn him into radical journalism. Accordingly, in the early months of 1820 much of its political coverage focused upon Cato Street and its aftermath: but, as the affair subsided and Carlile turned his enforced leisure to profitable effect, the content of the *Republican* increasingly embraced broader theoretical issues. In September 1820 Carlile gave prominence to a review which in retrospect may be seen as marking a stage of some significance in his personal political development.[5] The article concerned was an extensive review and critical development of a recent pamphlet by one Harrison Wilkinson: *The Principles of an Equitable and Efficient System of Finance*. Though proposing that payments be made to the indigent 'that would place them all in cottages, with gardens, and pigs, and cows', Wilkinson in no way called for a radical redistribution of property. His central proposal was for the abolition of the existing system of taxation, and its replacement by a

3 For other indications of the breadth of awareness of Spence at this time see G. Ensor, *Radical Reform: Restoration of Usurped Rights* (1819), 57; R. Davenport, *A Practicable, Easy and Safe Plan for Checking the Increase of Pauperism* (1823), 10; R. Owen, *The Life of Robert Owen, Written by Himself* (1858), i. 227.

4 T. Evans, *A Brief Sketch of the Life of Mr Thomas Spence, Author of the Spencean System of Agrarian Fellowship or Partnership in Land* (1821), J. W. Hudson, *A History of Adult Education* (1851), 49. A. Davenport, *Claremont; Or the Sorrows of a Prince. An Elegiac Poem* [1820], and *Queen of the Isles* [1820].

5 Richard Carlile, 'Mr Harrison Wilkinson, on Finance, Taxation, and Tithes', *Republican*, 22 Sept. 1820.

single 'equitable tax' upon land and funded property. These ideas were not in themselves remarkable, except perhaps for their author's apparent ignorance of the circulation of single-tax proposals in radical circles since at least the 1790s. Furthermore, though Wilkinson reiterated his views in a further publication a year later, their impact outside of the *Republican* seems to have been limited.[6]

The pamphlet, though, was a convenient peg upon which Carlile could hang an article which had to be written in the difficult conditions of Dorchester Gaol. He enthusiastically endorsed Wilkinson's strictures upon the tax system, that it was inequitable and discriminated against working people by forcing up the price of staples and the few available luxuries. Carlile commended, too, the principle of an equitable tax, which would draw finance for government from those most capable of paying it; but he went on to develop three lines of criticism. First, he rejected the notion that funded property should be subject to the single tax, since this involved an affirmation of the moral and legal right to such property, rights which Carlile like many other radicals held not to exist. He also pointed out that such a tax, by provoking the allegation that the Government was reneging on interest payments, would stiffen opposition to fiscal reform. In Carlile's view, 'land, and the land only' was 'the only tangible property'. The funds should therefore be abolished and former holders allowed a claim upon Crown and Government land, in so far as conditions permitted. Secondly, he reiterated a familiar argument that no innovation of such fundamental significance could realistically be expected of an unreformed Parliament: 'A discussion of the subject may be all well enough preparatory to removing that corrupt and corrupting influence that sways the English government, but until that government can be placed on a proper and respectable basis, nothing will be, nothing can be done.'

Carlile then turned to a third criticism, less central to the issue, but one to which he devoted disproportionate attention: 'The equitable tax now proposed, is the same thing, with a few exceptions and modifications as the plan called Spencean … certainly the most simple and the most equitable system of society and government that can be imagined.' It was a matter of 'common justice' to draw attention to the close parallels between Spenceanism and Wilkinson's proposals. Indeed, he stopped only just short of alleging that the one had been plagiarized by the other. The arguments of Thomas Evans's *Christian Policy* 'are assimilated to those now under review'. The Spencean plan had been 'run down without examination', the Spenceans themselves had unwisely deviated from it, and it was eminently

6 H. Wilkinson, *The Principles of an Equitable and Efficient System of Finance; Founded upon Self-evident, Universal, and Invariable Principles* (1820), 59 and *passim*; id., *Property against Industry: Or an Exposition of the Partiality, Oppression, Inequality, and Injustice, of the Present System of Finance* (1821).

suited to immediate adoption by the emerging republics of Latin America. It was vain, however, 'to urge it against the prejudices of those who have established properties in this country'. Hence Carlile argued for a single equitable tax on land as the most effective social and financial strategy for a reformed Parliament to pursue: the owners of large estates, much of them wastes and parkland, would be forced to give them up, or else ensure that they were productively farmed so as to pay for the equitable tax. This incentive to full cultivation was in turn a guarantee of fuller employment, which would also be effected by the increased demand for goods and produce no longer taxed and hence cheaper.

Thereafter, the 'equitable tax' was a recurring feature of Carlile's political programme. Later the same year he argued that the pressing need for this fiscal reform was the most urgent reason for calling a National Convention, and he returned to the issue on many subsequent occasions.[7] As late as 1833, when he had virtually completed his estrangement from the mainstream of the radical movement by his stringent criticism of Owenism and trade-unionism, Carlile still returned to the land question and, citing Spence as his prime authority, reiterated the merits of equitable taxation:

> The sentiment of Thomas Spence, that THE LAND IS THE PEOPLE'S FARM, is incontrovertible by any other argument than that of the sword. The land cannot be equitably divided among the people; but all rent raised from it may be made public revenue, and to save the people from taxation.[8]

In his last years Carlile still expounded the cause against 'Agrarian monopoly and usury … the two master evils of society'. It was one of the few issues, perhaps the only one, consistently advocated by him throughout his career. Less than four years before his death he engaged in a heated exchange with Bronterre O'Brien on the subject of the land: 'Here is a subject worth thinking, worth talking, worth writing, worth printing, worth a Convention. Universal Suffrage, in the present state of mind, and church, and kings, and priests and lords, is all humbug and trickery compared with it.' Again he repeated the 'people's farm' shibboleth, concluding: 'I am for getting the rent paid to the right landlord. How go you to work?' Carlile's enduring agrarian stance is in marked contrast to the development of those opinions which increasingly alienated him from many elements within radicalism. It has gone unnoticed and unremarked among his biographers;

7 e.g. *Republican*, 1 Dec. 1820; 18 July, 9 Aug., 20 Sept., 4 and 18 Oct., 20 Dec. 1822; 22 Oct. 1824; in 1832 the election address Carlile prepared for his abortive attempt to contest the Ashton-under-Lyne parliamentary seat included a proposal for a property tax, 'parochially assessed and gathered', J. Wiener, *Radicalism and Freethought in 19th Century Britain* (1983), 182.

8 Editorial, 'Politics', in *Gauntlet*, 10 Feb. 1833. About the same time Carlile also made clear what before he had only implied, that 'the equitable property tax should be a progressive one, i.e. a property tax, the percentage of which shall increase with the amount of property taxed', *Gauntlet*, 21 Apr. 1833.

and it leads one to doubt the veracity of such tags as 'an ardent believer in political economy and the virtues of competition'. Though accurate up to a point, that is manifestly not an adequate summary of his political views.[9]

It is the source of these views, rather than their implications for the intellectual biography of Carlile, which is of the most interest here. They confirm the extent to which agrarian ideas permeated all quarters of radicalism at this time, ideas often of a Spencean inclination. They also raise two interrelated questions pertinent to the study of Spenceanism: what connections, if any, did Carlile have with Spencean radicals? And why did he prefer to cite them, rather than Thomas Paine, in defence of the 'equitable tax'?

It is improbable that Carlile was unfamiliar with Paine's advocacy of a form of single tax: it is to be found not only in his pamphlet *Agrarian Justice* of 1797, but also in the earlier and wider-circulated *Rights of Man* (1791). As publisher of Paine's work, in prison with time for reading, and above all as Paine's most eminent disciple, Carlile would certainly have been aware of his arguments for fiscal reform. One is led to conclude that he regarded Spence and Evans as more authoritative on this issue, and significantly as more familiar to his readership. It is clear that Carlile did not blindly follow Spence into this area: but it is reasonable to suggest that he regarded Spencean theories as central to the development of radical ideas about land and taxation. Carlile's actual contacts with the Spenceans were limited, with the exception of Davenport, of which more below. Following Cato Street he claimed both Davison and Edwards had tried to involve him in an unspecified conspiracy. He was certainly well acquainted with the latter, whose Fleet Street premises adjoined his own, and whom he commissioned to sculpt a bust of Thomas Paine. Carlile also realized in retrospect how 'Thistlewood tried very hard to make companions of Mr Sherwin and myself'.[10]

However, in other respects Carlile's relationship with the Spenceans was slender. He had been most active as a journalist, rather than as a platform orator or agitator; and he worked on papers (*Sherwin's Weekly Political Register* and the *Republican*) to which Blandford, Davenport, and Wedderburn alone of the group contributed. Wedderburn was imprisoned with Carlile in Dorchester Gaol, and had himself advocated the Spencean single tax in his 1817 journal, *Axe Laid to the Root*, Carlile, though, wrote in October 1820 that 'I am as much debarred from communication with Wedderburn, as I am with any person in London, and more so: for I doubt whether I could pass a private communication to him.' About the time that

9 *Operative*, 18 (3 Mar. 1839); I. J. Prothero, *Artisans and Politics in Early Nineteenth Century London* (1979), 242. For biographical details of Carlile see Wiener, *Radicalism*; also G. D. H. Cole, *Richard Carlile* (1943); E. Royle, *Radical Politics, 1790-1900* (1971); and id., *Victorian Infidels* (1974).

10 *Republican*, 3 and 10 Mar., 28 Apr. 1820.

Carlile reviewed Harrison Wilkinson, Thomas Evans did become involved in a committee organized to defend the free-thinker and sustain his family and the *Republican*. This is a more promising association, but cannot have endured beyond his release from gaol, since Evans apparently died very soon after.[11] It is not, however, necessary to establish close personal contact between Carlile and any of the Spenceans to explain the agreement of their views on the single tax. Despite the relative numerical weakness of the Spenceans, their ideas had circulated widely and to good effect. Through the space he gave to Allen Davenport in the pages of the *Republican*, Carlile helped to ensure that they continued to do so.

When Davenport resumed writing it was for the successor of the journal whose editor had first encouraged him to write. The occasion of his return to print was his donation of a 'Poet's Mite' to the relief fund for Carlile and his family. He included with it a typical short poem: more significantly, this accompanied a letter in which he criticized Carlile for failing to advocate 'an Agrarian Government' along with his other political proposals. The letter, a short whimsical restatement of the Spencean platform, contrasts sharply with Carlile's writing: more verbose and inclined to a Utopian outlook, but with a perception of the roots of social inequality lacking in Carlile. Equality of property is the only basis for true human happiness, for the relationship between landless and the landed is that of slave to master, entailing spiritual as well as social and economic deprivation: 'Men who are excluded from the land, or the profits therefrom, are like beautiful and blooming flowers suddenly snatched from their genial beds ... they fade, wither, and prematurely die.' In conclusion, Davenport made a familiar Spencean affirmation: 'I have no doubt that it was the Agrarian fellowship in land that presented to the minds of the ancients the idea of Paradise.'[12]

Davenport's intervention in the discussion of agrarian ideas previously sustained only by the editor of the *Republican* initiated a string of correspondence the size and sophistication of which far exceeded the promise of this initial, slight letter. This correspondence is of some interest because of the identity of the protagonists; but rather more interest adheres to it because of the insight it offers into the kind of agrarian ideas circulating within the radical movement in this period of reassessment and renewal, and for its own contribution to this process. This discussion of agrarian and related issues preceded the co-operative phase of the labour movement, and is eloquent testimony to the need to consider radical

11 *Axe Laid to the Root*, 3 (Nov. 1817), 44-5; *Republican*, 20 Oct. 1820; cf. *Republican*, 3 May 1822, where Carlile states that he never attended Wedderburn's Hopkins Street Chapel; B. B. Jones, 'The Peoples First Struggle for Free Speech and Writing', *Reasoner*, 5 June 1859, cf. E. Royle, *The Infidel Tradition from Paine to Bradlaugh* (1976), 25.

12 A. D[avenport], 'To Mr R. Carlile', *Republican*, 20 Sept. 1822.

politics through the history of the ideas it generated, as well as for the institutions it nurtured.

At the core of this discussion lay the contributions made by Davenport to the *Republican*, and Carlile's replies to them; but there followed contributions from, among others, Francis Place. It must in fairness be added that the initial Davenport-Carlile exchange was protracted partly because of the prolixity of the former, and partly because both men became drawn into what were essentially semantic arguments, each defending himself as a matter of high principle. As Carlile conceded on one occasion, 'there is more difference between us in words and sound, than in sense and meaning'.[13]

The fundamental difference in the outlook of the two rested on the conception of nature. Carlile was more evidently the urban man: his view of nature and of agriculture was strictly functional, and centred on the essential role of labour in cultivation. The land may bear fruit, but through no fault of the cultivator it might not. 'It is clear', thought Carlile, 'that Dame Nature cares nothing about us. We must take care of ourselves in spite of her.' By contrast, Davenport adhered to a more idealistic conception:

> A man who possesses land, has only to put his grain into the ground and leave it to the creative hand of nature, who will not fail in due time, by a mysterious operation, to raise it up and multiply it fifty, or an hundred fold; and this is all performed in the absence of the labourer.

Land is the source of all life, upon it all men can, and ultimately must, subsist. Therefore it should be the people's 'common farm'. Men without land, or at least its profits, are (to recall a remark quoted earlier) like flowers wrenched from their parent bed. Davenport's position is most vividly conveyed in his claim: 'Nature owns the peasant.' Indeed, this Marylebone cobbler persistently reveals a peasant-like consciousness of the natural world, and faith in its rejuvenative properties.[14] In a contemporary context this is not so remarkable; it is rather Carlile's dispassionate, even dismissive, attitude which was unusual. This he extended even so far as to reject 'nature' as a conceptual term for political discourse. 'What are natural rights?' he hypothesized; 'Ask yourself the question, try it every way, and you will find it to be the right of conquest.' That land is 'the very foundation' of society and property is clear from empirical observation, and needs no metaphysical justification. Therefore to appeal to 'nature', 'natural' rights, or 'natural' justice for the right to the land is fatuous. Such an appeal may only rest on equity, on the integral right to fair dealing which derives from one's status as a human being.

13 *Republican*, 1 Oct. 1824.

14 Ibid.

Carlile was passing beyond the deistic philosophy of the Enlightenment to unabashed infidelism: 'Though I have long and often used this word *nature*, I begin to see it to be one of those words which ignorance fashions to cover its nakedness.'[15]

In practical terms Carlile's apostasy was of little immediate consequence as far as agrarian policy was concerned. He and Davenport were unanimous in their insistence that the merit of 'agrarian government' lay in its securing a balance of power within society between all its constituents. Davenport held that the wider the distribution of land within a society, the more equitable its government: 'This balance is founded on the principles of Nature: no human power can alter it …' In his principal statement in the *Republican* Davenport expanded on this:

> As estates become little kingdoms, the working people of every country become beggars and slaves. Harrington is perfectly correct, when he says, that a free people are no levellers; for all the levelling business must be done before a people can be free.[16]

Spence too, of course, had advanced the view that the equitable distribution of property was needed to ensure just government. But here his disciple breaks away from him by not advocating parochial government, but implying instead that agrarian equality may be implemented and administered at the level of national government. His reason for so doing was derived from his enthusiastic support for a national convention: Carlile had already stated the immediate task of the latter would have to be to implement the 'equitable tax'. Davenport's break in this direction is more decisive, and made with greater clarity, than Evans's a few years earlier in *Christian Policy*. The result is still obviously 'Spencean', but leaves behind the anarchical structure of Spence's ideal society, for a 'common wealth [that] shall hold their land as joint stock'.

Ultimately Davenport and Carlile parted company over the means by which equitable distribution of property, and hence power, was to be achieved. 'This is what is wanted,' wrote Carlile. 'Your AGRARIAN EQUALITY all centres in this desired balance of power … and that, it seems to me, can only be acquired, by a far more extensive equal knowledge than exists at present.' Thus far Davenport agreed, but the shoemaker's enthusiasm for 'agrarian equality' was absolute: in January 1825 Carlile was moved to a tetchy rebuttal:

> If I know anything of the general disposition of the readers of 'The Republican', it is, that they do not want, *more last words* about

15 Ibid., 1 Oct. 1824, 4 Oct. 1822.

16 Davenport, 'Reflections on Agrarian Justice, Being a Reply to Mr Carlile's Objections to an Agrarian Government', ibid., 18 Oct. 1822; 'Agrarian Equality', ibid., 1 Oct. 1824.

> 'Agrarian Equality' ... no one disputes its worth, as far as it can be carried, when practicable ... Our duty is to employ ourselves in undermining the hideous structure now existing, and the moment we have accomplished this first necessary object, then, to begin to discuss the best plan for the new structure. To be quarrelling about the new plan, and to leave the old rubbish to remove itself, is not wisdom, in my judgement.[17]

However, the debate not only continued but widened in scope and participants Shortly after Allen Davenport had made his most thorough exposition of the subject, he was joined by James Penny of Huddersfield in attacking existing property rights. Penny specifically berated William Cobbett for defending the claim of landed proprietors to their holdings. Property in land, he suggested, should be a life interest only: on the death of the owner it should be returned to the 'common stock'. This was a central plank in the Spencean platform. Carlile seized the opportunity to clarify the extent to which he supported it, given the situation of contemporary English society: 'I wish one of our common-stock gentlemen would tell us how a common stock is to be divided among a people hourly fluctuating as to numbers and identities, other than by raising all tax or revenue as rental?' This was the first time that the Malthusian motif had been introduced into the *Republican*'s pages in connection with the land question. Carlile was not at this juncture a Malthusian: while affirming that contraception ought positively to be encouraged, he reiterated the popular belief that Britain could support considerably more than its current population (ten times more, he estimated). In his view, the level of population only seemed to pose a threat because of the large proportion within it of unproductive placemen, clergy, lawyers, and aristocrats: eliminate them, 'and you will find no redundant population'. In a society ordered upon the principle of equitable taxation 'no man would hold more land than he could cultivate, improve, and turn to some advantage'.[18]

Carlile's rebuff to the Huddersfield agrarian drew the approving notice of Francis Place, who was, however, very much less inclined to dismiss the Malthusian threat. Place felt that Carlile was right to object to Penny's proposals, commenting, 'there is a notion among men that all their wants arise from the unequal division of land, and this blinds them to the other causes of their degradation', but he rejected the equitable tax as unfairly singling out one group, proposing instead that revenue should be raised from a levy on luxuries.[19]

---

17 Davenport, 'Reflections on Agrarian Justice, Being a Reply to Mr Carlile's Objections to an Agrarian Government', 1 Oct. 1824. Carlile, 'To Allen Davenport', ibid., 14 Jan. 1825.

18 Ibid., 22 Oct. 1824.

19 Place, ibid., 12 Nov. 1824. The article continues over two further issues, 19 Nov. and 17 Dec., the latter also having Carlile's reply.

The understandably high degree of interest in the repeal of the Combination Acts about this time, coupled with Carlile's burgeoning interest in Freemasonry since his release from prison, led to a lull in the discussion of the land and related matters in the *Republican*. Davenport for a while shifted his allegiance to the *Trades Newspaper*, where he engaged in an interesting proposal for 'bread' wages.[20] Among his opponents in that exchange was Richard Hassell, Carlile's imprisoned shopman and a former Dorset carter. The young Hassell embraced Malthusianism far more readily than did his employer. When Davenport resumed writing for the *Republican* it was in an attempt to refute Hassell once more, this time on the subject of Malthusian population theory. Their exchange was in itself unremarkable, but it was part of a wider (and widening) discussion that had considerable implications for agrarianism. To the broad outline of this debate we now turn.[21]

Inevitably bound up as it was with the thorny issues of the Poor Law and emigration, 'Malthusianism' was perhaps the central, social issue preoccupying radicalism in these decades. More than any other body of ideas, Malthusian economics was an affront to the belief system prevalent in the early industrial working class. Agrarian concepts of nature and society lay at the core of this system; and the extent to which radical attitudes to Malthusianism have been discussed without reference to agrarianism is a measure of the failure to understand either.

Quite simply, it was only a matter of time before the two became entangled. Spence had never referred to Malthus. This partly reflects the degree to which he had formulated all his ideas before 1798, the year *An Essay on the Principle of Population* was first published; but it also indicates how the impact of Malthus on radical theorists, with the singular exception of Godwin, was retarded, gaining impetus only in the post-war depression, and as discussion of the Poor Laws grew in volume. Cobbett was primarily responsible for introducing Malthus to a popular audience, and it is quite likely that the Spenceans first became aware of him through the reading aloud of the *Political Register* at their weekly meetings. By the end of 1817, however, the parson was being read in his own right at division meetings, and the immediate reasons for this are not hard to identify. First, Thomas Evans in his *Christian Policy the Salvation of the Empire* published the previous year had attacked 'the priest of paganism'

20 *Trades' Newspaper and Mechanics' Weekly Journal*: Davenport, 'Proposal for Bread Wages', 11 Sept. 1825; 'Bread Wages', 4 Dec. 1825; see also replies by Hassell (2 Oct., 6 Nov. 1825), defences by Campbell (16 Oct., 27 Nov., 11 Dec. 1825), and further attacks by Hassell and Place (1 Jan. 1826).

21 R. H., 'On the Poor Laws', *Republican*, 4 Aug. 1826; A. Davenport, 'To the Editor of the Republican', ibid., 25 Aug. 1826; R. H. 'To Mr Allen Davenport', ibid., 8 Sept. 1826. For Hassell, who was to die shortly after, see Carlile's obituary of him, ibid., 17 Nov. 1826; also Royle, *Victorian Infidels*, pp. 36-8, 143, and Wiener, *Radicalism*, *passim*.

and his 'just, natural, equitable, merciful, Christian, quiet mode of starvation'. Second, and more significantly, in a revised edition of the *Essay* Malthus had attacked the Spenceans.[22]

He did so in the course of a general critique of 'systems of equality'; they destroyed 'those stimulants to exertion which can alone overcome the natural indolence of man'; increase of population would soon outstrip production with consequent impoverishment which could only be prevented 'by means infinitely more cruel than those which result from the laws of private property, and the moral obligation imposed on every man by the commands of God and nature to support his own children'. Clearly Malthus intended his readers to infer from these remarks that infanticide was the only recourse of those who opposed him. With increasing awareness of contraception a different, and brighter, inference might be drawn — essentially the same one that lay beneath the surface throughout the *Essay*, though unintended by the author. Malthus reposed complete confidence in his argument, 'founded on the principle of population', expressing the view 'that it is not only ... generally and uniformly confirmed by experience, in every age and in every part of the world but is so pre-eminently clear in theory, that no tolerably plausible answer can be given to it.'[23] But the particular criticism he urged against equality of property was no different from his general forecast of the fate awaiting contemporary society if his *Essay* went unheeded; even though he added that egalitarianism brought poverty much nearer, this was an argument by no means unique to Malthus. However, he stated the inevitability of the onslaught of poverty with great force:

> In any system of equality, either such as that proposed by Mr Owen, or in parochial partnerships in land ... [what] is to prevent the division of the produce of the soil to each individual from becoming every year less and less, till the whole society and every individual member of it are pressed down by want and misery?

In a cryptic footnote, Malthus selected Thomas Evans rather than Owen to demonstrate the absurdity of egalitarian claims: Evans estimated the nation's annual rental at £150 million, approximately treble the real amount in Malthus's opinion: even so its equal division among the population would yield no more than £4 per head per year, 'not more than is sometimes given to individuals from the poor's rates; a miserable provision! and yet constantly diminishing.'[24]

22 HO 40/8(4), fo. 170 (report of 'H'), fo. 173 (report of 'A'), 15 Dec. 1817. T. Evans, *Christian Policy the Salvation of the Empire* (2nd edn., 1816), 18, 5. T. R. Malthus, *An Essay an the Principle of Population* (5th edn., 1817), vol. ii, Bk. 3, ch. 3, pp. 276-81.

23 Malthus, *Essay* (5th edn.), ii. 267-7, 279.

24 Malthus, *Essay* (5th edn.), ii. 280, 281 n.

Malthus's arguments were quickly taken up in critiques of agrarian polity, the *Quarterly Review* drawing particular attention to it in its essay upon the revised edition of the *Essay on Population*. Within a few years they were exercising radicals as well: at issue among them, though, was not the alleged tendency of the population inevitably to increase, but rather the capacity of nature to sustain such an increase should it occur. Carlile and Davenport, for example, readily conceded the fact of population growth, and it was Davenport — rather than Carlile — who first openly endorsed contraception on feminist grounds.[25] At the root of the agrarian case against Malthus lay a concept of a fertile and abundant nature.

It was a commonplace of radical thought that under rational cultivation, 'produce becomes superabundant', to use a term from the *Co-operator*. Speeches, letters, resolutions, and articles of the period abound in estimates of the soil's productive capacities. Often these were directed specifically at Malthusian principles; but their origins can be traced to earlier radical homage to the fertility of nature, for example in Paine's *Age of Reason*: 'Do we want to contemplate [God's] munificence? We see it in the abundance with which he fills the earth. Do we want to contemplate his mercy? We see it in his not withholding that abundance from the unthankful.'

'Tillage is a trade that never fails', thought Spence, a statement that was closely echoed in the *Black Dwarf* some seven years later: 'The earth is the only barterer with whom we can always make a profitable exchange.' William Godwin, in his early critique of the principle of population, developed a similar argument:

> Three fourths of the habitable globe are now cultivated. The improvements to be made in cultivation, and the augmentations the earth is capable of receiving in the article of productiveness, cannot, as yet be reduced to any limits of calculation. Myriads of centuries of still increasing population may pass away, and the earth be yet found sufficient for the support of its inhabitants.[26]

Godwin's global perspective was generally reduced to a national one among artisan radicals. Thomas Single, of Mile End, developed this view in a *Trades Newspaper* article headlined 'ABUNDANCE IN THE COUNTRY TO SUPPORT THE PEOPLE — FOLLY OF THE ANTI-POPULATIONISTS': 'Look at the quantity of land we have, and no country in the world need wish for a more fertile soil. The climate too is as fine, and as healthy, and as productive of all our real wants, as any in the habitable globe.'

25 Review of Malthus, 'On Population', *Quarterly Review*, 17 (July 1817), 401; A. Davenport, 'To the Editor of the Republican', *Republican*, 25 Aug. 1826, pp. 220-3.

26 *Co-operator*, 16 (1 Aug. 1829); T. Paine, *Age of Reason* (1915 edn.; 1st edn. 1793), 14; 'A Dream', *Spence's Songs*, iii [?1811], 2; *Black Dwarf*, 3/1 (1819), 2; W. Godwin, *Enquiry Concerning Political Justice* (3rd edn., 1798; repr. 1976), 769.

The *London Dispatch*, an early Chartist periodical, warmed to a similar theme in an ostensibly innocent column offering gardening tips. The productivity of potatoes, it suggested, could be improved substantially if the flowers were removed immediately they appeared: 'One discovery of this kind is worth a thousand Malthusian volumes against population. The resources of nature are unbounded.' The Suffolk Chartist and later self-styled 'apostle' of the Communist Church, Goodwyn Barmby, was even more emphatic:

> Nature is not to be exhausted because some political economist in his closet, fancies that the population of the earth will increase at a ratio so quick that food will be unable to be found for them. By all the powers of an increased, a compound and scientific agriculture; by all the recovered wastes, deserts, and swamps of this wide world; by all the exhaustless capacity and ingenuity of the mind of man; by the most grand and sacred idea of God as Love and Good; by all these we say is the Malthusian given the lie — is he called liar to his face.[27]

Though the anti-Malthusian position was usually argued with less abandon than the foregoing, one of the features of the debate was an enthusiasm for estimating the productive potential of the soil. Three and a half acres will easily support a family of five, estimated Charles Hall. As little as a third to half an acre, in Owen's view, could support a person if brought into garden cultivation. 'There was no need for apprehension for at least two hundred years to come', argued the *Poor Man's Guardian*; 'There is land in Great Britain and Ireland sufficient (if properly cultivated) to sustain five times the present population. Some say a great deal more, but we choose to be under the mark.' Hetherington, on another occasion, suggested the land could support four times the present population, adding, 'The fault is not in Nature's population, but in the monopoly of a bad social system.' Carlile on the other hand, for all his sympathy with Malthusianism, inclined to a multiple of ten, as has already been noted. An alternative approach was to calculate the amount of land available to support the current population. The middle-class co-operator George Penn, writing on behalf of the London Co-operative Trading Fund Association, produced what was perhaps the most optimistic estimate of 150 acres for each family of five. Thomas Single arrived at a figure of 18 acres per person; 'Equality', writing in the *Poor Man's Guardian*, thought 10; 'Aristides' of Birmingham claimed 1 acre under potatoes could yield up to seven and a half times the needs of the one man needed to cultivate it. Most surprising of all (at least to the modern reader nurtured on his

27 *Trades Newspaper*, 2/65 (8 Oct. 1826); *London Dispatch*, 48 (13 Aug. 1837); 'The Land and the Poor; Or Communization and Emigration', *Promethean*, 2 (Feb. 1842). Further implications of the idea of material abundance are discussed in N. W. Thompson, *The People's Science* (1984), esp. pp. 181 ff.

reputation as a voice of reason) is William Lovett's claim in 1831 that not only were there 3 acres per head of population, but also that if properly cultivated, only one was required, to support a family of four.[28]

Such statistics now seem patently spurious: but they were rooted in a long-established pattern of underestimating Britain's population. Richard Price, for example, believed the nation's inhabitants had diminished by as much as a quarter in the first eighty years of the eighteenth century. Even Malthus himself, it is instructive to recall, considerably underestimated the population of Britain in the first edition of his *Essay*.[29] Censuses from 1801 did not convince all: Cobbett's trenchant doubt is well known, less so that it was shared by others, notably Henry Brougham who openly questioned the evidence for growth provided in the first two censuses. Succeeding decades still found certain radicals dubious as to census evidence, as they were of almost anything emanating from the Government. A notable indication of this may be found in William Benbow's pamphlet *Grand National Holiday* (1832). Here it is suggested that a census of the people's own should be conducted during the general strike Benbow proposed:

> Over population, our Lords and Masters say, is another cause of our misery. They mean by this, that the resources of the country are inadequate to its population. We must prove the contrary, and during a holiday take a census of the people, and a measurement of the land, and see upon calculation, whether it is not an unequal distribution, and a bad management of the land, that make our Lords and Masters say, that there are too many of us.[30]

The purpose of citing examples of population estimates is not to adjudicate between them, but to emphasize the strong conviction in such circles at this time that 'mother earth' (as a City radical put it) 'remains, thanks to the bounty of Divine Providence, still ready to minister to Britain's prosperity, and give scope to the industry of Britons'.[31] Men such as Lovett and Hetherington were hardly cranks on the periphery of the movement. Their conviction, and that of those like them, did not rest on

28 C. Hall, *Effects of Civilisation on the People in European States* (1805), 301-2; R. Owen, *The Revolution in the Mind and Practice of the Human Race* (1849), 121; *PMG* 95 (30 Mar. 1833); *London Dispatch*, 40 (18 June 1837); *Republican*, 22 Oct. 1824; *WFP* 192 (14 Mar. 1829); *Trades Newspaper*, 8 Oct. 1826; 'Equality', in *PMG* 192 (7 Feb. 1835); *Pioneer*, 13 (30 Nov. 1833); Lovett, speech at the seventh quarterly meeting of the BAPCK, *Penny Paper for the People*, 15 Jan. 1831.

29 R. Price, *An Essay on the Population of England, from the Revolution to the Present Time* (2nd edn., 1780), 29; Malthus, *Essay on the Principle of Population* (1798), ch. 2, p. 23: 'The population of the Island is computed to be about seven millions.' The most reliable calculations now put the population of Britain, excluding Ireland, at 9.7 million in 1791 and 10.7 million in 1801: P. Deane and W. A. Cole, *British Economic Growth, 1688-1939* (2nd edn., 1969), 8.

30 *Parliamentary Debates*, xxi. 181 (18 Jan. 1812); W. Benbow, *Grand National Holiday and Congress of the Productive Classes* (1832), 9.

31 B. Wills, letter to editor, *WFP* 220 (26 Sept. 1829).

spurious calculation alone: it was born of that semi-mystical and peasant-like consciousness of Nature and her fecundity already noted in Davenport; and it clearly echoed the eighteenth-century 'moral economy' which ascribed dearth and distress to middlemen and speculators rather than to genuine paucity. It thrived, too, on a mutually sustaining relationship with contemporary radical economics, according to which unequal exchange and distribution of goods were fundamental deficiencies in the present system. The influential, self-styled 'moral economist' William Thompson observed:

> That savage tribes, ignorant of the means of production, disinclined to labour, should be overtaken by want were a matter of no surprise; but where art and nature had run, as it were, a race of emulation in the prodigality of their gifts, to intelligent and industrious millions, that these millions should be disenabled from enjoying these products of their own creation — this is the mystery, this the astounding spectacle. To what but to *a vicious distribution* of wealth can this extraordinary phenomenon be attributed?[32]

Only the savage is 'disinclined to labour'. The working classes, by contrast, 'do not in the least repine at having to labour all their days'. From this and a belief in nature's munificence, the organ of the Grand National Consolidated Trades Union deduced:

> It is a known fact, that every individual labourer can produce more than three times as much as is necessary for himself and his family; and it becomes, in consequence, an inference, either that every man who works ought to be in possession of abundance of the products of labour, or that it is consumed by those who do nothing. That the latter is the case, no one who knows anything of the state of this country will deny: and, what is monstrous, the non-producer lives in the midst of abundance, whilst the producer is confined to the least possible allowance.[33]

Thus did radicalism's long-established antagonism to old corruption, and to those who revelled in luxury at the people's expense, reinforce criticism of political economy. Both lent weight to the view that material abundance was readily attainable in spite of all appearances. In practical terms, though, popular agrarianism was no less reliant on the minutiae of debate about agricultural methods. Agrarian radicals, no less vulnerable than socialists subsequently were to anything calling itself science, were much influenced by (and themselves developed further) the contemporary

32 W. Thompson, *An Inquiry into the Principles of the Distribution of Wealth most Conducive to Human Happiness* (1824), pp. xvi and 413.

33 *Associate*, 5 (1 May 1829), 30; *Pioneer*, 1 (7 Sept. 1833), 6.

vogue for spade husbandry. Spade cultivation was deeply entrenched in the literature of scientific agriculture. The origin of this can perhaps be discerned in Jethro Tull's emphasis upon the repeated 'division' and 'pulverization' of the soil, processes he held to be as effective as manure, or more so, for improving the fertility of the soil, as Tull believed manures easily poisoned plants if inexpertly applied. This view was by no means defunct even in the second half of the nineteenth century, and while it did not necessarily involve the complete rejection of ploughing, it provides, in its denial of any particular utility for manuring, an informative parallel to spade husbandry.[34] The main source of interest in the latter, however, came from those whose primary intention was less to maximize agricultural production than to minimize the social effects of static demand for labour. 'A pamphlet on the Poor Laws', observed the Revd Sidney Smith, 'generally contains some little piece of favourite nonsense, by which we are gravely told this enormous evil may be perfectly cured. The first gentleman recommends little gardens; the second cows; the third a village shop; the fourth a spade'.[35] Robert Owen cannot be divorced from this kind of paternalist stance, and indeed his *Report to the County of Lanark* (1821) fits directly into this tradition, both in its general objectives and in some of its specific recommendations — spade husbandry included. Owen was, though, by no means primarily responsible for introducing spade husbandry to a popular, radical audience. Its attraction was all the greater for it being one of the few objects of complete unanimity between the great radical figures of the day: Cobbett, Owen, and, later, Feargus O'Connor. At one and the same time spade husbandry appeared capable of breaking the fetters on nature's fecundity, of absorbing so-called 'surplus' labour, and of providing a form of work which was healthful and even ennobling:

> Look to THE LAND. Theorists declare and practicists admit, that the cultivation of the land, by that simple machine, the *spade*, tends to increase the produce to a degree which amply covers the extra expense incurred in the wages of human labourers. … Let the culture of the land be conducted on garden principles, excluding from the service of their community all unnecessary horses … *prove the* PLOUGH *a nuisance*, show that PROFIT attends the culture of the land by the SPADE, and the face of nature changes. Go on, invention! Fling a bundle of rags into the mill, and receive it at the other end a volume of sermons! Double and quadruple the manufactures of Birmingham and Sheffield, of Manchester and Glasgow! Let ten men in each place suffice to manage their miraculously perfected operations — who cares? THERE IS THE LAND! There is the SPADE! and over sixty million acres will well support sixty

34 T. H. Marshall, 'Jethro Tull and the New Husbandry of the 18th Century', *EHR* 1st ser., 2/1 (1929-30), 44-5; A. Burnett, *Tillage: A Substitute for Manure* (1859).

35 *Edinburgh Review*, 33 (1820), 31-2.

> millions of inhabitants, including the full complement of well paid governors and instructors, of manufacturers and commercial labourers, superintendents, providing the same means of paying off the national debt to boot![36]

Other advocates of spade cultivation were more restrained in their enthusiasm, yet scarcely less ambitious in their predictions of its potential; and always such claims were attended by reminders that these were 'scientific arrangements'. This emphasis on scientific husbandry, with the explicit corollary that considerable *skill* was assumed in its execution, may have helped overcome prejudice among skilled industrial workers against agricultural work. No less attractive was the manner in which spade husbandry conformed to the Lockian paradigm of dignity in labour, Feargus O'Connor's *Practical Work on the Management of Small Farms*, written in 1843 but drawing heavily on the technical and political literature of the previous two decades, captured this sentiment vividly: 'When I see a man with his foot upon his spade, I think I recognise the image of his God, and in him that character which even the Malthusian deigns to assign him — A MAN STANDING ON HIS OWN RESOURCES ... In his own little holding he recognises the miniature of nature.'[37]

The corollary of the abiding belief in the fecundity of nature was a willingness to perceive industrial production, if properly organized, as inherently tending to similar ends. This belief in 'the potentiality of material abundance' is most apparent in the writings of Owen and Johannes Etzler. Rural settings were cardinal elements in the communitarian vision of both: but Arcadia alone could not redeem mechanization. Machine production was reconcilable with agrarian fundamentalism only provided that labour's control over machinery was as tangible as spade husbandry allowed over agricultural production. Davenport and George Petrie thus advocated that 'manufacturing machinery [be] made public property'. The principle that the land 'is the exclusive property of no man, but the common indefeasible right of all, is in a moral and rational point of view, strictly applicable to machinery'.[38]

On the other hand, agrarianism was as readily compatible with what might be termed a Luddite posture: commitment to a quasi-industrial economy of small producers. Even the popularity of Owenite communitarianism did little to dent this, witness the Chartist Land Company. The scale of an agrarian society, as much as its pastoral setting, rendered it attractive, together with the facility of self-dependence. This

36 *Pioneer*, 21 (25 Jan. 1834).

37 F. O'Connor, *A Practical Work on the Management of Small Farms* (1843), 40.

38 J. F. C. Harrison, *Robert Owen and the Owenites in Britain and America* (1969), 68; A. Davenport, *The Life and Literary Pursuits of Allen Davenport* (1845), 11; 'Agrarius' [G. Petrie], 'Good and Evil of Machinery', *Man*, 8 (25 Aug. 1833), 57.

was an article of faith among the advocates of freeholds, parochial control, and nationalization alike. In order to appreciate the dimensions of this more fully it is helpful to examine one statement in detail: Bronterre O'Brien's very first editorial in a paper he intended precisely for the discussion of social and theoretical issues, *Bronterre's National Reformer*. The editorial commences with a highly physiocratic statement of what O'Brien construed economic virtue to be. Leaving aside the moral and physical value of agricultural labour, it is the most productive and essential of all economic activity: 'Its prosperity can alone yield the means of reproduction and prosperity to all the rest ... The surplus of agricultural product is REAL CAPITAL which sets the artisans and handcraftsmen to work.' O'Brien had consistently drawn attention to the land question as being integral to social reform, ever since his entry into political journalism in 1831. Reading Jefferson reinforced his views:

> 'There are three ways', says the immortal Jefferson in his memoirs, 'by which a nation enriches itself; namely conquest, commerce, and agriculture, The first is brigandism, the second is chicane and swindling; the third alone is legitimate and compatible with the happiness of other states.'

However, unlike Jefferson, O'Brien, while reaffirming his strictures on commerce, extended his approval to manufacturers though emphatically not to

> the system which would first make this paramount to agriculture, and then bestow all the advantages of both on an upstart moneyed aristocracy, who, in drawing you off the land, have made you more abject slaves to their cupidity, than your forefathers ever were to the feudal barons of the middle ages.

Finally, in a passage which anticipates much that was later to flow from the pen of Feargus O'Connor, O'Brien concluded with an affirmation of the three key virtues of agrarian society: scale, setting, and self-dependence.

> Let us as little as possible exchange the healthful and harmonizing pursuits of the field for the withering and demoralizing occupations of the factory. Every human being ought by rights to be taught agriculture, and as Mr Loudon says, 'to be master of a garden to walk in', and the perfection of society will be when in addition to that consummation being obtained, every individual of society will also know some one trade well, with as much division and subdivision of labour as you like.[39]

---

39 Bronterre's *National Reformer*, 1 (7 Jan. 1837), 4. Jean Claudius Loudon was a prolific author of horticultural texts, e.g. *A Manual of Cottage Gardening, Husbandry, and Architecture* (1830); *The Suburban Gardener* (1838); and *The Suburban Horticulturalist* (1842). Though these were aimed, as

It is clear from these final words that O'Brien believed that de-skilling, seemingly integral to changes in industrial production, would cease to pose a threat to labour if the latter could also be relocated on the land. As much as it anticipates the arguments (and even phraseology) of O'Connor, this editorial is also a summation of more than a decade's discussion within radicalism in which the land was conceived as the primary means by which economic change could be tempered and redirected to labour's advantage (but not, note, reversed). In slump, land was a refuge; in boom, recreation; and at all times a guarantee of full employment. Once more we recall the speech of Dr Watson at Spa Fields, or Davenport's filial attachment to nature as revealed in the *Republican*. Some years later the Spencean tailor George Petrie expressed the same, reminding an NUWC audience 'that they were starving and naked, and now let them look to their mother earth'. Such statements are a recurring feature of the period, and it would seem superfluous to duplicate them. It is, however, useful to remind ourselves that this concern with, and faith in, the restorative powers of the land, was not held by men alone. As the opinions of women were less frequently recorded, the following extract from a speech at the Charlotte Street Institution has particular interest:

> I stand here as a woman, an *operative*, and a mother, to enter my feeble protest against the present oppressive and unjust condition of the producing classes ... It is my conviction that the great remedy for poverty amongst the operative class, is the possession of land; for land is the rich mine from which all wealth proceeds; it is the source and foundation, we may say; the garden of all production, the twin brother of labour; consequently its nearest relative.[40]

The notions at work here, as in the O'Brien editorial, hinge on more than simply the physical and moral benefits of agricultural labour. A crucial consideration is independence from a wage contract and the cash nexus, together with the materialistic concepts of success, failure, and happiness these impose. These substantive qualities readily combined with the mystique of land and nature, and the dignity of labour. The popular conception of the land as 'the garden of all production' and 'the twin brother of labour' clearly influenced popular political and economic analysis: the language of the natural rights of labour was suffused with agrarian imagery; this in turn reinforced the affinity radical theorists felt with Locke. A complementary conceptual division which became established in those years was that of 'natural' and 'artificial' society and rights. The obvious point of reference here is Thomas Hodgskin's *Natural*

their titles suggest, at a middle-class audience, the author had definite radical views — see e.g. a letter in Carlile's *Union* 8 (14 Ian. 1832).

40 *PMG* 85 (19 Jan. 1833); *Official Gazette of the Trades Unions*, 6 (12 July 1834).

and Artificial Rights of Property Contrasted, first published in 1832. Hodgskin's posthumous reputation was secured by Marx's discovery of him: his contemporary influence rested not so much on his now most widely known publication, an expensive pamphlet 'not intended for the poor', to quote its author, but rather upon 'small publications ... very widely circulated' (Place) which made use of his ideas and terminology. The *Poor Man's Guardian*, thanks to O'Brien, was arguably most important in this respect, and it is interesting to note that Hodgskin himself presented a copy of *Natural and Artificial Rights* to the paper with 'a very flattering note in testimony of our exertions'.[41] The consequence was not exactly as Hodgskin intended. The central purpose of his writing — to promote a pure *laissez-faire* climate in which the Lockian right to individual property might flourish — was eclipsed by the felicitous phraseology of his title and key concepts, which closely accorded with current modes of radical thinking about class legislation and property. Eventually this categorization of property rights was extended to embrace many more aspects of social organization. It was in the promotion of the Chartist Land Plan that the artificial-natural dichotomy achieved greatest dominance, especially in the rhetoric of Feargus O'Connor: 'With my operations I will thin the artificial labour market by employing thousands who are now destitute, and constituting an idle reserve to enable capitalists to live and make fortunes upon reductions of wages.'[42]

'Natural' and 'artificial' became central to O'Connor's vocabulary, and they link his thought, likewise the Chartist Land Plan as a whole, to the long-established strategy, in which all agrarian schemes participated, of promoting labour's relative scarcity. The swiftness with which the concept of artificiality was assimilated into the radical vocabulary indicates the strength of popular confidence in labour's potential, not to promote its interests within industrial capitalism (which to a considerable extent presupposed capitulating to it), but to step outside it and in effect to 'unmake' it. The basic rationale of all land schemes, co-operative farms, home colonies, and Chartist estates rested on the central assumption that a strategic withdrawal of labour from the 'artificial' to the 'natural' economy would undermine the basis on which low wages rested. In this they were at one with the organized trades with their objective of controlling entry to a craft, and thus maintaining wage levels. Through a return to what could be seen as first principles, however, agrarianism embraced all labour — beyond the skilled and semi-skilled trades — with its appeal further

41 T. Hodgskin, *The Natural and Artificial Rights of Properly Contrasted* (1832), p. iii; Place, BL Add. MS 27791, fo. 270; *PMG* 64 (1 Sept. 1832), 87 (2 Feb. 1832), 90 (23 Feb. 1832), 95 (30 Mar. 1832), 98-9 (20, 27 Apr. 1832). Quotation from issue no. 87.

42 *NS*, 12 Aug. 1848. For other examples of this usage see ibid., 27 May 1843, 17 May 1845, 30 Jan. 1847, 1 Jan. and 18th Mar. 1848; also O'Connor, *Practical Work*, esp, pp. 19-20.

enhanced by an allegedly dramatic potential for improving the quality of life:

> The withdrawal … of so large a number of labourers from the market of labour, would benefit all the employed artisans, by causing a rise in their wages: and the persons themselves so disposed, would gradually acquire comfort, improved habits, and intelligent minds.[43]

This, then, was the ideological context of the flood of practical proposals for operations upon the land which began to emerge in the 1820s. On to an apparent solution to the problem of labour's 'idle reserve' were grafted the attractions of natural scale, setting, and self-dependence. Faith in the fecundity of nature, in partnership with honest labour, sustained the whole.

43 'Co-operative Union the Only Effectual Remedy for National Distress', *London Co-operative Magazine*, ns 4/3 (1 Mar. 1830).

6

Precepts in Practice

In the 1830s travellers northwards out of London passed through an area just beyond Islington still known as Barnsbury Park. There, among half-built streets of suburban housing interspersed with market gardens and grazing land, the curious might have noticed six cottages, each with an acre of land surrounded by a white picket fence. Here a group of London tailors, shoemakers, and the like pursued their trades while sharing with their families and each other the task of cultivating the land. There were works by Cobbett in the residents' library of seventy volumes, while the advice of his *English Gardener* was put into effect at their school, 'run on co-operative principles'. The occupants of these 'Experimental Cottages' included, notably, the Scottish tailor George Petrie. An active trade-unionist and missionary for the GNCTU, Petrie wrote a column in the lively radical weekly *Man*, under the pseudonym 'Agrarius'. His articles in this widely-circulated paper are a useful guide to the opinions of those in whom radicalism and socialism merged. Landowners are the 'progeny of Norman adventures'; government as presently constituted is 'a foul usurpation'; the law of primogeniture is 'odious'. Trade unions are the 'focus for the fulfilment of our designs! Marriage is a 'desolating, barbarous and unnatural institution'.[1]

The remark about marriage gives an important clue to the political opinions of 'Agrarius'. Petrie was not merely a radical and trade-unionist, but much influenced by Owenism. Yet he preferred to describe himself as a 'Spencean and Republican', while living in a community whose pattern of settlement closely paralleled the estates of the Chartist Land Plan a decade later, rather than the projected colonies of Owen's new moral world. In its modest scale the Barnsbury Park Community was arguably more typical of popular agrarianism than either the official Owenite community, Harmony Hall, or the Chartist Land Plan; and in merging

1 The best description of the community is given in the *People's Hue and Cry*, 19 (10 Aug. 1834). See also *Crisis*, 2/22 (8 June 1833) and 2/35-6 (31 Aug., 7 Sept. 1833), and *Lancashire and Yorkshire Co-operator*, May 1832, suppl., p. 2, and Sept. 1832, p. 15. 'Agrarius' quotations from *Man*, 7 and 21 July, 18 Aug. and 1 Dec. 1833.

elements of traditional radicalism, trade-unionism, socialism, and Spenceanism, Petrie was probably a more typical working-class politician than those who can be neatly labelled with just one or two of those categories. The cluster of ideas loosely described by historians as 'Owenism' had many constituents. Numerous nostrums and ideals were given, in Foxwell's felicitous phrase, 'resonance and asylum' in Owenism. Spenceanism was not the least of them.[2]

London followers of Owen first projected a community as early as 1821. The 'family union' at Spa Fields was established by the Co-operative and Economical Society. Some members of the twenty or so families in the community continued in employment outside it. Others (milliners, blindmakers, tailors, cutters, and shoemakers are mentioned) worked within it. It was defunct by 1824, when George Mudie — its prime mover — joined the Scottish Owenite community at Orbiston.[3] Its members do not seem to have actively aspired to settle the land, but the Spa Fields colony is of interest for the present study because it set a precedent for experiments outside the 'official' Owenite movement, the participants in many of which did set out to get back to the land. It is now recognized that the use of the term 'Owenite' has often been too lax: it has been applied to associations and to people who operated entirely without Owen's imprimatur (and, often, his knowledge), and who not unusually were antagonists of mainstream 'Owenism', in so far as the latter can be defined with any validity. Indeed, Owen was never in control of most of the activities of 'Owenism'. 'The labour exchange movement, for instance ... developed a momentum of its own to which he merely responded.' A significant part of the momentum, as far as communitarianism was concerned, derived from radical agrarianism. The 'urge for acres', identified by Garnett in his study of the Owenite communities as part of their legacy, was not a consequence of communitarianism. Rather, the latter was partly the product of popular agrarianism. The activities detailed hereafter, therefore, are not selected on the basis of being Owenite, or socialist (many were neither), but as illustrations of the attempted practical application of agrarian precepts.[4]

The first practical land scheme promoted during the 1820s emerged with the London Co-operative Society's *Articles of Agreement for the*

---

2 H. S. Foxwell, introd. to A. Menger, *The Right to the Whole Produce of Labour* (1899), p. xxvii; cf. p. xciv.

3 The main contemporary source is the community's own paper, the *Economist* (1821-2). It is well covered by secondary writers, e.g. W. H. G. Armytage, *Heavens Below* (1961), 92-5; D. Hardy, *Alternative Communities in 19th Century England* (1979), 43-6; J. F. C. Harrison, *Robert Owen and the Owenites in Britain and America* (1969), 168-9; R. G. Garnett, *Co-operation and the Owenite Socialist Communities in Britain, 1825-45* (1972), 41-5.

4 I. J. Prothero, *Artisans and Politics in Early Nineteenth Century London* (1979), 245; Garnett, *Co-operation*, p. 33.

Formation of a Community on Principles of Mutual Co-operation, within Fifty Miles of London, published in 1825. One acre per member was the ideal: 'The land', wrote an anonymous co-operator, 'we will lay out and cultivate with the threefold view to health, abundant produce, and embellishment'. The following spring an advertisement was placed in the Society's own *Co-operative Magazine* for between 500 and 2,000 acres of land, to rent or purchase.[5] Shares, at £10, were beyond the means of most working people, and in any case the planned community never materialized. The Society's enduring contribution to English radicalism was in the field of education and the dissemination of information. Among the contributors to its *Co-operative Magazine* was Allen Davenport.[6]

The failure to proceed beyond advertising for land initiated a process within the movement which would be repeated many times in the future, a process whereby agrarian enthusiasts seceded from a parent body to attempt practical operations of their own. The result in this instance was the London Co-operative Trading Fund Association, its primary objective being 'to enable the Shareholders to buy or rent land, in order to obtain from it, by their united skill and labour, whatever they can rationally desire, and as nearly as possible at the cost price, namely, the labour expended in the production'. Significantly the Association numbered among its members Charles Jennison, one of the most active of the former Spencean Society, very soon elected to the Association's committee; also Davenport's close friend William Devonshire Saull, a City wine merchant, lecturer, and frequent patron of radical groups. A third member, among several from the Finsbury Spencean-Owenite axis, was the shoemaker Robert Wigg from Hoxton. The principal initiators of the Association, however, were three relative newcomers to metropolitan radicalism, the brothers Phillip and George Skene, and G. C. Penn.[7]

Whilst relations with the London Co-operative Society remained amicable, the members of the Association seem particularly to have been motivated by their frustration at the failure to implement declared agrarian objectives. The trading function referred to in its title was intended to be only an interim stage. Soon, however, the Association found itself imitating the Society's educational activities, and indeed superseding them. It advertised its willingness to provide speakers for meetings to promote co-operation, adding as it did so Penn's passionate plea: 'Why should poverty exist? Why should anyone able and willing to work, be in want?

5 London Co-operative Society, *Articles of Agreement* (1825), title-page (also repr. as app. to J. Gray, *Lecture on Human Happiness* (1825)); *Journeyman and Artizan's London and Provincial Chronicle*, 2 (19 June 1825); *Co-operative Magazine*, 4 (Apr. 1826). Further information may be found in Prothero, *Artisans*, pp. 240-1 and 246, and Harrison, *Robert Owen*, *passim*.

6 A. Davenport, 'Co-operation', *Co-operative Magazine*, 10, 11 (Oct., Nov. 1826).

7 London Co-operative Trading Fund Association, *Regulations* [1828], 1; cf. The Association's *To the Operative Classes* [1828].

The earth is large enough — there are 150 acres of land to every five persons, men, women and children together.' It was a measure of Penn and his comrades' earnestness of purpose that he suggested in all seriousness that clay-and-turf igloos would be both a practicable habitation for an incipient community, as well as an improvement on existing urban housing.[8]

In accordance with its growing didactic function the group changed its name in May 1829 to the British Association for Promoting Co-operative Knowledge (BAPCK). Although a London organization, the BAPCK was the focal point, as Dr Prothero reminds us, of 'an impressive and important national movement' in touch with nearly 500 societies by the spring of 1831. It was remarkable not least for the array of political luminaries that it gathered together — William Lovett, James Watson, John Cleave, and Henry Hetherington, for example. 'This gallery of London artisans', writes the historian of the Owenite movement, 'had read Owen, Thompson, Minter Morgan and Gray, and were prepared to try to put the principles of co-operation into practice'.[9] One further name needs to be added, that of Spence. Consider the following keynote address issued by the BAPCK in 1830:

> Permit us, then, fellow countrymen, to suggest to you, whether the real cause of destitution is not discoverable in our ignorance, and in the consequent arrogant assumption of a rapacious aristocracy, who claim as their exclusive property nearly all the land in the kingdom, and which enables them to place the whole of the working population in the position of slaves, by making their labour a marketable commodity … The iniquity of this unjust and exclusive possession of land would be of little consequence to the labouring population did it not enable the landowners, as they impudently term themselves, to wrest from the industrious workman the whole produce of his labour … The question is, can the labouring population devise any efficient plan to emancipate themselves from such a state of degradation? Every man must perceive that property now holds labour in complete subjection.[10]

This address 'to the Labourers, Mechanics, and Artisans of the United Kingdom', is a particularly forceful statement of a key facet of BAPCK policy. Its signatories are worthy of note: Hetherington, Lovett, George Petrie, Benjamin Warden, William McDiarmid, Thomas Powell, and Thomas Croley. The first two of course need no introduction, though the

8 'Co-operative Trading Associations', *WFP* 192 (14 Mar. 1829); letter to the editor, ibid. 219 (19 Sept. 1829).

9 Prothero, *Artisans*, p. 243; Harrison, *Robert Owen*, p. 200.

10 'Address of the British Association for Promoting Co-operative Knowledge to the Labourers, Mechanics and Artisans of the United Kingdom', *Political Letters and Pamphlets*, 31 Dec. 1830 ('A Letter to the Rt. Hon. Wilmot Horton'), 16.

extent to which both were committed (for at least a significant part of their careers) to thorough-going agrarian reform is often overlooked. Like Petrie, Warden, a master saddler, was active within the Finsbury Spencean group; and like Hetherington, he was a former member of the Freethinking Christians, the Unitarian sect closely connected with Spenceanism.[11] William McDiarmid was a printer and staunch agrarian, who had recently urged provincial co-operators to return to the land as soon as feasible.[12] Powell, one of Hetherington's shopmen, was an early secretary to the BAPCK, later a Chartist leader in his native Wales, and subsequently the promoter of the Tropical Emigration Society. He, too, lectured at the Finsbury chapel run by the Spencean-Owenite circle, and was also (with Allen Davenport) an officer of the free-thinking Anti-Persecution Union.[13]

It is clear from both the origins of the BAPCK and its public statements, especially the address of 1830, that its members believed the importance of land to the working classes to be a crucial matter to publicize. Although practical schemes were limited, there were no lack of material to this effect in the co-operative press. It is difficult, however, to tease out calls for land from the more-generalized call for communities. This is what makes the BAPCK address all the more remarkable. It isolates ownership of land as a cause for concern in its own right, and not just as the location for proposed communities. In doing so it draws on the key Spencean idea that property in land is the basis of both political and economic power. Owenism was indeed a place where Spenceanism found asylum and resonance.

Whatever the constraints upon forming agrarian communities, and for London co-operators these were geographical as well as financial, evidence can be advanced to suggest a greater number of local initiatives than is customarily supposed. The ambitious and well-documented Orbiston community in Scotland was closely followed by a more modest project in the West Country. In 1826 the Devon and Exeter Co-operative society established a community, first near Rockbeare close to the city, and then after the withdrawal of their initial sponsor, at a farm near Honiton. Like so many similar experiments it was short-lived and beset by financial difficulties.[14] Yet it was soon followed by several further initiatives. Towards the end of 1828 some Brighton co-operators, meeting as the

---

11 H. Hetherington, *Principles and Practise Contrasted* (1828), 6.

12 *WFP* 272 (25 Sept. 1830), McDiarmid was a member of the Metropolitan Co-operative Society, *PMG* 39 (10 Mar. 1832).

13 *PMG* 66 (15 Sept. 1832); D. Williams, *John Frost: A Study in Chartism* (1939) 104, 158-9. On the Tropical Emigration Society see G. Claeys, 'John Adolphus Etzler', *English Historical Review*, 101 (Apr. 1986), 351-75.

14 *Co-operative Magazine and Monthly Herald*, 7 (July 1826)-9 (Sept. 1826); F. Podmore, *Robert Owen* (1923 edn.), 377-9; G. J. Holyoake, *The History of Co-operation* (1906), 71; Harrison, *Robert Owen*, p. 170; Hardy, *Alternative Communities*, pp. 46-8.

'Benevolent Fund Association', leased 28 acres at Hurstpierpoint nine miles from the town. Some members, otherwise unemployed, cultivated the land as a market garden, the produce being sold at the Society's Brighton store. Within a year strong differences of opinion arose over whether those actually working the land should receive a differential dividend. The dispute was resolved, irrevocably, by the Society's agent absconding to America with part of the funds.[15]

The Co-operative Society founded by Birmingham Owenites in November 1828 also had strong agrarian leanings. Like other associations with the ultimate objective of settlement upon the land, it traded as a consumer co-operative for an interim stage. Unlike many co-operative trading ventures, however, it paid no dividend. 'Nothing in the way of profits of trade, or any part of the capital, shall ever be divided among the members, as Community of Property in Land and Goods is the great object of this Society.' The Birmingham co-operators, unusually among the smaller provincial schemes, left a fairly comprehensive indication of their occupations:

> Brassfounders, jewellers, silversmiths, jappaners, platers, gilt-toy makers, wire-workers, button-makers, screw-drivers, saddlers, hothouse manufacturers, rule-makers, gun-makers, engravers, wood-turners, book-binders, pocket-book makers, Britannia metal workers, shoe-makers, tailors, millers, bakers, etc.[16]

Even given the economic basis of Birmingham society, the list was weighted heavily towards skilled craftsmen — underlining not only that the Society's objectives appealed particularly to workers who valued independence and control of production highly, but also that membership of such organizations was a costly undertaking. Birmingham co-operators paid a 4*d.* weekly subscription, were debarred from joining other societies, and were expected to buy all provisions from the Society store without benefit of dividends. These sacrifices, however, enabled the Society very quickly to acquire several acres on the outskirts of Birmingham for members to cultivate. As the tobacconist William Pare, later an Owenite and co-operator of national importance, and one of the founders, wrote: 'I conceive it to be of the greatest importance for the societies to rent and cultivate land, as soon as possible. For the produce of the land there is always a good market in the members of the Society, and its cultivation may often give employment to members in want of work.'[17]

---

15 Armytage, *Heavens Below*, pp. 89-91; *Associate* 1 (Jan. 1829)-6(Oct. 1829). See also Garnett, *Co-operation*, pp. 51-2.

16 *Address Delivered at the Opening of the Birmingham Co-operative Society, November 17, 1828, by a Member. To which is Added the Laws of the Society* (1828), p. 32, rule 39; *WFP* 266 (11 Aug. 1830).

17 *Co-operative Magazine*, Mar. 1829, p. 65.

Close behind the Brighton and Birmingham experiments, two London schemes were initiated. The Westminster Co-operative Association, under the leadership of John Cleave the largest group of metropolitan co-operators, acquired land at Addington near Croydon in Surrey, where unemployed members were able to work.[18] Also south of the Thames, the Lambeth Co-operative Trading Union promoted a bakery-cum-land society, the Lambeth General Union. Its objectives were the provision of unadulterated food, a school for members' children, a library, and,

> ... from the savings which may result from their association, the means of purchasing for every member a small portion of land, whereupon he may erect a cottage, to which, in the evening of Life, he may retire, and by raising provisions for his own use upon the land, find some light and beneficial occupation in the cultivation of his own freehold, instead of spending his last days in the workhouse. These benefits are to be obtained by the skill and labour of the members, and will be ten times the sweeter in the enjoyment, under the consideration that the owners will be indebted for them to their Creator and themselves only.[19]

In so far as mainstream Owenism was concerned the Lambeth enterprise was decidedly heterodox, but the familiar hallmarks of popular agrarianism are here: self-help, self-dependence, the dignity of labour on the land, and the certainty of a ready reward from it.

Further agrarian schemes were initiated in both London and the provinces during the 1830s. A powerful stimulus behind such initiatives was the community at Ralahine, County Clare, Ireland. It was able to claim considerable success, and in turn the attention and admiration of English co-operators, during the years 1831-3. Managed by a young Owenite from Manchester, Edward Craig, it received extensive coverage in the English co-operative press, especially *Crisis* and the *Lancashire and Yorkshire Co-operator*, of which Craig had been editor until moving to Ralahine. The community's untimely demise in 1833 did little to quench its inspirational qualities, since the loss of the estate at Dublin gaming-tables by the landlord could scarcely be blamed upon the communitarians themselves.[20]

The period when Ralahine appeared to be enjoying every prospect of future success was one of considerable growth for the co-operative society movement in England, which expanded from fewer than 100 societies in 1829 to as many as 500 in 1832. Very little, however, can be gleaned about them beyond the scantiest evidence for their existence; yet it is clear that

18 *WFP* 217 (5 Sept. 1829).

19 *WFP* 197 (25 Apr. 1829); see also 206 (20 June 1829) and 226 (7 Nov. 1829).

20 The literature on Ralahine is extensive: there is a full bibliography attached to the best secondary account, R. G. Garnett's. See also Cormac Ó Gráda, 'The Owenite Community at Ralahine, County Clare, 1831-1833: A Reassessment', *Irish Economic and Social History*, 1 (1974), 36-48.

the siren-call of the land was not lost amidst the enthusiasm for co-operative trading, manufacture, and labour exchange. The experience of Manchester's Economical Co-operative Trading Society was typical:

> On the 28th of August, 1830, eight of us agreed to form a Co-operative Trading Society, and to pay 1£ each as a share, at no less than threepence per week ... With this capital we began to buy sugar, soap, and candles, which we retailed to ourselves and others; and we soon found encouragement to purchase other articles ... we found our profits accumulating fast. We now bought some leather and employed one of our members to make and mend shoes for us, which we found very beneficial. Then we bought stockings, worsted, linen, and flannel, manufactured by our Co-operative brethren. We then came to the unanimous resolution to begin manufacturing some good, stout, fast ginghams ... We have now thirty-six members, amongst whom are spinners, warpers, weavers, dyers, joiners, hatters, shoe-makers, tin plate workers, etc. indeed we are all workers like so many bees, and what can prevent us working our way to that land which would, with our industrious efforts, yield us abundance of every thing we stand in need in this world[?]

According to John Heaton, 'a plain working man' of Huddersfield, societies at Dewsbury, Leicester, Loughborough, Pemberton, Rochdale, and Rossendale, besides his own, were all similarly working their way to the land.[21] A year later Worcester co-operators were likewise poised, whilst at Worsley a society acquired a small portion of land primarily for the better education of members' children. Meanwhile the secretary of a society at Little Bolton looked forward with confidence to being 'able to command a capital to almost do anything in reason we think proper, and as the LAND lies before us we are determined at once to go up and possess it!'[22] A return to the land was also canvassed (and quite possibly acted upon) during the Lancashire spinners' strike of 1831. Fellow spinners in Glasgow, for example, were asked by one of the relief committee to contribute to a fund

> for the purpose of placing their starved brethren upon the lands in this country, as labour would otherwise remain a drug in the market ... He proceeded to detail the method of purchasing land, and locating operatives in farms of about five acres each, at rent of about £9 per annum, recommending 'clay built and thatched biggins'.[23]

The following year, again in Manchester, a 'Social Community

21 *Lancashire and Yorkshire Co-operator*, 3 (Oct. 1831), 1-2 for William Shelmerdine, storekeeper, Manchester; 4-5 for Heaton.

22 *Lancashire and Yorkshire Co-operator*, 12 (4 Feb. 1832), 3; ibid., *NS* 4 (June 1832), 10 (Nov. 1832).

23 *Voice of the People* (Manchester), 29 Jan. 1831, speech of James Nish.

Company' commenced an agrarian experiment on Chat Moss, acting on the proposition that 'Co-operators would affect but little towards their amelioration were they not allowed to cultivate the LAND for themselves'.[24]

The probability that the initiatives here listed were not isolated occurrences is considerably strengthened by evidence from this time of private individuals acquiring land, or utilizing waste and common, motivated by the same instinct as the co-operative societies. The 1831 Lancashire spinners' strike seems to have stimulated precisely such a move, which assumes 'institutional' form only because of the strike committee's appeal through the press. Evidence for personal initiatives is, by the very nature of such enterprise, scanty. Four unemployed Manchester fustian cutters took 'a good HOUSE and a plot of LAND, in Failsworth', but have only been recorded for posterity because as members of an 'Owenian Society' they were able to appeal through the co-operative press for orders. One John Smith, a discharged soldier with a family of eight, took an acre to cultivate by spade husbandry for local markets in Frimley, Surrey. We know this because he happened to write to the radical weekly *Cosmopolite*, urging its readers to follow his example.[25] So too did Edward Lance, a surveyor and occasional lecturer on agricultural topics at mechanics' institutes. He privately promoted a spade husbandry colony near Lewisham, Kent, advertising for Owenites impatient for communitarian life to join him.[26]

The formation of new groups and proposals by aspiring communitarians, impatient at the tardiness (as they saw it) of the mainstream of the movement in returning to the land, was especially obvious in London. The same restlessness which had created the BAPCK out of the London Co-operative Society and Trading Association gave rise in the spring of 1830 to the First London Manufacturing Community in Old Street Road. Skene, James Watson, Wigg, Jennison, and Davenport were founder members, the last soon assuming the office of storekeeper: 'We manufactured boots, shoes, brushes, etc., and for a time, our little establishment inspired us with the most ardent hopes, that it would realise our fondest anticipations, and convince the world of the superiority of the co-operative principle over that of competition.'[27] To further this purpose,

24 Dixon, speech at Eccles, *Lancashire and Yorkshire Co-operator, NS* 3 (May 1832), suppl., p. 1. See also A. E. Musson, 'Ideology of Early Co-operation in Lancashire and Cheshire', *Transactions of the Lancashire and Cheshire Antiquarian Society*, 68 (1958), 117-38, repr. in id., *Trade Union and Labour History* (1974), ch. 8.

25 *Lancashire and Yorkshire Co-operator, NS* 3 (May 1832), supp., p. 3; *Cosmopolite*, 26 (1 Sept. 1832).

26 *Cosmopolite*, 9 (5 May 1832) and 14 (9 June 1832); *Crisis*, 1/25 (25 Aug. 1832), 100. Lance was the author of several agricultural works, including *The Golden Farmer* (1831), dedicated to 'Scientific and Mechanics' Institutes', from which this biographical information is taken.

27 A. Davenport, *The Life and Literary Pursuits of Allen Davenport* (1845), 59-60.

Davenport composed a Co-operator's Catechism published in the group's journal, *The British Co-operator*, in July 1830. The catechism was reprinted about the same time in *The Associate*, headed by an engraving of an Owenite 'parallelogram' community in a lush, sylvan setting. By the time of the Third Co-operative Congress in April 1832, Jennison was acting as the Manufacturing Community's secretary. At the same congress another group of disgruntled co-operators, the Central Association, was represented by Petrie and William Benbow (the latter always a focus around whom those disenchanted with Owen organized). The Association met at Benbow's Theobalds Road Institute.[28]

George Petrie's participation at this time in the successful Barnsbury Park scheme well illustrates the impatience at Owen's dilatoriness felt by some enthusiasts for agrarianism. It is also unusual among the smaller communities for being fairly well documented. Yet, not surprisingly, it has been neglected in labour historians' concentration upon Owen and the larger communitarian projects. The community had been created in October 1831 by Pierre Baume, a French *émigré* and deist. His Society for Promoting Anti-Christian and General Instruction had for a brief time been an important focus for Finsbury radicals, much patronized by members of the Spencean circle. It was based at the Optimist Chapel, 33 Windmill Street, along with Baume's printing and bookselling premises. All three were acquired in the autumn of 1831 by the young James Watson when, to quote a Home Office informer, Baume 'turned Farmer'.[29]

The project was an attempt to put into practice the precepts of agrarianism, close to the heart of the metropolis. As George Petrie wrote shortly before joining the community:

> The great evil to be regretted (and is even acknowledged by the legislators themselves) is, that the great bulk of the people have been decoyed from the land and agricultural pursuits into cities and large towns, and there are compelled to submit to their masters' terms, having no alternative. Let them resolve to return to their lawful inheritance; let them take small allotments of land, and act on the principle we are pursuing.[30]

28 'The Co-operator's Catechism', *British Co-operator*, 4 (July 1830), 73-6, repr. in *The Associate and Co-operative Mirror*, 10-12 (1830). *Proceedings of the Third Co-operative Congress* (1832); Prothero, *Artisans*, p. 246, details the antagonism between the Central Association and the main Owenite co-operative movement.

29 HO 64/11, fo. 177; Prothero, *Artisans*, esp. pp. 260-1, has collected most of the available information about the Optimist Chapel. Two products of the press under Baume survive in HO 64/16: *Speech of a Frenchman, on the Proposed Bill for the Dissection of Human Bodies* (1829), and *A Revolution in England is Unavoidable* [1830]; Baume's translation of the 'Marseillaise' is in HO 64/17, and his magazine *The Optimist* also in HO 64/16.

30 G. Petrie, *Carpenter's Political Letters and Pamphlets*, 5 Mar. 1831, p. 24, repr. in the *Lancashire Co-operator*, 2 (25 June 1831), 6. Two delegates were sent to the 1832 Co-operative Congress; see

From Barnsbury Park Petrie wrote many of his 'Agrarius' articles in *Man*. 'One of the more successful journals of the decade with an estimated circulation of twelve thousand', *Man* was edited by Petrie's close friend Richard Egan Lee, who also printed pamphlets by Allen Davenport, another contributor to the paper. Petrie was also the author of some spirited and by no means negligible poetry, and a leader of the metropolitan tailors.[31] In 1832, as a missionary for the GNCTU, he undertook an extensive provincial tour embracing Banbury, Oxford, Coventry, and Liverpool. His early death in 1836 robbed radicalism, and the Spencean circle particularly, of a talented and energetic leader and publicist. Dedicated to the last, Petrie bequeathed his skeleton to William Devonshire Saull's private museum, where later for London Chartists it was to be the object as much of homage as of scientific curiosity.[32] The circumstances of his death are best left to the decent obscurity of a footnote.[33]

Financially, the Barnsbury Park community appears to have depended on Baume's personal investment — on which the return, he claimed in 1837, was £200 per year, a sum best regarded with caution. As a distinctive communitarian scheme the Experimental Gardens appear to have ended about the time of Petrie's death. The cottages and land survived intact, albeit engulfed by subsequent building development, until the 1860s. By that time, however, Baume had left London, first for Manchester and thence to the Isle of Man. He died in 1875, leaving a substantial fortune to Manx charities.[34]

Proceedings.

31 J. H. Wiener, *The War of the Unstamped* (1969), 183. There were at least two editions of Petrie's *Works*, 1836 and 1841, both edited by Lee; for the metropolitan tailors and Petrie's involvement see T. M. Parssinen and I. J. Prothero, 'The London Tailors' Strike of 1834 and the Collapse of the Grand National Consolidated Trades Union', *International Review of Social History*, 22 (1977), 64-107.

32 For Petrie's GNCTU activities see Parssinen and Prothero, 'The London Tailors' Strike', and HO 64/19, 17 and 26 Mar. 1834; *NS*, 31 Oct, 1846, p. 3 (description of Saull's collection).

33 R. E. Lee, 'Biographical Memoir of George Petrie', in his edn. of the latter's *Works* (1836), 12, claimed Baume deliberately hastened his death: in the 2nd edn. (1841) he implies the use of poison. William Lovett, *Life and Struggles* (1876; new edn. 1967), 41, thought Petrie's fatal mental collapse was occasioned by his wife's enthusiastic acceptance of Owenite marriage doctrine. The two theories may not be incompatible: after Petrie's death his wife and Baume became involved in a vitriolic exchange with Lee over the rights to publish the posthumous *Works*. Whatever the truth, Baume was quickly ostracised from London politics; Owen described him as 'totally unworthy of confidence' (Co-operative Union Ltd., Manchester, Owen Collection, no. 920).

34 Baume to Owen, 30 June 1837, Owen Collection, no. 920; S. Roberts, *The Story of Islington* (1975), 87. Details of Baume's life can be found in the *Dictionary of National Biography* and in Holyoake, *History of Co-operation* (1875), i. 220, 349- 51, ii. 401-5. There are several letters in the Owen Collection, nos. 375, 916, 920-3. Baume has been connected with Bromley, the disciple of Owen who leased to him the premises at 277 Gray's Inn Road first used for the National Equitable Labour Exchange, see A. Abrahams, 'No. 277, Gray's Inn Road', *Antiquary*, 44 (1908). See also R. Cooter, *The Cultural Meaning*

A further small community, also well documented, was formed in London shortly after Barnsbury Park. Thirty-two members of the Philosophic Land Association leased premises in Cromer Street (off the northern end of Gray's Inn Road) to form an interim community. They boasted a chapel, schoolroom, and regular social meetings. It is clear that they were enthusiasts, disgruntled with Owen and, in particular, with the labour bank system, which they saw as a diversion from getting back to the land. Their leader, William Cameron, a Scottish tailor, had been an enthusiast for community ever since 1822 when he joined the Edinburgh Practical Society. At that point he revered Owen, writing to him in 1823 in a decidedly apocalyptic strain, begging to be admitted along with his family to the proposed Motherwell community. By 1832 Cameron had settled in Spa Fields, London, where he agitated for the speedy establishment of a model community; then, frustrated, he advanced his own plan, 'having for its primary object the attainment of land':

> Mr Owen is of the opinion that any attempt on the part of his followers to reduce the system into practice would be attended with evil consequences, and is for the present impracticable, and will continue to be so until a public opinion is created in its favour, which is tantamount to saying, 'Live, horse, and you will get grass!'[35]

The formation of the Philosophic Land Association and its attendant community was accorded considerable publicity in *Cosmospolite* (a radical weekly later merged with *Man* and of a similar political hue), and accompanied by a pamphlet in which Cameron expanded on his differences with Owen. Entitled *The First Trumpet*, it drew from Carlile the gleeful verdict that 'as it calls for practical rather than theoretical proceedings it will be deemed heterodox'. The project seems to have drawn to a close by 1836, when we find Cameron supporting the Friendly Community Society, another breakaway group. By the 1840s he was a supporter of the Chartist Land Plan, and (in the company of Benbow and Thomas Preston) an outspoken critic of building society promotion.[36]

Preston was one of the former members of the Society of Spencean Philanthropists who held aloof from co-operation, apparently believing that

---

of Popular Science (1984), *passim*.

35 Cameron to Owen, 5 Aug. 1823, Owen Collection, no. 359; Cameron, 'Practical Co-operation', *Cosmopolite*, 1/17 (30 June 1832). Owen declined to print this article in *Crisis*, see *Cosmopolite*, 1/21 (28 July 1832), but advertisements were accepted later, see *Crisis*, 1/25 (25 Aug. 1832), 100. See also *Lancashire and Yorkshire Co-operator*, *NS* 2 (Sept. 1832), 14-15.

36 *Cosmopolite*, 2/32 (13 Oct. 1833); *Isis*, 28 Apr. 1832. I have been unable to locate a copy of Cameron's *The First Trumpet, and Address to the Disciples of Robert Owen of Class No.4, on the Importance and Necessity of Speedily Establishing a Bond of Union of Mutual Interests for Gradually Carrying into Operation the New Science of Society* (1832). A *Second Trumpet* was advertised by the same author in *NMW*, 13 Dec. 1834; *NMW*, 19 Nov. 1836; *NS*, 2 Sept. 1843; *NS*, 21 Aug, 1847.

any community scheme attempted in advance of full political emancipation was doomed to fail. While Davenport, Jennison, John Hunter, Mee, and Petrie were all active co-operators, Blandford, George, Harris, Palin, and Walker, as well as Preston, were not. Yet all the latter were involved in the National Union of the Working Classes (NUWC) and/or subsequently Chartism. It is in the NUWC that one may most readily observe members of the Spencean circle acting in concert to ensure that property and the land remained live issues. A key strategy here was to ensure that the Finsbury group they dominated was in the vanguard of radical discussion. It was Finsbury which, at the height of the Reform Bill crisis, petitioned the House of Commons to confiscate the estates of recalcitrant peers. It was Finsbury that furnished the majority of the committee of the Victim Fund in 1833, the organization which above all others sustained the campaign for an unstamped press. And, in the same year, it was Finsbury which dominated the NUWC subcommittee appointed to organize the campaign for a national convention. Petrie, Mee, Bailey, and Preston, all from Finsbury, were members, along with Lee, who although a south Londoner clearly belonged to the Spencean rump. The general meeting which passed the motion securing this tactic was engineered by Petrie and Lee, closely supported by John George and John Simpson — the latter not a member of the Spenceans though, interestingly, later secretary and treasurer of the Camberwell branch of the Chartist Land Company.[37]

It was this subcommittee that organized the public meeting in May 1833 which culminated in the infamous Cold Bath Fields incident, in which two metropolitan policemen were killed during the tumultuous dispersal of the crowd. The coroner's jury at the ensuing inquest returned a controversial verdict of 'justifiable homicide'. The incident became a *cause célébre* to rank alongside Spa Fields and Cato Street. Indeed, it bears more than superficial affinities with them. A proposal to attack the Bank of England and the Tower had been mooted by Petrie a few days before. The self-styled 'leveller' James Mee, former secretary of the Archer Street Spencean division, was actually speaking when police charged the meeting; he had been proposed from the floor by Richard Lee. Had the meeting proceeded it was to have considered a petition itemizing 'the most prominent of the evils under which we are now suffering'. These were 'individual appropriation of the soil, which is the natural right of all'; the law of primogeniture, 'by which the spurious portion of society are fastened like leeches upon the industry of the country'; the funding system; and 'hereditary and exclusive legislation'. The latter category included enclosure, mortmain, game and trespass laws.[38]

---

37 J. R. M. Butler, *The Passing of the Great Reform Bill* (1914), 303; Prothero, *Artisans*, p. 295, and id., 'Chartism in London', *Past and Present*, 44 (1969), 80 and 87; *PMG* 100 (4 May 1833).

38 BL Add. MS 27797, fos. 11-16. Earlier in 1833 'the laws of property' had been the subject of extensive

Both Lee and Mee were arrested for their part in the incident. In the furore that erupted before they were acquitted, Preston, George, and Davenport were among the fiercest critics of the police's conduct. The incident is best understood as a belated and ill-conceived attempt by the Spencean circle to act on the same strategic principles that had been pursued in 1816-20. It is also distinctly possible that the authorities over-reacted to the demonstration, having been unnerved by the spectacle (well documented in intelligence reports) of so many Spencean enthusiasts once again in collusion.[39]

Far more important for the sustained vitality of Spenceanism was the commitment of key adherents to a broad policy of political education. They were amongst the most indefatigable speakers and lecturers in radical London. Sometimes they could be found speaking every night, effectively covering all the week's principal public meetings in the capital.[40] This, and their continued contributions to the press, helped to ensure that agrarian issues were not eclipsed in the developing movement, and that the memory of Spence was kept alive. The 'Principles, Spencean and Republican' of *Man*, for example, were widely acknowledged; so too was the gritty determination of Preston, Davenport, and George — despite advancing years — in the cause of truth. A testimonial committee organized for the 69-year-old Preston in 1837 formed an important link with a new generation of radical politicians: Davenport and 'Republican George' were among the collectors; Charles Neesom, soon to become prominent as a Chartist and free-thinker, acted as treasurer; the young G. J. Harney held office as secretary.[41] The testimonial was well merited. In the 1830s Preston had significantly stepped up his involvement in the popular movement and lent his weight to a number of causes, having overcome considerable personal difficulties (he had raised a family of seven single-handed since 1807, and was now the main source of support for his fifteen grandchildren). He joined the campaign for the unstamped press, speaking at meetings in support of Cleave and Hetherington when they were arrested in 1835. With James Walker, another member of Dr Watson's circle and a

---

discussion within the NUWC, largely promoted by the Spencean group, who provided speakers for every class in London in Jan. and early Feb.; see the official announcement of meetings and speakers, *Working Man's Friend*, 26 Jan. 1833.

39 There are numerous press reports on the incident, but see esp. *The Times*, 14 May 1833 (examination of Lee); *PMG* 100 (4 May 1833)-102 (18 May 1833). Preston and George, *PMG* 103 (25 May 1833); Davenport, letter to the editor, *Working Man's Friend*, 1 June 1833. See also Prothero, *Artisans*, pp. 295-6, and G. Thurston, *The Clerkenwell Riot* (1967).

40 e.g. *PMG* 76 (17 Nov. 1832), *PMG* 88 (9 Feb. 1833); *Working Man's Friend*, 26 Jan. 1833.

41 *Standard*, 10 Sept. 1833, quoted in *PMG* 120 (21 Sept. 1833). Preston testimonial, *London Dispatch*, 52 (10 Sept. 1837); Neesom had joined the Spenceans in 1818-19 and in his own words 'was very nearly implicated' in Cato Street: see M. Chase, 'Charles Neesom', in J. Bellamy and J. Saville (eds.), *Dictionary of Labour Biography*, viii (1987).

participant in the Cato Street defence committee, Preston also busied himself promoting the ideas of Alexander Milne. The latter had published yet another breakaway Owenite plan in 1834, under the title of *The Millenium or Happy Social Circle*. It was 'an improvement of Spence and Owen's plan, by going direct to Capital & Income', according to an informer who heard Preston speak on it at Walker's Coffee House.[42] About the same time Preston put forward a plan of his own. His Prestonian Society was closely modelled on Spencean ideals, but tempered also with Paine's *Agrarian Justice*. The main features were compulsory state acquisition of one acre in forty upon a landowner's death, thereby ensuring a peaceable resumption of the land into private property; old age pensions paid from a levy upon those in work; and a death duty on property of all kinds at 6*d*. in the pound. By 1836 a Prestonian Association was meeting in the Sir John Barleycorn, Booth Street, Spitalfields; there was possibly a further group meeting in Club Row, Bethnal Green. Thomas Preston was also involved, however, in activities reminiscent of earlier years: frequently seen in the company of Julian Thistlewood, promising 'to revenge his father's death'; and keenly anticipating 'a Successful Triumph of the cause of the people when the Struggle commences as he is certain it is on the Eve'. Robert Wedderburn also resurfaced about this time, at one of Robert Taylor's exuberantly disreputable diabolic 'services', held at William Benbow's Institute in Theobalds Road.[43]

Preston's boisterous and avowedly unrespectable radicalism isolated him from some in the movement. Even his tolerant associate Davenport thought him half mad and a drunkard, while Carlile lampooned him in the *Republican*. Yet in many respects Preston was a very typical figure, albeit of a strand within radicalism more usually ignored by historians: unskilled rather than skilled, revolutionary rather than gradualist, intemperate rather than respectable. Preston had almost vanished into the opaque society of tavern radicalism in the 1820s and his base remained there until his death in 1850. He therefore made little lasting impression on the more formalized organization of the metropolitan work-force. In terms of an enduring and tangible contribution to the survival of Spencean radicalism, Allen Davenport especially was far more important. The publication of his *Life, Writings, and Principles of Thomas Spence*, printed by Lee, in 1836 was particularly significant, Davenport's biography of Spence brought both men before a new audience, at the same time reinvigorating old

42 *PMG* 181 (22 Nov. 1834). The content of 'Preston's Plan' can be judged from subsequent attempts to promote it, *NS*, 31 Oct. 1840 and 18 Jan. 1845. Julian Thistlewood's reappearance was brief; for the rumour that he had been involved in 1830 in the Revolution in Paris see *WFP* 272 (25 Sept. 1830).

43 HO 64/19-17, 20, 22, and 25 Mar. 1834. Milne's pamphlet was advertised in *Man*, 2/20 (18 May 1834): 'It exhibits a Legal and Practical Plan for annihilating Poverty and Poor Rates, and making even the lowest grade of mankind Comfortable and virtuous. The plan wants only to be known to be approved of, and to be generally approved of to be acted upon immediately.'

connections. His association with George Julian Harney, for example, dates from this point; while Francis Place at last publicly associated himself closely with the views 'of my old and esteemed friend, Thomas Spence'. Shortly after the *Life* was published, a dinner marking Spence's birthday was held at the Eastern Institution, Shoreditch — a co-operative educational institute managed by Jennison. Charles Neesom chaired the evening, and Davenport and John George addressed the 'numerous and highly respectable' assembly, which concluded its proceedings by singing some of Spence's songs.[44]

In the biography of his mentor Davenport expressed profound regret that Spence had been eclipsed by Owen, when 'the Spencean system ... is the very foundation' of Owen's proposals. Davenport and his associates did much to redress this. By the summer of 1838 Bronterre O'Brien, in an article surveying recent developments in radical politics, could declare:

> The SPENCEAN doctrine is not only preached, but details for its practical working are brought prominently to public view. The people, who never before the Reform Bill, seriously canvassed the landlord's title to his share of the land, but who merely complained of his legislatorial interference with that portion of its produce which belongs to the nation, now discover that so long as the title exists, so long will the prejudicial interference continue.[45]

In effect, Davenport and his Spencean associates were making a significant contribution to the processes which impelled radicalism forward and created within a section of the Chartist movement a climate of opinion considerably in advance of orthodox Owenism. The formation in 1836-7 of the East London Democratic Association exemplifies this process. The Spenceans Waddington, Ireland, Neesom, Preston, and Jennison (the earliest meetings were held at the Eastern Institution) were all involved, besides Davenport, its founding president.[46]

However, the detailing of Spencean activity in the mid-1830s should not be permitted to obscure the extent to which there was a more general surge of interest in agrarian projects from this time. Enthusiasm for land schemes of one kind or another paralleled, rather than was supplanted by,

---

44 *Cleave's Weekly Police Gazette*, 30 July 1836; *NMW*, 30 Apr. 1836.

45 *NS*, 16 June 1838.

46 A. Davenport, *The Life, Writings, and Principles of Thomas Spence* (1836), 22-3; East London Democratic Association, *Prospectus* (1837), repr. in D. Thompson, *The Early Chartists* (1971), 55-6; London Democratic Association, *Constitution* (1838), copy in HO 44/52. At least two others, who had been associates of the Spenceans, joined the Association: Thomas Ireland and Samuel Waddington, cf. *London Dispatch*, 38 (4 June 1837), HO 42/180, 21 Sept. 1818. J. Bennett, 'The London Democratic Association 1837-41: A Study in London Radicalism', in J. Epstein and D. Thompson (eds.), *The Chartist Experience* (1982), 87-119, is the best secondary source on the Association. See also *London Mercury*, 4 June-23 July 1837.

growth in trades organization. The NUWC itself spawned 'a Society, formed for the purposes of Renting Land, purchasing stock, etc., with a view to the mutual support and protection of its members when out of Employment'. These objectives it shared with the Friendly and Protective Agricultural Association, formed in September 1833 and based in Covent Garden. James Tucker, the secretary, was an enthusiastic Owenite who had campaigned in 1829 for all the London co-operative societies to combine for the purchase of an estate near London.[47]

The Halfpenny-a-Week Land Club was another similar society, slightly better documented. The title was taken from a suggestion made by a carpenter, H. Tipper of the 5th Lodge of the Federated Society of Operative Builders, and a BAPCK Council member, for a weekly levy of ½*d.* on every workman's wage, the accumulated funds to be used to purchase land and stock to enable the unemployed to settle. This was shortly before the great builders' strike of 1834. The Club not only weathered the latter but appears also to have acquired property; at any rate, in 1835 it was able to offer a cottage, a quarter-acre of land, and livestock to the next of kin of one of the Tolpuddle martyrs. Assistance was also offered to the widow of Charles Pendrill, the Spencean and unwitting abettor of the spy Oliver. Some connection with Freemasonry is implied in a printed reply from Hetherington to Tipper. The Club is an aspect of the otherwise well-documented builders' movement which is largely a mystery, but the pedigree of its principle, 'Let the labour of the labourer be first applied to land', is unmistakable.[48]

The Halfpenny-a-Week Land Club is but one of the indications of an increase in agrarianism from 1834. The debate surrounding the poor law contributed to this. A meeting of trades delegates in January 1835 suggested a policy of agrarian co-operation:

> viewing the absolute necessity OF THE CONNECTION of the various Trade Societies to employ their unemployed, to possess Land, as one of the only fundamental elements which Man is heir to, we hereby resolve, that the Organ of each Society, as are employing their unemployed members, shall call a meeting, for the purpose of drawing up such plans as shall give the utmost confidence in any ulterior arrangements.

The extent of the response to this resolution is unclear. The Grand Lodge of the United Operative Tailors resolved that 'Man must return to the breast of his mother earth for nurture. The land, his unalienable right, must

47 *PMG* 24 (3 Dec. 1831); *Crisis*, 3/11 (9 Nov. 1833); *WFP* 210 (18 July 1829).

48 *Man*, 14 (13 Oct, 1833); *PMG* 153 (10 May 1834); *Crisis*, 4/5 (10 May 1834), 4/8 (31 May 1834), 4/12 (28 June 1834); *NMW*, 13 Dec, 1834; *PMG* 204-5 (2, 9 May 1835); BAPCK, *Report of the Committee, and Proceedings at the Fourth Quarterly Meeting* (1830), 10. In 1841 Tipper was a supporter of Goodwyn Barmby's Central Communist Propaganda Society, see *NMW*, 25 Sept, 1841.

again be his.' The brass-workers certainly acted on these sentiments and acquired land: 'being only partially or half employed in their regular trade of brass-working, they will fill up their time in tillage of land'.[49]

A rather different venture, closer to the heart of mainstream Owenite thinking, dates from the same time: the Social Land Community of Friends to the Rational System of Society, founded in March 1834. Its foundation demonstrated yet again the impatience of Owenites to set up a community: it operated at first from Presley's Coffee House, John Street, without Owen's personal imprimatur. Its officers, however, were close to Owen: the treasurer, Samuel Austin, was formerly secretary of the National Equitable Labour Exchange; the secretary, Frederick Bate, was a wealthy patron of the movement who subsequently bankrupted himself in financing Harmony Hall. In 1836, changing its title to the National Community Friendly Society, it succeeded as the parent body of Owenism. Its new secretary, Anthony Peacock, was a Finsbury Owenite and, as it happens, Charles Jennison's next-door neighbour.[50] The Social Land Community also traded in real property, and among London socialist organizations was far from unique in doing so. The National Land Equitable Labour Exchange, the similarly titled rival organization to Owen's labour bank, which William Bromley started in the premises it vacated in 1833, was connected in some way with property speculation. Bromley was possibly an associate of Baume, whose Experimental Gardens at Barnsbury Park cannot be exempted from possible commercial overtones. Like Baume, Bromley was involved in counter-Owenite socialism, promoting Thomas Macconnell as a lecturer to rival the Social Institute in Charlotte Street; Macconnell was yet another Finsbury radical and an occasional lecturer at Benbow's Theobalds Road Institute.[51] Another socialist organization trading in real property about this time was the First London Community Society; whether this was connected with the similarly titled Manufacturing Society, founded in 1830 with its strong Spencean input, it is impossible to say. In November 1838 the First London announced that it was 'about to make a practical experiment upon the land'. With the addition of small loans from members, it would be investing its accumulated capital in a lease upon

> ... a few acres of ground near London, the greater part of which it is intended to under let for the building of cottages at a ground rent. On the part reserved, it is intended to build and establish an Industrial School, and to form a summer resort for members and their friends,

49 *PMG* 189 (17 Jan, 1835); *Official Gazette of the Trades Unions*, 14 and 21 June 1834.

50 *Crisis*, 3/27 (1 Mar. 1834), 4/7 (24 May 1834); Garnett, *Co-operation*, p. 145; *NMW*, 6 May 1837, 7 Nov. 1840.

51 A. Abrahams, 'No. 277, Gray's Inn Road', p. 132. Biographical details of Macconnell from his *Lecture on the Signs of the Times* (1832), title-page; cf. Garnett, *Co-operation*, p.140; *Crisis*, 2/2 (19 Jan. 1833).

> together with the benefit of a country residence, should the health of the members require such a restorative.[52]

In making available grounds mainly for summer recreation the Society was continuing an authentic popular tradition, declining in London owing to the capital's phenomenal growth but still thriving elsewhere. Such blatant participation in the market for real property would seem to put the First London Community Society beyond the pale of radicalism, and still more of socialism, but the volatility of land prices on urban margins arguably forced such a strategy on radical groups hoping to settle their members on the land. In their commercial undertakings, societies like the First London presaged the Freehold Land Movement of the late 1840s and 1850s, one of the most significant elements in the growth of both building societies and suburban development, which grew from the interaction of Chartism, advanced liberalism, and popular agrarianism. English radicalism was Janus-headed in its stance on property. A Spencean-inspired tradition that expounded the uniqueness and importance of land could as well underpin arguments in favour of working-class participation in the land market, as those aiming to remove land from the commercial market altogether. This was particularly so, given the chequered history of communal-ownership experiments. It is plausible, also, that workers in centres of particularly rapid urbanization (and therefore escalating prices) were fearful of impending and permanent exclusion from property ownership.

The year 1838 witnessed two further agrarian ventures on the periphery of the Owenite movement. Of the first, the Association for the Internal Colonisation of Tradesmen and the Poor, virtually nothing is known.[53] Of the second, the community at Manea Fen, Cambridgeshire, considerably more can be discovered: it published its own newspaper, *The Working Bee*, for some eighteen months, engendered considerable debate within the radical press generally, and has duly been remembered by secondary authorities. What has not been appreciated is the extent to which the Hodsonian Community (named after its founder) adhered to fundamental agrarian tenets, which included an explicit avowal of the influence of Spence. Accordingly, the Manea Fen community was, for many disgruntled agrarians within the Owenite movement, a symbol of considerable potency, Davenport applied in 1839 to be admitted, but was turned down as the community had shoemakers enough for the moment. His enthusiasm undimmed, he wrote regularly for the *Working Bee* in the autumn of 1840, including a three-part history of the Owenite movement which made *inter alia* a swingeing attack on socialist branch culture for too often losing sight of the land, the one essential ingredient of progress. All

52 *Star in the East*, 24 Nov. 1838.

53 *London Dispatch*, 25 Mar. 1 Apr. 1838.

socialist schools should have land attached, he said, and urban groups should establish Halls of Science for agriculture and natural sciences in country areas. [54]

Davenport's opinions were wholly in line with the tone of the *Working Bee* and its parent community, which revived the Spencean slogan 'The land is the people's farm', and published frequent editorials on agrarian issues along with letters from fellow enthusiasts throughout the country. 'Before the bulk of the nation will be well fed and clothed — we must have the land … the only means that can effect the change desired', wrote a Christian socialist from Manchester, adding that the land was 'a very essential point of the blessings promised' at the millennium. Benjamin Warden praised the community as 'The Advanced Guard of Social Reformers', and used the *Working Bee*'s columns to attack what he perceived as a trend toward autarchy in Owenism, as well as the inept handling of the Queenwood project. Both he and Davenport helped organize support for Manea Fen among sympathetic socialists in London, through the establishment of 'Branch No. l' of the Hodsonian community in the East End.[55]

Manea Fen was not the sole agrarian scheme in East Anglia. In a concentration of radical activism which has never been noticed, still less explained, the Hodsonian Community operated alongside branches of United Advancement Societies in Wisbech, March, Peterborough, and Lincoln. The first of these in fact pre-dated Manea, and like the other three seems to have drawn heavily on the skilled artisans of its prosperous market town for support. The specific form of the United Advancement Societies, however, was the product of the energies of James Hill, a local landowner, banker, and Owenite sympathizer. In January 1838; in the paper he edited, *The Star in the East*, Hill had welcomed the formation of a Wisbech Working Men's Association. Simultaneously, though, he called for the institution of a land society. Hill, who was already experimenting with rational education at an infant school he conducted in Wisbech, had very definite views on the benefits of rational cultivation:

> Nature furnishes the materials with which food, clothing and lodging may be increased to an indefinite extent … Millions of millions of acres

54 Useful secondary accounts of the community may be found in Armytage, *Heavens Below*, pp. 145-64; Harrison, *Robert Owen*, p. 171; Hardy, *Alternative Communities*, pp. 49-53; B, Taylor, *Eve and the New Jerusalem* (1983), pp. 252-8. Davenport, 'The Rise, Progress, and Probable Results of the Social System', *Working Bee*, *NS* 1/20, 26, 30 (17 Oct., 28 Nov., 26 Dec. 1840). See also ibid., *NS* 1/21-2, 25 (24, 31 Oct., 21 Nov, 1840) Davenport's application to join the community is recorded ibid. 1/20 (30 Nov. 1839).

55 Spencean influence, *Working Bee*, 1/1 (20 July 1839), NS 1/10, 11 (8, 15 Aug. 1840); 'A Christian Socialist', 'The Land — The Land', ibid., *NS* 1/16 (19 Sept. 1840); Warden, ibid., *NS* 1/18 (3 Oct. 1840). See also ibid. 1/4 (10 Aug. 1839), *NS* 1/9, 12 (1, 22 Aug. 1840). Branch No. 1, *Social Pioneer*, 2 (16 Mar. 1839); see also ibid. 4 and 5 (30 Mar. and 6 Apr. 1839) for further letters by Warden.

> of land are yet uncultivated, and are a storeroom inexhaustible for the supply of FOOD. The application of chemical science, to that part of the earth, which is brought under cultivation, will admit of its productive-powers being rendered much more effective.[56]

It seemed that Hill was to have the most prominent forum possible in which to demonstrate his theories when, in 1837, his Wretton Hall estate was selected as the site for the first official Owenite community in England. However, his insistence that he personally should manage the colony was unacceptable to Owen and the National Community Friendly Society, who withdrew their support. James Hill remained sufficiently loyal to Owen, though, to lampoon almost weekly 'the Manea (alias maniac) scheme'. Simultaneously, he promoted his own agrarian experiment, whose inception was celebrated in May 1839 by a 'Festival, to celebrate the commencement of the redemption of the land by peaceable means into the hands of its rightful Owners, the people — the only True lords of the soil'.[57]

It was not successful. In spite of their promoter's ambitions, the United Advancement Societies' support rested principally on their routine functioning as consumer co-operatives. Membership declined as dividends fell under the impact of purchasing and stocking the land. It is unclear if Hill was a proponent of an agrarian version of 'philanthropy plus five per cent', or whether he found his personal ownership of the colony's land morally offensive, but the community foundered largely because it owned the land it occupied. The bitter irony under which the forty or so communitarians of nearby Manea Fen laboured, on the other hand, was that, however truly they had returned to the land, they still were merely tenants. In 1841 the project broke up amid bitter recriminations when William Hodson withdrew his support. Yet, quite apart from Harmony Hall (which survived, albeit precariously, from 1839 until 1845),[58] there were still further attempts to put into practice Owenite and agrarian precepts. James Hill himself, having moved to London, was engaged in one such venture. His National Land and Benefit Building Society of 1845-7 enjoyed the support of some notable radical figures, including William Carpenter, Bronterre O'Brien, Goodwyn Barmby, and the former Spencean Charles Neesom. The Society, which was quickly eclipsed by the Chartist Land Plan, was as much part of the building society movement of the 1840s and 1850s as it was of agrarianism; though more correctly, perhaps, it should be seen as an amalgam of the two, similar to the Freehold Land

---

56 *Star in the East*, 20 Jan., 10 Feb., 3 Mar., 11 Aug. 1838; 13 Apr. and 23 Nov. 1839

57 Ibid., 7 Oct, 1838, 13 and 27 Apr. 1839; see also Armytage, *Heavens Below*, pp. 142-3; Garnett, *Co-operation*, p. 152.

58 Harrison, *Robert Owen*, *passim*; Garnett, *Co-operation*, pp. 165-213; Hardy, *Alternative Communities*, pp. 53-8.

Societies.[59]

In Lancashire at this time Elijah Dixon, one of the veterans of the 1832 Chat Moss land scheme, was involved with other Mancunian co-operators in floating a Christian Co-operative Joint Stock Company to locate members on the land. Enthusiasts in two other cities, Liverpool and Leeds, formed communities in Wales. The first, at Pant Glas near Dolgellau, was short-lived; but the Leeds Redemption Society's Carmarthenshire estate, founded in 1845, survived ten years — a not inconsiderable achievement. Like Manea Fen, it attracted considerable interest from London reformers and a supportive metropolitan society was formed in 1847. A separate co-operative society of Religious Socialists in the capital had been founded in 1840 'for the purpose of purchasing and cultivating such a quantity of land as would employ some of our poor brethren as may be out of work, and also to provide an Asylum for ourselves and for our children'.[60]

Land schemes were, as in the 1820s and 1830s, again under discussion within trade societies in this decade. The issue was discussed at length among Sheffield metalworkers in 1843, the same year that it was revived within the metropolitan tailors' union. Coventry ribbon weavers formed the bulk of the membership of a Labourers' and Artizans' Co-operative Society, which cultivated land provided by Charles Bray, a local manufacturer and wealthy Owenite, until 1862 when it was replaced by a Garden Society.[61] In 1845 Manchester smallware weavers chose to concentrate their resources upon a land scheme in preference to a co-operative store. The National Association of United Trades, formed the same year, devoted considerable discussion to agrarian proposals, and a National Association for the Employment of Surplus Labour in Agriculture and Manufactures was formed in consequence. Among other trades organizations, the Oldham spinners' union acquired 8 acres for its unemployed members to cultivate as a market garden; and the Yorkshire wool-staplers likewise took a farm at this time. Similarly, East London cordwainers, meeting at the Standard of Liberty in Brick Lane, formed a society to attain 'land for those who get no work at their trades, instead of

---

59 See the Society's paper *The Commonweal* (1845-6), edited by Hill; BL, Place Collection, Set 56, Jan.-Dec. 1845, fo. 405, and Jan.-Aug. 1846, fo, 247; *NS*, 21 June 1845; *NMW*, 17 May 1845 and 19 July 1845; *Lloyds Weekly London Newspaper*, 15 June 1845; *National Reformer*, 11 (12 Dec. 1846), 14-17 (2-30 Jan. 1847), and 26 (27 Mar. 1847).

60 Harrison, *Robert Owen*, pp. 171-2; *Spirit of the Times* and *Weekly Tribune* carried regular reports on the Redemption Society and its estate, 1849; London Branch, *Spirit of the Times*, 8 (28 Apr. 1847). The fullest account of the Redemption Society is given by J. F. C. Harrison, *Social Reform in Victorian Leeds: The Work of James Hole, 1820-1895* (1954).

61 J. Salt, 'Trades Union Farms in Sheffield', *Notes and Queries*, 206 (1961); *The Life Boat*, 1 (2 Dec. 1843); Coventry Perseverance Co-operative Society, *Jubilee History* (1917), 22 — see also Harrison, *Robert Owen*, pp. 240-1.

them getting a bit of bread and cold water at the workhouse'.[62]

Twelve months later, however, this 'Boot and Shoemakers Mutual Protection Society' dissolved itself and invested all its capital in shares of the Chartist Land Plan.[63] This documented example suggests that the Chartist plan, because of its almost gargantuan proportions, absorbed much energy that might otherwise have found an outlet in small-scale agrarian projects. Indeed, Feargus O'Connor himself seems to have envisaged Chartism implementing a strategy of this diffused nature when in May 1840 he called for the establishment of 'Associations, throughout the whole kingdom, to be called Chartist Agricultural Associations — Five Acre Associations — or Landed Labour Associations'. Within three months of this initial call, one Working Men's Association at least was considering the formation of 'an Agrarian Company'.[64] At this earliest and most critical stage, the nascent concept of a Chartist land scheme drew heavily on grass-roots support: William Hill, the Hull Swedenborgian, initiated coverage in depth of land issues in the *Northern Star* during his editorship, a strategy shared by its publisher Joshua Hobson, himself editor in 1843-4 and publisher also of O'Connor's pamphlet of 1841 *'The Land' the Only Remedy for National Poverty and Impending National Ruin*.[65] Much has been made of the opposition to the Land Plan encountered by O'Connor from the other Chartist leaders: less appreciated is the extent to which the scheme enjoyed support from those who, whilst their national reputations were slender, were locally figures of considerable eminence. James Leach, the Manchester radical bookseller was one such; William Beesley, 'the Lion of North Lancashire', was another; from Yorkshire one might mention James Arran of Bradford, as well as from Huddersfield, initially, Hobson; and in the South, Thomas Frost of Croydon. In London the Owenite T. M. Wheeler was central to the success of the plan, whilst the Spenceans Allen Davenport and Thomas Preston were also influential in gathering support. It was provincial support of this nature which largely secured approval for the plan at the Birmingham Convention of 1843.[66]

62 *NS*, 18 and 25 Jan. 1845; NAUT business is reported throughout the paper at this time. See also J. Belchem's important study 'Chartism and the Trades, 1848-1850', *English Historical Review*, 98 (July 1983), esp. p. 573. J. Foster, *Class Struggle and the Industrial Revolution* (1974), 232; S. and B. Webb, *The History of Trades Unionism* (1894), 161.

63 *NS*, 24 Jan. 1846.

64 O'Connor, *NS*, 16 May 1840; Cirencester Working Men's Association, ibid., 29 Aug. 1840.

65 *NS*, 25 Apr. 2 and 9 May, 20 June 1840; F. O'Connor, *'The Land', The Only Remedy for National Poverty and Impending National Ruin* (Labourer's Library, nos. 2 and 3; 1841). For Hobson's subsequent rift with O'Connor over the conduct of the Land Plan see *NS*, 6 and 20 Nov. 1847, also a scrapbook of cuttings (mainly from the *Manchester Examiner*) in the Goldsmiths' Library, University of London.

66 Beesley, *NS*, 29 Oct., 5 Nov. 1842; Arran, 31 Oct. 1840; Davenport, 21 Nov. 1840, 29 Aug. 1846; Davenport, 'The Social Sun', *Reasoner*, 1 (1846), 158. Preston, *NS*, 30 Sept., 1843. On Wheeler see W. Stevens, *A Memoir of Thomas Martin Wheeler* (1862), 25; J. Bellamy and J. Saville (eds.), *Dictionary of Labour Biography*, vi (1982), 266-9. T. Frost, *Forty Years' Recollections* (1880), 96.

Because of a tendency to see the Land Plan as a largely unheralded eruption, to be credited almost exclusively to O'Connor (or, rather, blamed on him), the extent of early support for an agrarian scheme has gone unnoticed. This is not to devalue O'Connor's importance, but rather to establish more satisfactorily the origins of the scheme. Though in many respects the Land Plan evolved under the influence of factors peculiar to the mid-1840s and to the Chartist movement in what might be described as its post-euphoric phase, that it happened at all can be seen as the consequence — almost the culmination — of the popular agrarian tradition.

The Chartist Land Plan was thus no maverick episode in the history of British working-class movements.[67] Its uniqueness lay not in its aims and objectives, but in its scale: at its peak some 70,000 members subscribed weekly to shares at £2.10*s*. which entitled them to participate in ballots for allotments of land. Each cottage smallholding was to be one of hundreds, on estates bought on behalf of the plan; and each was to pay an economic rent into a central fund from which land for further smallholdings was to be purchased. The scheme's huge success (in terms of the support it attracted) was hardly anticipated at the outset, and can only be ascribed to the strength of the agrarian tradition, and to the vision of a new social and economic order which the Land Plan shared with Chartism as a whole. The Chartists 'have commenced the Agrarian Revolution', wrote Davenport; 'The Jubilee is come at last.' Almost inevitably, *Jubilee* was used to describe the opening celebrations for the 'People's first Estate', O'Connorville in Hertfordshire.[68]

O'Connor's initial intention, though, was that the plan should be a practical demonstration of the power of spade husbandry; of the virtues of independent labour; of the social and economic importance of the family unit; and of the fallacies of Malthusianism. In short, it was to be a prototype of the kind of society which would be universally viable once the Charter was law. The application for registration under the Friendly Societies' Act explained:

> OBJECTS OF THE SOCIETY: to purchase land on which to locate such of its members as may be selected for that purpose to demonstrate to the working classes of the kingdom — firstly, the value of the land, as a means of making them independent of the grinding capitalists; and, secondly to shew them the necessity of securing the speedy enactment of the 'People's Charter', which should do for them nationally, what this

67 There is a considerable literature on the plan, though the need remains fully to integrate its history with that of Chartism generally: J. MacAskill, 'The Chartist Land Plan', in A. Briggs (ed.), *Chartist Studies* (1959); J. Saville, intro. to R. G. Gammage, *History of the Chartist Movement* (new edn., 1969), 128-37; A. M. Hadfield, *The Chartist Land Company* (1970); Hardy, *Alternative Communities*, pp. 75-105.

68 *Reasoner*, 1/10 (6 Aug. 1846); *NS*, 22 and 29 Aug. 1846.

> society proposes to do sectionally: the accomplishment of the political and social emancipation of the enslaved and degraded working classes.[69]

No such glib formula, however, could be found to satisfy the Registrar of Friendly Societies, the principal objection being that the plan was effectively a lottery. Since registration was refused, William Prowting Roberts, the miners' attorney who also acted for the plan, advised an application for joint-stock company status. Theoretically the requirements of the relevant act were straightforward: applications must be accompanied by the names, addresses, and occupations of the subscribers of at least 51 per cent of the share capital. For most business undertakings a handful of names sufficed. For the Chartists' 'National Land Company', in which few held multiples of even two shares, the consequences were disastrous. Tens of thousands of names, in alphabetical order, were required, with a stamp duty of £3.15*s*. due on every hundred. 'The number of names overcame us', explained W. P. Roberts's clerk.[70] From the Chartist perspective the episode was further evidence of the iniquities of class legislation. In spite of comprehensive legal reforms — arguably, partly because of them — the law was inherently inimical to working-class associational forms. The Land Plan was certainly not alone in confronting this, but arguably it was here that the confrontation was most dramatic.

However, the failure to secure legal recognition was not the cause of the scheme's demise, though it certainly increased its problems. It was the sheer scale of the enterprise that so unnerved critics and, ultimately, supporters alike. The share capital originally subscribed was adequate for the purchase of land for, at most, just 500 holdings. Success would have been most likely given good land close to expanding markets, but the very cost of such a commodity put it beyond reach; and in any case a tradition which laid such emphasis on the appeal of an honourable subsistence, was little-attuned to agricultural realities. Secondly, success depended on detailed actuarial management. O'Connor was neither capable of this, nor prepared to delegate the responsibilities he so cheerfully accumulated. This was fatal: the return from rentals was vastly overestimated; the period of years in which all the shareholders might be accommodated was not the 15 claimed, but more likely 75 or 115.[71] Most humiliating of all the results of this mismanagement was an attempt to increase rents to raise capital. The company was wound up in 1851, amid recriminations, financial and legal chaos, and a collapse of confidence in O'Connor, who had ruined both his private fortune and his mental and physical health in the plan's promotion.

Surveying the tattered remnants of the plan in 1858, Wheeler, its first

69 *NS*, 3 May 1845.

70 SC National Land Company, 6th Report, *PP* 1847-8 (577), xix, evidence of Chinery, q. 186.

71 SC National Land Company, 1st Report, *PP* 1847-8 (398), xix, evidence of Finlaison, q. 4541.

secretary and himself an allottee at O'Connorville, yet managed to find grounds for optimism about its long-term significance:

> Instead of being a failure, it has proved a signal success. Land which had heretofore been considered a question affecting landholders or Farmers alone, suddenly became the paramount question of the day and pre-eminently the People's question, the rage for manufactures and commercial speculation had disinherited man from his birthright, the projection of the Land Company rekindled the ancient flame, and reknit the ties which bound the labourer to his mother earth.[72]

Whatever the exaggeration Wheeler brought to his appraisal, the Chartist Land Plan had dramatically fathomed the depths of working people's continuing attachment to the land. It was not the case, however, that it had renewed ties which had been completely severed, as the present study should have made clear. The Chartist Land Plan, through the human energies and organizational resources upon which it capitalized, gave shape to deeply rooted popular feeling. O'Connor and his associates found, as it were, the angel in the marble.

72 T. M. Wheeler, leader article, *National Union*, (5 Sept. 1858), 33.

7

Designed for the Support of Mankind

Art thou poor but honest man,
        Sorely oppress'd and a' that,
Attention give to the Chartist plan,
        'Twill cheer thy heart and a' that
        For a' that and a' that,
Though landlords gripe and a' that,
        I'll show thee, friend, before we part,
The rights of man and a' that.

The rights of man then's in the soil,
        An equal share and a' that,
For landlords no one ought to toil —
        'Tis imposition and a' that,
        Yes a' that and a' that,
Their title-deeds and a' that,
        How'er they got them, matters not,
the land is ours for a' that.

Cursed be he who shall remove
        The poor man's bounds and a' that,
Or covet aught should he improve
        His house, or stock, and a' that,
        Yes, a' that and a' that
His cattle, goods, and a' that,
        Could but be mortgaged for a term,
Till Jubilee and a' that.

Brave Chartist has shewn the way to fix,
        Man's happiness and a' that,
His freedom with his interest mix,
        Their Charter plan will shew that,
        Yes a' that and a' that,
Divide the rent, and a' that,
        What God has gave all should enjoy,
And all the world should know that.[1]

1 *The Chartist Song* [c.1840] BL 1875.D.5(41); cf. 'The Spencean Plan for a' that', *Spence's Songs*, ii.

One can but speculate who, about 1840, was responsible for republishing as a broadside ballad Thomas Evans's 'Spencean Song' of *c.* 1811, with amendments confined merely to substituting 'Chartist' for 'Spence' or 'Spencean' throughout. It is vivid testimony, though, to the vitality at grass-roots level of agrarianism, and the Spencean ideas at its core. Interpretation of the 'back to the land' element in radical politics has usually hinged on seeing it as anachronistic — the product of a retarded class consciousness and insufficient awareness of industrialism. Agrarianism was not, though, a mutant throwback to pre-industrialism, even if the rural ambience of early nineteenth-century Britain was a key factor underpinning popular 'land consciousness'. Agrarianism was very much the product of, and a response to, the increasing capitalization of industry. It sought a material platform from which industrialization might be ameliorated and directed to labour's advantage. At the same time patterns of migration, urban growth, and economic expansion continued tangibly to link labour with the land. However, this was no longer merely a labour force, but a working class with access (albeit precarious at times) to material resources for self-education and political organization, sustained by a burgeoning tradition of democratic agitation. All this both made possible, and further validated, the search for 'a new life, intense and unconfined'.[2]

This is not to accuse the English working class of naïve Utopianism. Throughout this period the working class refused to be confined: confined at the work-place to wage labour, and to subordinate roles in the processes of production; confined at elections merely to the hustings; confined in their leisure time to those associational forms bearing the imprimatur of 'respectability', and for recreation to officially designated 'public' open spaces.

> Have we not seen the commons of our fathers enclosed by insolent Cupidity, — our sports converted into crimes, — our holidays into fast days? The green grass and the healthful hay-field are shut out from our path. The whistling of birds are [*sic*] not for us — our melody is the deafening noise of the engine.

In every sense, therefore, popular politics was centred upon an ideology of exclusion.[3] What lent to radicalism generally, and to its explicitly agrarian variants particularly, a sense of urgency and optimism, even in the mid-1840s, was a perception of economic and political exclusion being the consequences of very recent processes, continuing, but not predestined and immutable.

One indication of radicalism's awareness of the immediacy of change

2 W. Whitmore, 'Respite Hours', *Firstlings* (1852), 28, and see above, ch. 2.

3 *Pioneer*, 7 (19 Oct. 1833); G. Stedman Jones, 'Rethinking Chartism', in id., *Languages of Class* (1983) is the most recent and cogent analysis of radicalism as an ideology of exclusion.

was its perceptiveness regarding the shifting definition of property. This important issue, vast in itself, can only be touched on here. Spence's concept of property, derived from Locke (as was shown in Chapter 2), was one widely employed by other radicals; true property is an extension of the person, and upon it all 'rights of property' in goods and land must be contingent. The shipwrights' leader John Gast, a close associate of the Spencean group, expressed the matter succinctly in his pamphlet *Calumny Defeated*:

> ... the labor of the mechanic, stands upon a firmer basis, with respect to the originality of its right, than the right to landed property: in fact, that of the mechanic is physical, and consequently coeval with his existence: the other, at best, is but legal ... There was a time when such ownership of land did not exist: and its exclusive proprietorship depends wholly upon custom, sanctioned by the positive law of the country.[4]

'Property is but the creation of law' argued the *Poor Man's Guardian*; 'whoever makes the law has the power of appropriating the national wealth. The rich do at present make the law, therefore they are in possession of the national wealth. If they did not make the law they would not have the property.' Charles Neesom

> solemnly declared he never had the slightest idea of encroaching on any man's personal property, but the property which had been acquired by the plunder of the people, he would encroach on when he could because he knew it to be his. This might be treason to some, but he declared it was the honest sentiment of his heart. They (the working men) were not the despoilers of property, but the producers of it.[5]

When speaking of property, radicals also drew upon an attenuated but nevertheless lively concept of communal ownership. Opposition to enclosure, throughout this period always near the head of radical grievances, was one vehicle which kept concepts of communality very much alive. Communal ownership forms, as Edward Thompson has argued, endured far into the eighteenth century, both in law and in 'the denser reality of social practice'.[6] 'The Land is the People's Farm' slogan vividly summed up this tradition of looking at land, and of thinking about property. The historical reality (albeit receding) of a property system founded upon communally regulated use-rights, rather than upon absolute possession, considerably influenced English radical attitudes to the land.

4 J. Cast, *Calumny Defeated* (1802), 9.

5 *PMG* 206 (16 May 1855), ibid. 105 (8 June 1833).

6 E. P. Thompson, 'The Grid of Inheritance: A Comment', in J. Goody, J. Thirsk, and E. P. Thompson, *Family and Inheritance: Rural society in Western Europe, 1200-1800* (1976), 328-60.

Furthermore, as long as an awareness of such rights of usage survived, the theoretical concept of all land having once been held in common had an immediate historic reality. Radical analysis of property advanced from this material basis, powerfully reinforced by a reading of Locke which emphasized first his theory of property based on the historical veracity of the state of nature; and second the conviction that common ownership of both land and the goods of nature was itself an authentic form of property.[7]

It may be less obvious, though, how such an interpretation squares with that other radical theory of property, exemplified by Cobbett, which explicitly endorsed private ownership. Cobbett's theoretical stance on private property has to be teased out from some of his lesser-known works, notably the *Legacy to Labourers*.[8] Here and elsewhere his exaggerated deference to historical institutions such as feudalism, the medieval church, and the Elizabethan poor law, reflects not his shortcomings as a historian but his self-appointed function as a moral critic of contemporary society. Cobbett deployed his idealized vision of the past to expose the shortcomings of the present. He therefore endorsed private property in land, as long as there existed beside it a continuing framework of use-rights which both recalled and maintained in its essence the original state of nature, and thus permitted a property in the soil to those who, privately, possessed none. In Cobbett's thought natural right entitles all to a living, not to a plot or holding of the land *per se*. So long as work could be made available to all seeking it, at a rate of remuneration allowing a decent standard of living, the case for public ownership (of land or any means of industrial production) did not, Cobbett felt, stand up to scrutiny. However, as a natural corollary, obligations adhered to private property: hence Cobbett's favourable image of feudal society as a complex of mutual rights and obligations; and hence also his opposition to enclosure, which destroyed rights of usage and access to the land, while simultaneously extending private property beyond that socially acceptable optimum at which landholders might still fulfil their responsibilities to the community. The New Poor Law of 1834, of course, represented the landed establishment's ultimate abrogation of responsibility towards the people as a whole.

> God gave them life upon this land; they have as much right to be upon it as you have; they have a clear right to a maintenance out of the land, in exchange for their labour; and, if you cannot so manage the lands yourselves as to take labour from them in exchange for a living, give

7 This reading of Locke appears less wilful in the light of the examination of his thought by J. Tully, *A Discourse on Property: John Locke and his Adversaries* (1981), than it did in that of the earlier and prevailing critique by C. B. Macpherson, *The Political Theory of Possessive Individualism* (1962).

8 But see the excellent summary of Cobbett's views in a *Northern Liberator* editorial, 13 July 1839.

the land up to them; they are not to perish at any rate.[9]

An identical emphasis on the irrefutable rights of all to maintenance lay at the heart of the radical case for public ownership — the difference from Cobbett (and, it can be added, O'Connor) being that early advocates of public ownership saw no possible accommodation between landed and landless, no act of reciprocity equal to the loss of the land; yet there are points in Cobbett's writings at least, as in the passage just quoted, when he clearly implies that the situation has passed beyond the point at which any meaningful accommodation can be restored, precisely because of the extent to which labour is landless, and bereft of rights of ownership and access alike. In the minds of ordinary readers, therefore, radical views of landed property were likely to appear less incompatible than dispassionate analysis allows. We should beware, in any case, of imposing anachronistic expectations of coherence and consistency on radical economic thought at this time. Its key point was its radicalism, its seeking-out of the roots of injustice, and its vision of an economic and social order in which unmerited privilege was defunct.

Leaving innovative theorists like Spence aside, radical leaders were often remarkably flexible in their espousal of economic doctrines: thus Allen Davenport warmly supported the Chartist Land Plan; and O'Brien, one of the scheme's most implacable opponents, is several times on record as endorsing the virtues of smallholdings.[10] In this respect his ideas closely paralleled the views of the Chartist leader with whom he is most often contrasted: Feargus O'Connor. The Chartist Land Plan may well have been the negation of nationalization, but it was nevertheless a distinctively radical response to the growth of private property in land, identifying as Spence and O'Brien had done the need to devolve economic and political powers attendant on private ownership; at the same time it reaffirmed with Cobbett that private property might be acceptable if constrained by size and sense of social responsibility. The ostensibly Janus-headed stance of English radicalism, at once critical of private property in the soil and yet jealous for rights of property in land, is not problematic if we view it as a bid not for the ownership of the means of production, but rather for a control of them. In spite of their differences, then, it is possible to detect important underlying unities in the various advocates of agrarian reform: belief in the universal right to living out of the land; suspicion of centralized government; and a way of seeing property in land which was shaped by concepts of access and usage, rather than of absolute possession.

---

9 'The Fires', *Cobbett's Weekly Political Register*, 28 Feb. 1835, col. 536. See also his *Legacy to Labourers* (1835), especially letters 1, 2, 5, and 6.

10 *Northern Liberator*, 6 July 1839, and *Cheltenham Free Press*, 2 Mar. 1842, cited by M. Hobby, 'Chartism and the Land Plan in Gloucestershire', University of Wales (Swansea) MA dissertation (1980), 22.

In such a context, the rental basis of the Chartist Land Plan, an ostensible paradox often seized upon by its opponents, constituted no problem in principle for its shareholders and adherents.

Access and usage were not the sole unifying elements in agrarianism. At its core lay also a cluster of attitudes about land, labour, and nature, focusing upon the issues of status, independence, and control over the disposal of one's labour. Clearly these were attractive to artisans; these elements, however, were no less appealing to non-artisan groups, who likewise perceived and experienced industrialization as a threat to, or outright destroyer of, their status as independent producers, enjoying the control of production and, thus, of the organization of their daily life. Agrarianism was essentially an ideology of small producers. Among the attractions of a return, in some form, to the land was the potential extension or renewal of control over the means of production. The importance of this to those accustomed to independence, either directly and personally, or in a self-regulating community at the work-place, should not be underestimated (difficult, perhaps, in modern industrial society, which tends to see people as consumers rather than producers). Not the least heinous crime of the 'rebel of Nature', Thomas Malthus,[11] was the creation of a framework of reference in which ordinary people were stigmatized as consumers rather than accorded their customary role as producers. Behind the radical retort to Malthusianism lay faith not just in the fecundity of nature, but in labour's capacity to release and enhance it.

Malthus judged the relative reproductive capabilities of man and nature, and found nature wanting. Anti-Malthusianism of necessity therefore inclined, as was shown in Chapter 5, to emphasize the existence, or at very least immediate potentiality, of material abundance; and it opposed all restraints upon labour realizing it. One consequence of this, which grates against modern environmentalism, was a starkly utilitarian attitude to the land, and to the aesthetics of landscape. It has recently been argued with some force that the French lagged behind the English in appreciating the sublimity of wild nature. It depends, though, who or what is meant by 'English' here. For many of the working class untamed nature was unnatural. A marked resistance to the alleged aesthetic appeal of raw nature, paralleling eighteenth-century France, can be detected among nineteenth-century English radicals: they rejected an aesthetic based on untouched, unsubdued 'natural' nature, in favour of one emphasizing cultivation and productiveness.[12] 'The whole earth [should] be as the

11 A. Davenport, 'Agrarian Equality', *Republican*, 10/13 (1 Oct. 1824), 410.

12 D. G. Charlton, *New Images of the Natural in France: A Study in European Cultural History, 1750-1800* (1984). See also K. Thomas, *Marx and the Natural World: Changing Attitudes in England, 1500-1800* (1983); challenging though it is, this study draws overwhelmingly on polite, literary sources and thus exaggerates the extent to which the English felt either comfortable with, or favourably disposed towards, untamed nature by the end of the eighteenth century.

Garden of Eden', claimed Spence, referring to its abundant fertility rather than its association with lost innocence. Britain, wrote Robert Owen, 'must now become essentially agricultural', a view supported by O'Connor when he described the English landscape as barren compared with that of the Low Countries. 'Why are huge forests still allowed to stretch with idle pomp and all the indolence of eastern grandeur?' inquired Mary Wollstonecraft, 'Why does the brown waste meet the travellers' view, when men want work?'[13]

As the quotation from Wollstonecraft suggests, it was not the self-esteem of labour alone which validated the cultivated, at the expense of the uncultivated, landscape. William Benbow, in his influential *Grand National Holiday* proposal, developed this view at some length:

> The only class of persons in society, as it is now constituted, who enjoy any considerable portion of ease, pleasure and happiness, are those who do the least towards producing anything good or necessary for the community at large. They are few in number … And this fraction of society … is as *one* to *five hundred* when compared to the people who produce all the good things seen in the world. Notwithstanding the *one*, the *unit*, the mere *cypher* has all the wealth, all the power of the state, and consequently prescribes the way and details the manner, after which he pleases the 499 should live in the world. The 499 who create the state, who are its instruments upon all occasions, without whom it cannot go on for a single second, who dig deep, rise early, and watch late, by whose sweat and toil the whole face of nature is beautified — rendered pleasant to the sight, and useful to existence; — the 499 who do all this are reduced to less than nothing in the estimation of the *unit* who does no one thing, unless *consuming* may be called doing something.[14]

This concern that nature should effectively be harnessed for work reflected in part the uncertainties of labouring lives still often interspersed with periods of actual scarcity. The subsistence crises of 1794-6 and 1799-1801 were pivotal episodes in the experience of older radicals. Even to accept that unproductive landscapes might be part of the natural order was to offer a hostage to Malthusianism: human overlordship, it can be argued, has always been most vigorously asserted by those for whom it has been most precarious. There was another facet to the aesthetics of agrarianism, as Benbow powerfully argues, which linked it integrally to the fight against 'The Thing', Old Corruption. A non-productive landscape mirrored the non-productive part of humanity — idle, parasitic, and consumed in

13 T. Spence, 'A Dream', in *Spence's Songs*, iii [?1811], 19; *NMW*, 28 May 1842; *NS*, 11 Oct. 1845; M. Wollstonecraft, *A Vindication of the Rights of Men* (2nd edn., 1790), 148. Such views echo Locke, see *Second Treatise*, sections 36, 37, and 47.

14 W. Benbow, *Grand National Holiday and Congress of the Productive Classes* (1832), 4.

luxury. 'If there were no parks, and no pleasure grounds', argued Davenport, 'the whole face of the country would present to the eye cornfields, meadows, gardens, plantations of all kinds of fruit trees, etc., all in the highest state of cultivation.' 'NO LAND, if wanted for the People, SHOULD LIE IDLE', wrote 'Co-operatus'; 'SPADE-HUSBANDRY will soon turn *Parks* and *Pleasure Grounds* into one scene of fertility and abundance.'[15] 'Catius', addressing the members of the builders' union, was yet more explicit:

> How many thousands now feel the piercing sting of griping hunger, that pride may enjoy in cold exclusive selfishness its many follies, vices, even crimes, which by a sad perversion of ideas have been misnamed the harmless pleasure of the few. Such pleasures leave whole acres lying waste, that hound and horse may trample on the earth, which cultivated by now starving man, would gratefully repay in teeming bounty the labour he bestowed. It is such that hide the fair face of nature by unbecoming fence and towering wall ...[16]

Opposition to enclosure, like agrarianism very much concerned with issues about land distribution and access, was a sphere where agrarian and general radical ideologies particularly reinforced each other. It was a commonplace, in the early radical movement especially, that one of the prime purposes of enclosure was to construct pleasure grounds. The use of the sickle, 'Citizen' Richard Lee sarcastically observed in 1795, 'is daily declining; as *Gentlemen* of landed property are got into a way of parcelling out their land into Sheep-walks, Lawns, and Parks for deer to run about in'. In a lecture to the Society of the Friends of Liberty the same year, John Baxter (subsequently a Spencean) asked: 'Is not our Arable Land converted into Pasturage for the breed of Horses for pleasure (which have augmented to treble their number within these thirty years) ... ?'[17]

The claim that enclosure took place purely to abet the recreations of the rich was, if not palpably false, only a quarter-truth, but it followed logically from the anti-establishment emphasis of radicalism generally. Indeed, the very strength of this emphasis incapacitated agrarianism in the generation of any more subtle and far-reaching analysis of economy and society. The root of oppression was located, with absolute conviction, even mechanically, in a misappropriation of soil. From this politically enforced injustice all others grew. The *Northern Star* editorial, already quoted in the first chapter, was merely an unusually explicit statement of a general view.

---

15 Davenport, 'Reflections on Agrarian Justice', *Republican*, 18 Oct. 1822. For similar utilitarian attitudes see *WFP* 220 (26 Sept. 1829); *NMW*, 6 Aug. 1836 and 30 July 1842; 'Co-operatus', *No. 1. Division of Land. To the Peasantry* [*c*.1835]

16 *Pioneer*, 6 (12 Oct. 1833); cf. *Penny Paper for the People*, 15 Jan. 1831; and *British Co-operator*, 4 (July 1830).

17 *The Blessings of War* (?1795], 5; J. Baxter, *Resistance to Oppression, the Constitutional Right of Britons* [1795], 6.

> ... we consider that the monopoly of land is the source of every social and political evil ... every law which 'grinds the face of the poor' has emanated from this anomalous monopoly ... our national debt, our standing army, our luscious law church, our large police force, our necessity for 'pauper'-rates, our dead weight, our civil list, our glorious rag money, our unjust laws, our game laws, our impure magistracy, our prejudiced jury system, our pampered court, and the pampered menials thereunto belonging, are one and all so many fences thrown round the poor man's inheritance.[18]

Agrarianism's challenge, then, was to forms of property rather than of production. Hence the emphasis on opposition to enclosure: a further expropriation of the people's farm, denying natural and actual legal rights and reinforcing aristocracy and luxury; but enclosure was not, on the whole, ever seen as the specific consequence of the capitalization of agriculture. Proponents of smallholdings and of public ownership alike remained locked in fundamentally anti-landed-establishment postures. Even Spenceanism, which aimed at the most comprehensive reconstruction of the economy, was not inimical to small producer capitalists. On the contrary, it rather appealed to the latter: even farmers in the Spencean polity were the independent tenants, and not the managers, of the people's farm. Bronterre O'Brien, almost alone among non-communitarian radicals in developing a coherent case for the nationalization of land, was in the 1840s still advancing the case for smallholdings, and by implication small owners.

It is important, though, to avoid dismissing popular agrarianism for failing to accomplish what it never set out to do: that is, develop a socialist, or even a proto-Marxist, critique of capitalism. Radical agrarianism was a critique, and a powerful one, of Marx's so-called 'primitive accumulation', and of social relations of production, of the wage contract, the cash nexus, and the materialistic concepts of success, failure, and happiness entailed on them. 'It is a proud and peculiarly indigenous tradition that British socialism and radicalism have been concerned not only with structural shifts of economic and political power, but with the very quality and excellence of all dimensions of human existence.'[19] This evaluation of Owenite culture is valid for agrarianism also. The views of the English agrarians might be summed up not as 'back to the land', but as 'forward to the land as it would be'.[20] For, while 'God made the country, and man made the town', he had made it for particular purposes of which inertia was not

18 *NS*, 22 Mar. 1845; and cf. Jones, *Languages of Class*, pp. 152-3.

19 E. M. Yeo, 'Robert Owen and Radical Culture', in S. Pollard and J. Salt (eds.), *Robert Owen, Prophet of the Poor* (1971), 107-8.

20 Cf. Charlton, *New Images*, p. 192, on Rousseau.

one. It is because of this abiding emphasis upon the land, *in partnership with human agency*, as a productive force that the values which have been investigated here are more accurately termed *agrarian* than pastoral. Pastoralism, 'a puzzling form which looks proletarian but isn't', as William Empson remarked, is more properly applied to responses to urbanism and industrialism which sought escape in nature: either a nature unreconstructed by man, or a contrived Arcadia in which the natural order, not labour, is the producer.[21] While it is true that agrarianism was powerfully informed by popular belief in the mystique of nature, the relationship with labour which it posited was a mutually sustaining one. It is worth repeating the conclusion of Dr Watson's speech at the second Spa Fields meeting, 2 December 1816:

> We have been truly told that Trade and Commerce are at an end — but we still have the Earth — which Nature designed for the support of mankind — The Earth is capable of affording us all the means of allaying our wants and of placing Man in a Comfortable situation — If a Man has but a Spade, A Hoe, and a Rake and turns up his Mother Earth — He will be sure to find the means of averting Starvation.[22]

To a post-Marxian observer this is unpromising rhetoric with which to forge the revolutionary moment. That these were the sentiments used on a cold December day to raise a substantial crowd to the pitch at which they were prepared to march on the City and Tower of London has much to say about the centrality of agrarianism to the radical politics of early nineteenth-century England; and much to say, too, about contemporary working-class evaluation of the dignity of labour.

21 W. Empson, *Some Versions of Pastoral* (new edn. 1968), 6; see also R. Williams, *The Country and the City* (1973), *passim*.

22 HO 40/3(3), fos. 895-9.

Bibliography

1. MANUSCRIPT SOURCES

British Library, London (Department of Manuscripts), Place Papers, Add. MSS 27791, 27797, 27808-9, 27816-18, 27822, 27840, 27851, 35152.

British Library, London (Department of Printed Books), Place Collection, Sets 56, 60, and 64.

Co-operative Union Ltd., Manchester, Robert Owen Papers; George Jacob Holyoake Collection.

Devon County Record Office, Exeter, Sidmouth Papers.

Public Record Office (Chancery Lane), London:

Privy Council Papers, PC 1/23; PC 1/3117; PC 1/3526; PC 1/3535.

Privy Council Register, PC 2/140.

Treasury Solicitor's Papers, TS 11/45; TS 11/122; TS 11/97-208; TS 11/689, 939, 951, 953, 955, 958-9, 965, 966; TS 24/3.

Public Record Office (Kew), London:

Letters and papers on disturbances, 1816-22, HO 40/3-17.

Letters and papers, 1797-1822, HO 42/40-203.

Letters and papers, 1820-1, HO 44/1-8.

Secret Service Reports, HO 44/52.

Secret Service Reports, HO 64/11-19.

Police Correspondence, HO 65/1.

Letters and papers, HO 100/75.

Law Officers' Reports, HO 119/1.

2. UNPUBLISHED THESES

Claeys, Gregory, 'Owenism, Democratic Theory and Political Radicalism', University of Cambridge Ph.D. thesis (1983).

Donnelly, F. K., 'The General Rising of 1820: A Study of Social Conflict in the Industrial Revolution', University of Sheffield Ph.D. thesis (1975).

Hobby, M., 'Chartism and the Land Plan in Gloucestershire', University of Wales (Swansea) MA dissertation (1980).

HONE, J. ANN, 'The Ways and Means of London Radicalism, 1796-1821', University of Oxford D.Phil. thesis (1975).
MCCALMAN, IAIN D., 'A Radical Underworld in Early 19th Century London: Thomas Evans, Robert Wedderburn, George Cannon and their Circle, 1800-1835', Monash University, Ph.D. thesis (1984).
MARSHALL, PETER H., 'William Godwin: A Study of the Origins, Development and Influence of his Philosophy', University of Sussex. D.Phil. thesis (1976).
NEESON J. M., 'Common Right and Enclosure in 18th Century Northamptonshire', University of Warwick Ph.D. thesis (1977).
ROBINSON, F. J. G., 'Trends in Education in Northern England During the 18th Century: A Biographical Study', University of Newcastle Ph.D. thesis (1972).

3. PARLIAMENTARY PAPERS

Proceedings

Parliamentary History of England from the Earliest Period to the Year 1803 (1819 edn.).
The Parliamentary Debates from the Year 1803 to the Present Time (1817).
Hansard's Parliamentary Debates (1817-19).

Reports

Select Committee on Emigration from the United Kingdom, Second Report, *PP* 1826-7 (237), v.
Select Committee on Public Walks, *PP* 1833 (448), xv.
Select Committee on Education in England and Wales, *PP* 1835 (465), vii.
Reports from Assistant Hand-loom Weavers' Commissioners, part II, *PP* 1840 (43-11), xxiii.
Report by Mr Hickson on the Condition of the Hand-loom Weavers, *PP* 1840 (639), xxiv.
Enquiry into the Sanitary Condition of the Labouring Population, *PP* 1842 (HL), xxvii.
Select Committee on Commons Inclosure, *PP* 1844 (583), v.
Royal Commission on the Condition of the Framework Knitters, appendix, parts I and II, *PP* 1845 (618, 641), xv.
Select Committee on National Land Company, First Report, PP 1847-8 (398), xix; Sixth Report, *PP* 1847-8 (577), xix.
Select Committee on Public Libraries, *PP* 1849 (655), xviii.

4. NEWSPAPERS AND PERIODICALS

Associate, 1829-30; continued as *Associate and Co-operative Mirror*, 1830.

Axe Laid to the Root, 1817.

Black Dwarf, 1817-24.

British Co-operator: see *Co-operative Magazine and Monthly Herald*.

Bronterre's National Reformer, 1837.

Carpenter's Political Letters and Pamphlets, 1830-1.

Charter, 1839-40.

Cleave's Weekly Police Gazette, 1835-6.

Cobbett's Weekly Political Register, 1804-36.

Commonweal, 1845-6.

Co-operative Magazine and Monthly Herald, 1826-7; continued as *Co-operative Magazine*, 1828-9; *London Co-operative Magazine*, 1830; *British Co-operator*, 1830.

Co-operator, 1828-30.

Cosmopolite, 1832-3.

Crisis, 1832-4.

Economist, 1821-2.

English Chartist Circular, 1841-4.

Forlorn Hope, 1817.

Freemen's Magazine: Or, the Constitutional Repository, Containing, A Free Debate Concerning the Cause of Liberty (Newcastle), 1774.

Freethinking Christians' Magazine, 1811-14.

Gauntlet, 1833-4.

Gentlemen's Magazine, 1797-1815.

Giant Killer or Anti-landlord, 1814.

Gorgon, 1818-19.

Independent Whig, 1815-21.

Isis, 1832.

Journeyman and Artizan's London and Provincial Chronicle, 1825.

Lancashire Co-operator, 1831; continued as *Lancashire and Yorkshire Co-operator*, 1831-2.

Leeds Mercury, 1819.

Life Boat, 1843-4.

Lloyds Weekly London Newspaper, 1845.

London Chronicle, 1816-19.

London Co-operative Magazine: see *Co-operative Magazine and Monthly Herald*.

London Dispatch, 1836-8.

London Mercury, 1836-7.
Man, 1833-4.
Medusa, 1819-20.
Morning Chronicle, 1795.
National Reformer, 1846-7.
New Moral World, 1834-45.
New Times, 1818.
Northern Liberator, 1837-40.
Northern Star, 1837-52.
Official Gazette of the Trades Unions, 1834.
One Pennyworth of Pigs' Meat, first pub. 1793-5; 2nd edn. 1795; 3rd edn. 1796.
Operative, 1838-9.
Optimist, 1829.
Penny Paper for the People, 1830-1.
People's Hue and Cry, 1834.
Pioneer, or Grand National Consolidated Trades' Union Magazine, 1833-4.
Poor Man's Guardian, 1831-5.
Promethean, 1842.
Reasoner, 1846-61.
Reformists' Register, 1817.
Republican, 1819-26.
Shamrock, Thistle and Rose, or the Focus of Freedom, 1818.
Sherwin's Weekly Political Register, 1817-19.
Social Pioneer, 1839.
Star in the East, 1836-40.
Theological Comet, 1819.
The Times.
Trades' Newspaper and Mechanics' Weekly Journal, 1825-7; continued as *Trades Free Press*, 1827-8; *Weekly Free Press*, 1828-31.
Union, 1831-2.
Voice of the People, 1831.
Weekly Free Press: see *Trades' Newspaper and Mechanics' Weekly Journal.*
Working Bee, 1839-40.
Working Man's Friend, 1832-3.

5. CONTEMPORARY PRINTED SOURCES

The place of publication of books is London, unless stated otherwise.

A Brief Vindication of the Principles of Mr. Malthus, in a Letter to the Author of an Article in the Quarterly Review (1813).

Address and Regulations of the Society of Spencean Philanthropists; with an Abstract of Spence's Plan ... Published by Order of the Society (1815).

Address Delivered at the Opening of the Birmingham Co-operative Society, November 17, 1828, by a Member. To which is Added the Laws of the Society (Birmingham, 1828).

Address of the Society of Christian Philanthropists to All Mankind on the Means of Promoting Liberty and Happiness [1819].

Address of the Society of Spencean Philanthropists to all Mankind, on the Means of Promoting Liberty and Happiness (1817).

Aikin, John, *A Description of the Country from Thirty to Forty Miles around Manchester* (1795).

An Inquiry into those Principles Respecting the Nature of Demand and the Necessity of Consumption (1821).

At a Meeting of Real Friends to Truth Justice, and HUMAN HAPPINESS, IT WAS RESOLVED. That the Principles of CITIZEN SPENCE'S THEORY OF SOCIETY, are Immutable and Unchangeable as Truth and Nature on which they are Built ... (broadside) (1801).

Aylmer, Edward, *Memoirs of George Edwards, alias Wards, the Acknowledged Spy, and Principal Instigator of the Cato Street Plot* ... (1820).

Bamford, Samuel, *Passages in the life of a Radical* (2nd edn. 1844; new edn. 1967; repr. Oxford, 1984).

Baume, Pierre, *Speech of a Frenchman, on the Proposed Bill for the Dissection of Human Bodies, Delivered at the British Forum, Monday, 23 March, 1829.*

——— *A Revolution in England is Unavoidable, Since all Sound Politicians are of the Opinion that THINGS, both in Church and State, Cannot Remain Much Longer as they are!!!* [1830].

Baxter, John, *Resistance to Oppression, the Constitutional Right of Britons. Asserted in a Lecture delivered before Section 2 of the Society of the Friends of Liberty, on Monday, November 9th* [1795].

Benbow, William, *Grand National Holiday and Congress of the Productive Classes* (1832).

Bewick, Thomas, *A Memoir of Thomas Bewick, Written by Himself* (1st edn., Newcastle, 1861; new edn., Oxford, 1975 (ed. I. Bain), repr. 1979)

Blandford, E. J., *Prince Cobourg's Lamentation for the Loss of the Princess Charlotte* [1817].

The Blessings of War. Consisting of Extracts from Pigott's Political

Dictionary and Others [?1795].

BOGUE, DAVID, and BENNETT, JAMES, *History of Dissenters, from the Revolution in 1688, to the Year 1808*, 4 vols. (1809-12).

A Brief Account of the Church of God, known as Free-thinking Christians: Also, an Abstract of the Principles which they Believe, and the Laws of Church Fellowship they have Adopted (1841).

BRITISH ASSOCIATION FOR PROMOTING CO-OPERATIVE KNOWLEDGE, *Report of the Committee, and Proceedings at the Fourth Quarterly Meeting ... April 18th, 1830* (1830).

Britannia's Command to the Universe (broadside ballad) (1819).

BROWN, J., *Sixty Years' Gleanings from Life's Harvest* (Cambridge, 1858).

BURN, J. W., *Autobiography of a Beggar Boy*, ed. D. Vincent (1978).

BURNETT, ALEXANDER, *Tillage: A Substitute for Manure, Illustrated by the Principles of Modern Agricultural Science, and the Precepts and Practice of Jethro Tull* (1859).

COBBETT, WILLIAM, *Legacy to Labourers: Or, What is the Right which the Lords, Baronets, and Squires, have to the lands of England? In Six Letters Addressed to the Working People of England* (1835).

'CO-OPERATUS', *No. 1. Division of land. To the Peasantry* [*c*.1835].

DAVENPORT, ALLEN, *the Kings, or, Legitimacy Unmasked, A Satirical Poem* (1819).

——— *Claremont; Or the Sorrows of a Prince. An Elegiac Poem* [1820].

——— *Queen of the Isles* [1820].

——— *The Life, Writings, and Principles of Thomas Spence, Author of the Spencean System, or Agrarian Equality* (1836).

——— *The Life and Literary Pursuits of Allen Davenport ... written by himself* (1845).

DAVENPORT, RICHARD, *A Practicable, Easy and Safe Plan for Checking the Increase of Pauperism and the Evils Resulting from the Poor Laws* (Battle and Lewes, 1823).

DICKSON, R. W., *General View of the Agriculture of Lancashire: With Observations on the Means of its Improvement. Drawn up for the Consideration of the Board of Agriculture* ... (1815).

EAST LONDON DEMOCRATIC ASSOCIATION, *Prospectus* (1837).

ENSOR, GEORGE, *Radical Reform: Restoration of Usurped Rights* (1819).

Essay on Printing by a Spencean Philanthropists [*sic*] [1816].

EVANS, JOHN, *A brief Sketch of the Denominations into which the Christian World is Divided; Accompanied by a Persuasive to Religious Moderation* (1795).

EVANS, THOMAS, *Christian Policy the Salvation of the Empire* ... (2nd edn., 1816).

——— *Christian Policy in Full Practice among the People of Harmony ...*

to which are Subjoined a Concise View of the Spencean System of Agrarian Fellowship (1818).

——— *A Brief Sketch of the Life of Mr Thomas Spence, Author of the Spencean System of Agrarian Fellowship or Partnership in Land, with an Illustration of his Plan in the Example of the Village of Little Dalby, Leics; Accompanied with a Selection of the Songs sung in all the Sections of the Spencean Society* (Manchester, 1821).

Frost, Thomas, *Forty Years' Recollections: Literary and Political* (1880).

Gammage, R. G., *History of the Chartist Movement* (1854; new edn. 1969).

Gast, John, *Calumny Defeated: Or, a Compleat Vindication of the Conduct of the Working Shipwrights, During the Late Disputes with their Employers* (Deptford Bridge, [1802]).

Godwin, William, *Enquiry Concerning Political Justice and its Influence on Morals and Happiness* (3rd edn. 1798; new edn., Harmondsworth, 1976).

Hall, Charles, *Effects of Civilisation on the People in European States* (1805).

Heavisides, Henry, *The Centennial Edition of the Works of Henry Heavisides* (1895).

Hetherington, Henry, *Principles and Practice Contrasted; Or a Peep into 'The Only True Church of God upon Earth', Commonly called Freethinking Christians* (2nd edn., 1828).

Hodgskin, Thomas, *The Natural and Artificial Rights of Property Contrasted. A Series of letters ... to H. Brougham. By the author of 'Labour Defended against the Claims of Capital'* (1832).

Holt, John, *A General View of the Agriculture of the County of Lancaster* (1795).

Hone, William, *The Meeting in Spa-Fields. Hone's Authentic and Correct Account, at Length, of all the Proceedings on Monday, December 2nd; with the Resolutions and Petition of Nov. 15, 1816* (1816).

——— *The Riots in London. Hone's Full and Authentic Account, Containing ... Particulars of the Events in the Metropolis, on Monday, the 2nd of December 1816* (1816).

——— *Hone's Riots in London, Part II. With Most Important and Full Particulars ... Elucidating the Events of Monday, December 2, 1816. Including Original Memoirs and Anecdotes of Preston, Dyall, the Watson Family, Thomas Spence ... Showing the Real Occasion and True Character of the Tumults* (1816).

——— *Full Account of the Third Spa-Fields Meeting* (1817).

——— *Another Ministerial Defeat! The Trial of a Dog for Biting a Noble Lord* (1817).

——— *Official Account: Bartholomew Fair Insurrection and the Pie-bald Poney Plot!* (1817).

——— *Official Account of the Noble Lord's Bite* (1817).

Hudson, J. W., *A History of Adult Education* (1851).

A Humourous Catalogue of Spence's Songs [?1811].

Hunt, Henry, *Memoirs of Henry Hunt, Esq. Written by Himself, in His Majesty's Jail at Ilchester, in the County of Somerset* (1820).

Hutton, William, *The Life of William Hutton, F.A.S.S. Including a Particular Account of the Riots at Birmingham in 1791. To Which is Subjoined the History of his Family Written by Himself, and Published by his Daughter, Catherine Hutton* (1816).

Lance, Edward Jarman, *The Golden Farmer, Being an Attempt to Write the Facts Pointed out by Nature, in the Sciences of Geology, Chemistry and Botany* ... (1831).

Lawless, Valentine Brown (Baron Cloncurry). *Personal Recollections of the Life and Times, with Extracts from the Correspondence, of Valentine Lord Cloncurry* (Dublin, 1849).

London Co-operative Society, *Articles of Agreement for the Formation of a Community on Principles of Mutual Co-operation, within Fifty Miles of London* (1825).

London Co-operative Trading Fund Association *To the Operative Classes* [1828].

——— *Regulations* [1828].

London Corresponding Society, *The Report of the Committee of Constitution of the London Corresponding Society. (Printed for the Use of Members)* (1794).

——— *The London Corresponding Society Addresses the Friends of Peace and Parliamentary Reform* (1793).

Loudon, Jean Claudius, *A Manual of Cottage Gardening, Husbandry, and Architecture* ... (1830).

——— *The Suburban Gardener* (1838).

——— *The Suburban Horticulturalist* (1842).

Lovett, William, *Life and Struggles of William Lovett in his Pursuit of Bread, Knowledge and Freedom, with Some Short Account of the Different Associations he Belonged to and of the Opinions he Entertained* (1876; new edn. 1967).

Lowman, Moses, *Dissertation on the Civil Government of the Hebrews. In Which the True Designs and Nature of their Government are Explained. The Justice, Wisdom and Goodness of the Mosaical Constitution are Vindicated* (1740).

Macconnel, Thomas, *A Lecture on the Signs of the Times: Delivered in the Great Lecture Room of Robert Owen's Institution, Gray's Inn Road, on the Morning of November 18, 1832* (1832).

Mackenzie, Eneas, *A Descriptive and Historical Account of the Town and*

County of Newcastle upon Tyne, Including the Borough of Gateshead (Newcastle, 1827).

——— *Memoir of T. Spence. From Mackenzie's History of Newcastle* (Newcastle, 1826).

MALTHUS, THOMAS ROBERT, *An Essay on the Principle of Population as it Effects the Future Improvement of Society* … (1798).

——— *An Essay on the Principle of Population* … (5th edn., 1817).

MARAT, JEAN-PAUL, *The Chains of Slavery. A Work Wherein the Clandestine and Villianous Attempts of Princes to Ruin Liberty are Pointed out, and the Dreadful Scenes of Despotism Disclosed. To Which is Prefixed, An Address to the Electors of Great Britain* … (1774).

MARGAROT, MAURICE, *Proposal for a Grand National Jubilee: Restoring to Every Man his Own, and Thereby Extinguishing both Want and War* (Sheffield [1812]).

'A Master Shoemaker', 'My Life and Adventures', *Boot and Shoemaker*, 14 June-6 Sept. 1879.

More Reasons for a Reform in Parliament, Contained in Letters … (1793).

MURRAY, JAMES, *Sermons to Asses* (Newcastle 1768; new edn., London, Wm. Hone, 1817).

——— *Lectures to Lords Spiritual; Or an Advice to the Bishops, Concerning Religious Articles, Tithes, and Church Power, with a Discourse on Ridicule* (Newcastle, 1774).

——— *An Impartial History of the Present War in America; Containing an Account of its Rise and Progress, the Political Springs thereof, with its Various Successes and Disappointments, on Both Sides* (1778).

——— *Lectures upon the Book of the Revelation of John the Divine: Containing a New Explanation of the History, Visions, and Prophesies, Contained in that Book*, 2 vols. (Newcastle, 1778).

——— *Sermons for the General Fast Day* (Newcastle, 1781).

O'CONNOR, FEARGUS, *'The Land', the Only Remedy for National Poverty and Impending National Ruin; How to Get it; and How to Use it.* (Labourers Library, nos. 2 and 3; Leeds, 1841).

——— *A Practical Work on the Management of Small Farms* (1843; new edn. 1845),

OWEN, ROBERT, *Report to the County of Lanark* (1821; new edn., Harmondsworth, 1969)

——— *The Revolution in the Mind and Practice of the Human Race: Or the Coming Change from Irrationality to Rationality* (1849).

——— *The Life of Robert Owen, Written by Himself* (1858; new edn. 1967).

PAINE, THOMAS, *Age of Reason* (1793; new edn. 1915).

——— *Agrarian Justice: Opposed to Agrarian Law and to Agrarian Monopoly; Being a Plan for Meliorating the Condition of Man, by Creating in Every Nation a National Fund …* (1797; new edn. 1840).

Pellew, Henry, *The Life and Correspondence of the Rt. Hon. Henry Addington, First Viscount Sidmouth*, 3 vols. (1847).

Petrie, George, *The Works of George Petrie …*, ed. R. E. Lee (1836, new edn. 1841).

'Pindar, Peter', *Bubbles of Treason; Or, State Trials at Large, Being a Political Epistle from an Irishman in London to his Brother in Paris; and Containing a Humorous Epitome of the Charge, Evidence, and Defence* (1817).

Place, Francis, *The Autobiography of Francis Place, 1771-1854*, ed. Mary Thale (Cambridge, 1972).

Preston, Thomas, *The Life and Opinions of Thomas Preston, Patriot and Shoemaker, etc.* (1817).

Price, Richard, *An Essay on the Population of England, from the Revolution to the Present Time* (2nd edn., 1780).

——— *The Evidence for a Future Period of Improvement in the State of Mankind, with the Means and Duty of Prompting it, Represented in a Discourse Delivered … at the Meeting House in the Old Jewry* (1787).

——— *Observations on the Nature of Civil Liberty, and the Principles of Government, from Dr. Price's much Esteemed and Popular Essay, Published Anno 1776. With the Declaration of Principles, and Regulations of the Friends of Liberty United for Promoting Constitutional Information, the Only Means by Which a Reduction of Taxes, and the Enormous Price of Provisions can be Obtained; or Unjust and Unnecessary Wars Prevented* [?1794].

Proceedings of the Friends of the Liberty of the Press (1793).

Proceedings of the Third Co-operative Congress Held in London … On the 23rd of April 1832 … Reported and Edited, by Order of the Congress, by William Carpenter (1832).

Radcliffe, W., *Origin of the New System of Manufacture* (Stockport, 1828).

Reid, William Hamilton, *The Rise and Dissolution of the Infidel Societies in this Metropolis: Including the Origin of Modern Deism and Atheism; the Genius and Conduct of these Associations; their Lecture Rooms, Field Meetings, and Deputation; from the Publication of Paine's Age of Reason till the Present Period* (1800).

Richmond, Alexander B., *Narrative of the Condition of the Manufacturing Population …* (2nd edn., 1825).

Rose, William, *A Letter to the Rev. Wm. Douglas, M.A. Chancellor of the Diocese of Salisbury, Containing a Review of the Spencean Philosophy; and in Which its opposition to Scripture and Fact is Pointed out* (Salisbury, [1817]).

A Song for the New Dispensation. The Cry of the Oppressed (1819).

Southey, Robert, 'Parliamentary Reform', *Quarterly Review*, 31 (October 1816), 225-78.

Spence, Thomas, *The Grand Repository of the English Language: Containing Besides the Excellencies of All Other Dictionaries and Grammars of the English Tongue, the Peculiarity of Having the Most Proper and Agreeable Pronounciation of the Alphabetic Words Denoted in the Most Intelligible Manner by a New Alphabet* (Newcastle, 1775); facsimile reprint, ed. R. C. Alston (English Linguistics 1500-1800, 155; Menston, 1969).

——— *The Real Reading-made-easy; Or, Foreigners' and Grown Persons' Pleasing Introductor to Reading English, Whereby all Persons, of whatever Age or Nation, May soon be Taught, with Ease and Pleasure, to Read the English Language* (Newcastle, 1782).

——— *A Supplement to the History of Robinson Crusoe, Being the History of Crusonia, or Robinson Crusoe's Island, Down to the Present Time* … (English and phonetic edns., Newcastle, 1782).

——— *The Case of Thomas Spence, Bookseller, The Corner of Chancery Lane, London; who was Committed to Clerkenwell Prison, on Monday the 10th of December, 1792, for Selling the Second Part of Paine's Rights of Man* ... (1793).

——— *The Rights of Man, as Exhibited in a Lecture Read at the Philosophical Society, in Newcastle, to Which is now Added, an Interesting Conversation between a Gentleman and the Author, on the Subject of the Scheme. With the Queries Sent by the Rev. Mr J. Murray to the Society in Defence of the Same* … (1793).

——— *The End of Oppression; or a Quartern Loaf for Two-pence; Being a Dialogue between an Old Mechanic and a Young One. Concerning the Establishment of the Rights of Man* (lst and 2nd eds., 1795).

——— *A Letter from Ralph Hodge, to his Cousin Thomas Bull* [1795].

——— *A Fragment of an Ancient Prophecy. Relating, as Some Think, to the Present Revolutions, Being the Fourth Part of the End of Oppression* (1796).

——— *The Meridian Sun of Liberty; Or, the Whole Rights of Man, Displayed and Most Accurately Defined* … (1796).

——— *The Reign of Felicity, Being a Plan for Civilising the Indians, of North America; Without Infringing on their National or Individual Independence. In a Coffeehouse Dialogue, Between a Courtier, an Esquire, a Clergyman and a Farmer* (1796).

——— *Spence's Recantation of the End of Oppression* (1796).

——— *The Rights of Infants: Or, the Imprescriptable Right of Mothers to such a Share of the Elements as is sufficient to Enable them to Suckle and Bring up their Young. In a Dialogue between the Aristocracy and a*

Mother of Children, To which are Added by Way of a Preface and Appendix, Strictures on Paine's Agrarian Justice (1797).

——— *The Constitution of a Perfect Commonwealth. Being the French Constitution of 1794, Amended and Rendered Entirely conformable to the Rights of Man. By T. Spence, Author and Publisher of the Best Repository of Sound and Standard Politics, Entitled 'Pig's Meat'* … (lst and 2nd edns., 1798).

——— *The Restorer of Society to its Natural State in a Series of Letters to a Fellow Citizen, With a Preface Containing the Objections of a Gentleman who Perused the Manuscript, and the Answers by the Author* (1801; phonetic edn, 1803).

——— *The Important Trial of Thomas Spence for a Political Pamphlet Entitled 'The Restorer of Society to its Natural State', on May 27th, 1801, at Westminster Hall before Lord Kenyon and a Special Jury* (phonetic edn., 1803; 2nd edn., in English, 1807).

——— *Second Edition. A Receipt to make a Millenium or Happy World. Being Extracts from the Constitution of Spensonia* [1803].

——— *A Receipt to Make a Millenium or Happy World. Being Extracts from the Constitution of Spensonia* (4th edn. [1803]).

——— Something to the Purpose. A receipt to Make a Millenium or Happy World. Being Extracts from the Constitution of Spensonia [?1805].

——— *Spence's songs: Part the First* [?1811].

——— *Spence's songs: Part the Second* [?1811].

——— *Spence's songs: Part the Third* [?1811].

——— *Spence's Plan for Parochial Partnerships in the Land* … (1816).

STEVENS, WILLIAM, *A memoir of Thomas Martin Wheeler, Founder of the Friend in Need Life and Sick Assurance Society* (1862).

TAYLOR, WILLIAM COOKE, *Notes of a Tour in the Manufacturing Districts of Lancashire* (1841).

THOMPSON, WILLIAM, *An Inquiry into the Principles of the Distribution of Wealth Most Conducive to Human Happiness; Applied to the Newly Proposed System of Voluntary Equality of Wealth* (1824; new edn. 1850).

TILLY, W., *The Spencean Jubilee* [?1801].

The Trial of Edward Marcus Despard, Esquire, For High Treason, at the Session House, Newington, SURRY [*sic*] (1803).

Trial of James O'Coighley (1798).

The Trial of James Watson (1817).

The Trial of Robert Wedderburn (A Dissenting Minister of the Unitarian Persuasion) for Blasphemy, ed. Erasmus Perkins [i.e. George Cannon] (2 edns., both 1820).

The Trial of Thomas Hardy for High Treason … Taken Down in Shorthand by Joseph Gurney, 4 vols. (1794-5).

Watson, James, *The Rights of the People: Unity or Slavery* (lst and 2nd edns. 1818; 3rd edn., Manchester, 1819).

——— *More Plots, More Treason, More Green Bags. A Letter to Viscount Lord Sidmouth* (1819).

[Wedderburn, Robert], *Christian Policy; or Spence's Plan, in Prose and Verse. By a Spencean Philanthropist* (1818).

[———] *A Few Plain Questions for an Apostate* [1819].

Whitmore, William, *Firstlings* (1852).

——— *Gilbert Marlow, and Other Poems* (Cambridge, 1859).

Wilkinson, George Theodore, *An Authentic History of the Cato-Street Conspiracy; With the Trials at Large of the Conspirators, for High Treason and Murder; a Description of their Weapons and Combustible Machines, and Every Particular Connected with the Rise, Progress, Discovery, and Termination of the Horrid Plot* (1820).

Wilkinson, Harrison, *The Principles of an Equitable and Efficient System of Finance: Founded upon Self-Evident, Universal, and Invariable Principles* … (1820).

——— *Property against Industry: Or an Exposition of the Partiality, Oppression, Inequality, and Injustice, of the Present System of Finance: Demonstrating that Property is the Only Just Source of Revenue; and that all Taxes Ought to be Imposed on Property* … (1821).

Wilson, Walter, *History and Antiquities of Dissenting Churches and Meeting Houses, in London* …, 4 vols. (1810).

Winchester, Elhanan, *A Course of Lectures on the Prophecies that Remain to be Fulfilled, Delivered in the Borough of Southwark, as also, at the Chapel in Glass-House Yard in the Year 1790*, 4 vols. (1790).

Wollstonecraft, Mary, *A Vindication of the Rights of Men* (2nd edn., 1790).

The Wrongs of Man by Feudal Landlords [?1816].

Yelloly, John, *Some Account of the Employment of Spade Husbandry on an Extensive Scale in the County of Norfolk* … (1838).

6. SECONDARY PRINTED SOURCES

The place of publication of books is London, unless stated otherwise.

Abercrombie, David, *Studies in Phonetics and Linguistics* (1965).

Abrahams, Aleck, 'No. 277 Gray's Inn Road', *Antiquary*, 44 (Apr. 1908), pp. 128-34.

Adler, Georg, 'Der ältere englische Sozialismus und Thomas Spence', introd. to T. Spence, *Das Gemeineigentum am Boden* (Leipzig, 1904).

Allen, H. S., 'Jean-Paul Marat, M.D.', *Alumnus Chronicle* (University of St Andrews), 18 (Jan. 1936), pp. 30-9.

Anderson, Michael, *Family Structure in 19th Century Lancashire* (Cambridge, 1971).

Armstrong, K., (ed.) *Bless'd Millennium* (Whitley Bay, 2000).

——— (ed.), *The Hive of Liberty* (Whitley Bay, 2007).

Armytage, W. H. G., *Heavens Below: Utopian Experiments in England, 1560-1960* (1961).

Ashworth, William, *Genesis of Modern British Town Planning: A Study in Economic and Social History of the 19th and 20th Centuries* (1954).

Atkins, James, *The Tradesmen's Tokens of the Eighteenth Century* (1892).

Bachmann, Fritz, *Die Agrarreform in der Chartistenbewegung: Eine Historisch-kritische Studie über die Doktrinen des englischen Sozialismus von 1820-1850* (Berne, 1928).

Baxter, T. L., and Donnelly, F. K., 'The "Revolutionary Underground" in the West Riding; Myth or Reality?', *Past and Present*, 64 (1975), pp. 124-32.

Beal, J., *English Pronunciation in the Eighteenth Century: Thomas Spence's "Grand Repository of the English Language"* (Oxford, 1999).

Beedell, A. V., and Harvey, A. D. (eds.), *The Prison Diary (16 May-22 November 1794) of John Horne Tooke*, (Leeds, 1995).

Beer, Max, *A History of British Socialism*, 2 vols. (1919-20).

——— (ed.), *The Pioneers of Land Reform: Thomas Spence, William Ogilvie, Thomas Paine* (1920).

Behagg, Clive, 'Custom, Class and Change: The Trade Societies of Birmingham', *Social History*, 4/3 (Oct. 1979), pp. 455-80.

Belchem, John D., 'Henry Hunt and the Evolution of the Mass Platform', *English Historical Review* 93 (1978), pp. 739-73.

——— 'Chartism and the Trades, 1848-1850', *English Historical Review*, 98 (July 1983), pp. 558-87.

——— *'Orator' Hunt: Henry Hunt and English Working-class Radicalism* (Oxford, 1985).

Bell, Florence, *At the Works: A Study of a Manufacturing Town (Middlesbrough)* (1907; repr. 1985).

Bennett, J., 'The London Democratic Association 1837-41: A Study in London Radicalism', in Epstein and Thompson (eds.), *The Chartist Experience*, pp. 87-119.

Benson, John, *The Penny Capitalists: A Study of Nineteenth Century Working Class Entrepreneurs* (Dublin, 1983).

Benton, Philip, *The History of Rochford Hundred* (Rochford, 1867).

Bloch, Ruth H., *Visionary Republic: Millennial Themes in American Thought, 1756-1800* (Cambridge, 1985).

BONNETT, A., 'Thomas Spence, *Property in Land Every One's Right', Labour History Review* 74:1 (April, 2009).

——— 'The other Rights of Man', *History Today*, (September 2007).

BRONSTEIN, J. L., *Land Reform and Working-Class Experience in Britain and the United States, 1800-62* (Stanford, Ca., 1999).

BURNETT, JOHN, VINCENT, D., and MAYALL, DAVID, *The Autobiography of the Working Class: An Annotated, Critical Bibliography*, i. *1790-1900* (Brighton, 1984).

BUTLER, J. R. M., *The Passing of the Great Reform Bill* (1914).

BYTHELL, DUNCAN, *The Handloom Weavers: A Study in the English Cotton Industry during the Industrial Revolution* (Cambridge, 1969).

——— *The Sweated Trades: Outwork in Nineteenth Century Britain* (1978).

CAVE, K. (ed.), *The Diary of Joseph Farrington*, xvi (Yale, 1985).

CHADWICK, STANLEY, *'A Bold and Faithful Journalist', Joshua Hobson, 1810-1876* (Huddersfield, 1976).

CHAPMAN, JOHN, 'Land Purchasers at Enclosure: Evidence from West Sussex', *Local Historian*, 12 (1977), pp. 337-41.

——— 'The Parliamentary Enclosures of West Sussex', *Southern History*, 2 (1980), pp. 73-91,

CHARLTON, D. G., *New Images of the Natural in France: A Study in European Cultural History, 1750-1800* (Cambridge, 1984).

CHASE, MALCOLM S., 'Thomas Spence', and 'Charles Neesom', in J. Bellamy and J. Saville (eds.), *Dictionary of Labour Biography*, viii (1987).

——— 'Out of radicalism: the mid-Victorian Freehold Land Movement', *English Historical Review* 106 (1991).

——— (ed.), *The Life and Literary Pursuits of Allen Davenport, with a Further Selection of the Author's Work* (Aldershot, 1994).

——— '"We wish only to work for ourselves": the Chartist Land Plan', in M. Chase and I. Dyck (eds.), *Living and Learning: Essays in Honour of J. F. C. Harrison*, (Aldershot, 1996).

——— '"Wholesome object lessons": the Chartist Land Plan in retrospect', *English Historical Review* vol. 118 (2003).

CLAEYS, GREGORY (ed.), 'Four Letters between Thomas Spence and Charles Hall', *Notes and Queries*, 28/4 (Aug. 1981), pp. 317-21.

——— 'Documents: Thomas Evans and the Development of Spenceanism, 1815-16: Some Neglected Correspondence', *Bulletin of the Society for the Study of Labour History*, 48 (1984), pp. 24-30.

——— 'John Adolphus Etzler, Technological Utopianism, and British Socialism: The Tropical Emigration Society's Venezuelan Mission and its Social Context, 1833-48', *English Historical Review*, 101 (Apr. 1986), pp. 351-75.

Clarke, John, Critcher, Charles, and Johnson, Richard, *Working-class Culture* (1979).

Clephen, James, 'Jean-Paul Marat in Newcastle', *Monthly Chronicle of North-country Lore and Legend*, 1/2 (Apr. 1887), pp. 49-53.

Cole, G. D. H., *Richard Carlile, 1790-1843* (1943).

——— *A History of Socialist Thought*, i. *The Forerunners, 1789-1850* (1953; new edn. 1977).

Coleman, D. C., 'Proto-industrialisation: A Concept too Many' *EHR* 36 (1983), pp. 435-48.

Colley, L., *Britons: Forging the Nation, 1707-1837* (1992).

Collins, E. J. T., 'Migrant Labour in British Agriculture in the 19th Century', *EHR* 29 (1976), pp. 38-59.

Conkin, Paul K., *Prophets of Prosperity: America's First Political Economists* (Bloomington, Ind. 1980).

Cooter, Roger, *The Cultural Meaning of Popular Science: Phrenology and the Organisation of Consent in 19th Century Britain* (Cambridge, 1984).

Coventry Perseverance Co-operative Society, *Jubilee History* (Coventry, 1917).

Cragoe, M. and Readman, P. (eds), *The Land Question in Britain, 1750-1950* (Basingstoke, 2010).

Cunningham, Hugh, *Leisure and the Industrial Revolution, c.1780-c.1880* (1980).

Cunningham, William, *Growth of English Industry and Commerce in Modern Times*, 2 vols. (5th edn. Cambridge, 1910-12).

Cunliffe, J. and Erreygers, G. (eds.), *The Origins of Universal Grants. An Anthology of Historical Writings on Basic Capital and Basic Income*, (Basingstoke, 2004).

Dalton, Richard, and Hamer, Samuel, *The Provincial Token Coinage of the Eighteenth Century*, 3 vols. (1910-18).

Davidson, James West, *The Logic of Millennial Thought* (New Haven, 1977).

Davidson, John Morrison, *Concerning Four Precursors of Henry George and the Single Tax* (1900).

Davies, C. Stella, *A History of Macclesfield* (Manchester, 1961).

Davis, H. W. C., 'Lancashire Reformers, 1816-17', *Bulletin of The John Rylands Library*, 10 (Manchester, 1926), pp. 47-79.

Deane, P., and Cole, W. A., *British Economic Growth, 1688-1939: Trends and Structure* (2nd edn., Cambridge, 1969).

Dickinson, H. T., *Liberty and Property: Political Ideology in 18th Century Britain* (1977).

——— *The Political Works of Thomas Spence* (Newcastle upon Tyne,

1982).

Dinwiddy, J. R., 'The Black Lamp in Yorkshire, 1801-2', *Past and Present*, 64 (1975), pp. 113-23.

——— 'Charles Hall, Early English Socialist', *International Review of Social History*, 21 (1976), pp. 256-76.

Dyos, H. J., and Wolff, Michael, *The Victorian City: Images and Realities* (1973).

Elliott, Marianne, 'The "Despard Conspiracy" Reconsidered', *Past and Present*, 75 (1977), pp. 46-61.

Empson, William, *Some Versions of Pastoral* (new edn., 1968).

Epstein, James, *The Lion of Freedom: Feargus O'Connor and the Chartist Movement, 1832-1842* (1982).

——— and Thompson, Dorothy (eds.), *The Chartist Experience: Studies in Working Class Radicalism and Culture, 1830-60* (1982).

Feather, John, *The Provincial Book Trade in Eighteenth Century England* (Cambridge, 1985).

Foster, I., *Heronsgate: Freedom, Happiness and Contentment* (Rickmansworth, 1999).

Foster, John, *Class Struggle and the Industrial Revolution: Early Industrial Capitalism in Three English Towns* (1974).

Fraser, Derek (ed.), *A History of Modern Leeds* (Manchester, 1980).

Freemantle, A. F., 'The Truth about Oliver the Spy', *English Historical Review*, 47 (1932), pp. 601-16.

Gallop, G. I. (ed.), *Pigs' Meat: The Selected Writings of Thomas Spence Radical and Pioneer Land Reformer, With an Introductory Essay and Notes* (Nottingham, 1982).

Garnett, R. G., *Co-operation and the Owenite Socialist Communities in Britain, 1825-45* (Manchester, 1972).

George, Henry, 'Science of Political Economy', in *Complete Works*, vi (1904).

Goodway, David, *London Chartism, 1838-1848* (Cambridge, 1982).

Goody, J., Thirsk, J., and Thompson, E. P., *Family and Inheritance: Rural Society in Western Europe, 1200-1800* (Cambridge, 1976).

Green, F. E., 'The Allotment Movement', *Contemporary Review*, 114 (1918), pp. 90-7.

Hadfield, A. M., *The Chartist Land Company* (Newton Abbot, 1970; Aylesbury, 2000, new edition).

Hampsher-Monk, Ian, 'Civic Humanism and Parliamentary Reform: The Case of the Society of the Friends of the People', *Journal of British Studies*, 18 (1979), pp. 70-89.

Hardy, Dennis, *Alternative Communities in 19th Century England* (1979).

Harrington, James, *The Political Works of James Harrington*, ed. J. G. A.

Pocock (Cambridge, 1977).

HARRISON, J. F. C., *Social Reform in Victorian Leeds: The Work of James Hole, 1820-1895* (Leeds, 1954).

——— *Robert Owen and the Owenites in Britain and America* (1969).

——— *The Second Coming: Popular Millenarianism, 1780-1850* (1979).

HATCH, NATHAN O., *The Sacred Cause of Liberty: Republican Thought and the Millennium in Revolutionary New England* (New Haven, 1977).

HEATON, H., *The Yorkshire Woollen and Worsted Industries* (2nd edn., 1965).

HILL, CHRISTOPHER, 'The Norman York' in *Puritanism and Revolution* (1958).

——— *The World Turned Upside Down: Radical Ideas during the English Revolution* (1972; repr. Harmondsworth, 1975).

HILTON, B., *A Mad, Bad, and Dangerous People? England, 1783-1846* (Oxford, 2006).

HINDE, WENDY, *Castlereagh* (1981).

HOBSBAWM, ERIC, *Labouring Men* (1964).

HOLLIS, PATRICIA, *The Pauper Press: A Study in Working-class Radicalism of the 1830s* (Oxford, 1970).

HOLYOAKE, GEORGE JACOB, *The History of Co-operation* (1875; rev. edn., 1906).

HOWE, J. ANN, *For the Cause of Truth: Radicalism in London, 1796-1821* (Oxford, 1982).

HOUGHTON, W. E., *The Victorian Frame of Mind, 1830-1870* (Yale, 1957).

HOWARD, EBENEZER, *Garden Cities of Tomorrow* (1898; new edn. 1902).

HYNDMAN, H. M. (ed.), *The Nationalisation of the Land in 1775 and 1882. Being a Lecture Delivered at Newcastle-on-Tyne, by Thomas Spence 1775. Reprinted and Edited, with Notes and Introduction, by H. M. Hyndman, 1882* (1882).

JANOWITZ, A., *Lyric and Labour in the Romantic Tradition* (Cambridge, 1998).

JOHNSON, DAVID, *Regency Revolution: The Case of Arthur Thistlewood* (Salisbury, 1974).

JONES, DAVID, J. V., *Chartism and the Chartists* (1975).

JONES, GARETH STEDMAN, *Languages of Class: Studies in English Working Class History, 1832-1982* (Cambridge, 1983).

KASSON, JOHN F., *Civilising the Machine: Technology and Republican Values in America 1776-1900* (New York, 1976).

KEMP-ASHRAF, PHYLISS MARY, *Life and Times of Thomas Spence* (Newcastle, 1984).

KING, J. E. and MARANGOS, J., 'Two arguments for basic income: Thomas Paine (1737-1809) and Thomas Spence (1750-1814)' *History of*

Economic Ideas, 14: 1 (2006).

Knox, Thomas R., 'Thomas Spence: The Trumpet of Jubilee', *Past and Present*, 76 (1977), pp. 75-98.

——— 'Popular Politics and Provincial Radicalism: Newcastle-upon-Tyne, 1769-1785', *Albion*, 11/3 (1979), pp. 224-41.

Kramnick, Isaac, 'Republican Revisionism Revisited', *American Historical Review*, 87/3 (1982), pp. 629-64.

Lean, E. T., *The Napoleonists; A Study in Political Disaffection, 1760-1960* (1970).

Leeson, R. A., *Travelling Brothers: The Six Centuries' Road from Craft Fellowship to Trade Unionism* (1979).

Locke, John, *Two Treatises of Government*, ed. with introd. and app. crit. by Peter Laslett (Cambridge, 1960).

MacAskill, J., 'The Chartist Land Plan', in A. Briggs (ed.), *Chartist Studies* (1959), pp. 304-41.

McCalman, Iain D., 'Unrespectable Radicalism: Infidels and Pornography in early 19th century London', *Past and Present*, 104 (Aug. 1984), pp. 74-110.

——— 'Ultra-radicalism and Convivial Debating-clubs in London, 1795-1838', *English Historical Review*, 102 (Apr. 1987), pp. 309-33.

——— *Radical Underworld: Prophets, Revolutionaries and Pornographers in London, 1795-1840* (Cambridge, 1988).

Macpherson, C. B., *The Political Theory of Possessive Individualism* (Oxford, 1962).

Mansfield, Nicholas, 'John Brown; A Shoemaker in Place's London', *HWJ* 8 (Autumn 1979), pp. 128-36.

Marangos, J., 'Thomas Paine (1737-1809) and Thomas Spence (1750-1814) on land ownership, land taxes and the provision of citizens' dividend', *International Journal of Social Economics*, 35: 5 (2008).

Marshall, T. H., 'Jethro Tull and the New Husbandry of the Eighteenth Century', *EHR* 2/1 (1929-30), pp. 41-60.

Marx, Leo, *The Machine in the Garden: Technology and the Pastoral Ideal in America* (New York, 1964).

Massin, Jean, *Marat* (Paris, 1960).

Maxted, Ian, *The London Book Trades, 1775-1800: A Preliminary Checklist of Members* (Folkestone, 1977).

Menger, Anton, *The Right to the Whole Produce of Labour: The Origin and Development of the Theory of Labour's Claim to the Whole Product of Industry*, ed. H. S. Foxwell (1899).

Messner, A. 'Communication: land, leadership, culture and emigration: some problems in Chartist historiography', *Historical Journal* 42 (1999).

MORLEY, HENRY, *Memoirs of Bartholomew Fair* (1858; 2nd edn, 1874).

MORRIS, B., *Ecology and Anarchism* (Worcester, 1996).

MUSSON, A. E., 'Ideology of Early Co-operation in Lancashire and Cheshire', *Transactions of the Lancashire and Cheshire Antiquarian Society*, 68 (1958), pp. 117-38.

——— *Trade Union and Labour History* (1974).

NEUBURG, VICTOR EDWARD (ed.), *Literacy and Society* (1971).

NEIHUUS, HEINRICH, *Geschichte der englischen Bodenreformtheorien* (Leipzig, 1910).

O'GRÁDA, CORMAC, 'The Owenite Community at Ralahine, County Clare, 1831-1833: A Reassessment', *Irish Economic and Social History*, 1 (1974), pp. 36-48.

PACKER, I., *Lloyd George, Liberalism and the Land: the Land Issue and Party Politics in England, 1906-1914* (Woodbridge, 2001).

PARSSINEN, T. M., 'The Revolutionary Party in London, 1816-1820', *Bulletin of the Institute of Historical Research*, 45 (1972), pp. 266-82.

——— 'Association, Convention, and Anti-Parliament in British Radical Politics, 1771-1848', *English Historical Review*, 87 (1973), pp. 504-33.

——— 'Thomas Spence and the Origins of English Land Nationalisation', *Journal of the History of Ideas*, 34 (1973), pp. 135-41.

——— 'Thomas Spence', in J. O, Baylen and N. I. Gossman (eds.), *Biographical Dictionary of Modern British Radicals*, i. (Brighton, 1979), pp. 454-8.

——— and PROTHERO, I. J. , 'The London Tailors' Strike of 1834 and the Collapse of the Grand National Consolidated Trades Union: a Police Spy's Report', *International Review of Social History*, 22 (1977), pp. 64-107.

PHILP, M. (ed.), *The French Revolution and British Popular Politics* (Cambridge, 1991).

PIERSON, STANLEY, *Marxism and the Origins of British Socialism: The Struggle for a New Consciousness* (Ithaca, NY, 1973).

POCOCK, J. G. A., *Politics, Language, and Time* (New York, 1971).

——— *The Machiavellian Moment: Florentine Political Thought and the Atlantic Republican Tradition* (Princeton, 1975).

——— *Virtue, Commerce, and History: Essays on Political Thought and History, Chiefly in the Eighteenth Century* (Cambridge, 1985).

PODMORE, FRANK, *Robert Owen: A Biography* (1906; new edn, 1923).

POLLARD, SIDNEY, and SALT, JOHN (eds.), *Robert Owen, Prophet of the Poor: Essays in Honour of the 200th Anniversary of his Birth* (1971).

POOLE, D., *The Last Chartist Land Settlement: Great Dodford, 1849* (Dodford, 1999).

POTTER, DAVID M., *People of Plenty: Economic Abundance and the*

American Character (Chicago, 1954).

PREST, JOHN, *The Industrial Revolution in Coventry* (1960).

PRICE, RICHARD, *Masters, Unions and Men: Work Control in Building and the Rise of Labour, 1830-1914* (Cambridge, 1980).

——— 'Labour Process and Labour History', *Social History*, 8 (1982), pp. 57-75.

——— *Labour in British Society: An Interpretative Essay* (1986).

PROTHERO, IORWERTH J., 'Chartism in London', *Past and Present*, 44 (1969), pp. 76-105.

——— 'William Benbow and the Concept of the "General Strike"', *Past and Present*, 63 (1974), pp. 132-71.

——— *Artisans and Politics in Early Nineteenth Century London; John Gast and his Times* (Folkestone, 1979).

READ, DONALD, *Peterloo: The 'Massacre' and its Background* (Manchester, 1958).

READMAN, P., *Land and Nation in England: Patriotism, National Identity, and the Politics of Land, 1880-1914* (Woodbridge, 2008).

REED, MICK, 'The Peasantry of 19th Century England: A Neglected Class?', *HWJ* 18 (Autumn 1984), pp. 53-76.

ROBERTS, SONIA, *The Story of Islington* (1975).

ROE, MICHAEL, 'Maurice Margarot: A Radical in Two Hemispheres, 1792-1815', *Bulletin of the Institute of Historical Research*, 31 (1958), pp. 68-78.

ROSE, J., *The Intellectual Life of the British Working Classes* (2001).

ROYLE, EDWARD, *Radical Politics, 1790-1900: Religion and Unbelief* (1971).

——— *Victorian Infidels: The Origins of the British Secularist Movement 1791-1866* (Manchester, 1974).

——— *The Infidel Tradition from Paine to Bradlaugh* (1976).

——— *Robert Owen and the Commencement of the Millennium: A Study of the Harmony Community* (Manchester, 1998).

RUDKIN, OLIVE D., *Thomas Spence and his Connections* (1927; repr. New York, 1966).

SALT, JOHN, 'Trades Union Farms in Sheffield', *Notes and Queries*, 206 (1961), pp. 82-3.

SCHMITT, PETER J., *Back to Nature: The Arcadian Myth in Urban America* (New York, 1969).

SCRIVENER, M., *Poetry and Reform: Periodical Verse from the English Democratic Press, 1792-1824* (Detroit, 1992).

SCRUTON, WILLIAM, *Bradford Fifty Years Ago* (Bradford, 1897).

SEARBY, PETER, *Coventry Politics in the Age of the Chartists* (Coventry, 1964).

——— 'Chartists and Freemen in Coventry, 1838-1860', *Social History*, 2 (1977), pp. 761-34.

SHEPARD, LESLIE, *John Pitts: Ballad Printer of Seven Dials, London 1765-1844* (1969).

SHEPPARD, F. H. W., *Local Government in St. Marylebone, 1688-1835: A Study of the Vestry and the Turnpike Trust* (1958).

SHIELDS, ANTHEA FRASER, 'Thomas Spence and the English Language', *Transactions of the Philological Society*, 61 (1974), pp. 33-64.

SMITH, ALAN, 'Arthur Thistlewood: A Regency Republican', *History Today*, 3 (1953), pp. 846-52.

SMITH, D. M., The Hatting Industry in Denton, Lancs', *Industrial Archaeology*, 3 (1966), pp. 1-7.

SMITH, HENRY NASH, *Virgin Land: the American West as Symbol and Myth* (New York, 1950).

SMITH, J., 'James Murray (1732-1782): radical dissenter', *North East History* 32 (1988).

SMITH, OLIVIA, *The Politics of Language, 1791-1819* (Oxford, 1984).

SPERBER, HANS, and TRITTSCHUH, TRAVIS, *American Political Terms: An Historical Dictionary* (Detroit, 1962).

STANHOPE, JOHN, *The Cato Street Conspiracy* (1962).

STEVENS, JOHN, *England's Last Revolution: Pentrich 1817* (Buxton, 1977).

Stevenson, John, *Popular Disturbances in England, 1700-1870* (1979).

STORCH, ROBERT D. (ed.), *Popular Culture and Custom in Nineteenth Century England* (1982).

TAYLOR, ANTONY, '"Commons-Stealers", "Land-Grabbers" and "Jerry-Builders": Space, Popular Radicalism and the Politics of Public Access in London, 1848-1880', *International Review of Social History* 40 (1995).

TAYLOR, BARBARA, *Eve and the New Jerusalem: Socialism and Feminism in the 19th century* (1983).

THALE, MARY (ed.), *Selections from the Papers of the London Corresponding Society 1792-1799* (Cambridge, 1983).

Thomas, Keith, *Man and the Natural World: Changing Attitudes in England, 1500-1800* (1983).

Thomas, William, *The Philosophic Radicals: Nine Studies in Theory and Practice, 1817-1841* (Oxford, 1979).

THOMPSON, DOROTHY, *The Early Chartists* (1971).

——— *The Chartists* (1984).

THOMPSON, EDWARD P., *The Making of the English Working Class* (2nd edn., Harmondsworth, 1968).

——— 'The Moral Economy of the English Crowd in the Eighteenth Century', *Past and Present*, 50 (1971), pp. 76-136.

Thompson, Noel. W., *The People's Science: The Popular Political Economy of Exploitation and Crisis* (Cambridge, 1984).

Thurston, Gavin, *The Clerkenwell Riot: the Killing of Constable Culley* (1967).

Torr, Dona, *Tom Mann and his Times*, i. *1856-1890* (1956).

Tully, John, *A Discourse on Property: John Locke and his Adversaries* (Cambridge, 1981).

Tuveson, Ernest Lee, *Redeemer Nation: the Idea of America's Millennial Role* (Chicago, 1968).

Verinder, Frederick, *Land for the Landless: Spence and 'Spence's Plan' (1775). With Neo-Spencean Appendix (1896) ... compiled by J. Morrison Davidson* (English Land Restoration League, 1896).

Vicinus, Martha, *The Industrial Muse: A Study of 19th century British Working Class Literature* (1974).

Vigier, François, *Change and Apathy: Liverpool and Manchester during the Industrial Revolution* (Cambridge, Mass., 1970).

Vincent, David (ed.), *Testaments of Radicalism: Memoirs of Working Class Politicians, 1790-1885* (1977).

Waters, Arthur W., *Notes Gleaned from Contemporary Literature, &c., Respecting the Issuers of the 18th Century Tokens, Struck for the County of Middlesex* (Leamington Spa, 1906).

Watkinson, Ray, 'Thomas Bewick, 1753-1828', in L. M. Munby (ed.), *The Luddites and Other Essays* (1971), pp. 11-32.

Webb, Sidney, and Webb, Beatrice, *The History of Trades Unionism* (1894).

Weiner, S. K., 'Public and private occasion in 1820s radical poetry: Paine commemorations and Davenport's *Muse's Wreath*', *Nineteenth-Century Contexts* 30: 4 (December 2008).

Welford, Richard, *Men of Mark 'twixt Tyne and Tweed*, iii (1895).

Wells, Roger, A. E., *Insurrection: The British Experience, 1795-1803* (Gloucester, 1983).

Wiener, Joel H., *The War of the Unstamped: The Movement to Repeal the British Newspaper Tax, 1830-6* (Ithaca, NY, 1969).

——— *Radicalism and Free Thought in 19th Century Britain: The Life of Richard Carlile* (New York, 1983).

Wilentz, Sean, *Chants Democratic: New York City and the Rise of the American Working Class, 1788-1850* (Oxford, 1984).

Williams, David, *John Frost: A Study in Chartism* (Cardiff, 1939).

Williams, Raymond, *The Country and the City* (1973; 2nd edn., St Albans, 1975).

Wilson, K., *The Sense of the People: Politics, Culture and Imperialism in England, 1715-85* (Cambridge, 1995).

Wood, Marcus, *Radical satire and print culture, 1790-1822* (Oxford, 1994).

Worrall, D., *Radical Culture: Discourse, Resistance and Surveillance, 1790-1820* (Detroit, 1992).

Wordie, J. R., 'Social Change on the Leveson-Gower Estates, 1714-1832', *EHR* 27 (1974), pp. 593-609.

Yeo, E. M., 'Robert Owen and Radical Culture', in Pollard and Salt (eds.), *Robert Owen, Prophet of the Poor*, pp. 84-114.

Zahler, Helen Sara, Eastern Working Men and National Land Policy, 1862 (New York, 1941).

Index

Also available from
Breviary Stuff Publications

Barry Reay, The Last Rising of the Agricultural Labourers, *Rural Life and Protest in Nineteenth-Century England*
£12.00 • 192pp *paperback* • 191x235mm • ISBN 978-0-9564827-2-3

The Hernhill Rising of 1838 was the last battle fought on English soil, the last revolt against the New Poor Law, and England's last millenarian rising. The bloody 'Battle of Bosenden Wood', fought in a corner of rural Kent, was the culmination of a revolt led by the self-styled 'Sir William Courtenay'. It was also, despite the greater fame of the 1830 Swing Riots, the last rising of the agricultural labourers.

Barry Reay provides us with the first comprehensive and scholarly analysis of the abortive rising, its background, and its social context, based on intensive research, particularly in local archives. He presents a unique case-study of popular mobilization in nineteenth-century England, giving us a vivid portrait of the day-to-day existence of the farm labourer and the life of the hamlet. Dr. Reay explores the wider context of agrarian relations, rural reform, protest and control through the fascinating story of *The Last Rising of the Agricultural Labourers.*

John E. Archer, 'By a Flash and a Scare', *Arson, Animal Maiming, and Poaching in East Anglia 1815-1870*
£12.00 • 208pp *paperback* • 191x235mm • ISBN 978-0-9564827-1-6

'By a Flash and a Scare' illuminates the darker side of rural life in the nineteenth century. Flashpoints such as the Swing riots, Tolpuddle, and the New Poor Law riots have long attracted the attention of historians, but here John E. Archer focuses on the persistent war waged in the countryside during the 1800s, analysing the prevailing climate of unrest, discontent, and desperation.

In this detailed and scholarly study, based on intensive research among the local records of Norfolk and Suffolk, Dr Archer identifies and examines the three most serious crimes of protest in the countryside — arson, animal maiming and poaching. He shows how rural society in East Anglia was shaped by terror and oppression in equal measure. Social crime and covert protest were an integral part of the ordinary life of the rural poor. They did not protest infrequently, they protested *all the time*.

Buchanan Sharp, In Contempt of All Authority, *Rural Artisans and Riot in the West of England, 1586-1660*
£12.00 • 204pp *paperback* • 191x235mm • ISBN 978-0-9564827-0-9

The leaders and most active participants in riot were rural artisans — skilled men working in non-agricultural employments. These artisans, particularly those in the major industries of seventeenth-century England located in the forested West, were largely wage-earners. Virtually landless cottagers who relied on the market for food, clothworkers and other artisans frequently engaged in food riots and attempted insurrections during times of depression or harvest failure. These artisans exploited the common waste of the royal forests. Enclosure of the forests by the Crown threatened the livelihood of those workers who depended on the forests for raw material and pasturage. The result was the Western Rising, a series of massive anti-enclosure riots which took place in Gillingham Forest on the Wiltshire-Dorset border, Braydon Forest in Wiltshire and the Forest of Dean in Gloucestershire. There were also concurrent riots in Leicester Forest, and Feckenham Forest, Worcestershire. A similar series of riots followed in the 1640s.

FORTHCOMING

Bob Bushaway, By Rite, *Custom, Ceremony and Community in England 1700-1880*
ISBN 978-0-9564827-6-1

Roger Wells, Insurrection, *The British Experience 1795-1803*
ISBN 978-0-9564827-3-0

Roger Wells, Wretched Faces, *Famine in Wartime England 1793-1801*
ISBN 978-0-9564827-4-7

www.breviarystuff.org.uk

Lightning Source UK Ltd.
Milton Keynes UK
UKOW05f1819200813

215691UK00001B/61/P